MEMOIRS
OF AN ACCIDENTAL AIRMAN

F. F. Rainsford

MEMOIRS OF AN ACCIDENTAL AIRMAN

F. F. RAINSFORD

with a foreword by
Lord Boothby

Thomas Harmsworth Publishing
London

ACKNOWLEDGEMENTS

Many people have helped me to write this book. I am grateful especially to:
Messrs J. & R. Chambers of Edinburgh for permission to use
material on Kenya first published in Chambers Journal in 1934;
Air Commodore Henry Probert MBE, MA, of the Air Historical
Branch of the Ministry of Defence;
Mr. Harry Hannam and Miss Joan McPherson of the Foreign
and Commonwealth Office Library;
Mr. Simon Partridge, OBE, for much help and encouragement
throughout;
Captain J. Henley, DSC, RN, for putting me right on naval
matters;
The Imperial War Museum for use of photographs;
and also the Ministry of Defence;
and most of all to my wife Audrey who has lived through much of
it, typed it all and whose suggestions have been invaluable.

FFR.

Rainsford, Frederick Fitzpatrick
Memoirs of an accidental airman.
1. World War, 1939-1945—Campaigns—Africa, North
2. World War, 1939-1945—Aerial operations, British
3. World War, 1939-1945—Personal narratives, British
I. Title
940.54′ 23′ 0924   D766.82

ISBN 0-948807-03-2

ISBN 0 948807 03 2

Printed in Great Britain by
The Bath Press, Avon

Foreword

I was pleased and proud when Air Commodore Rainsford, widely known to a host of friends in the Royal Air Force and in the Diplomatic Service as 'Turkey', asked me to write a Foreword to his book of Memoirs. It is not a Preface. I have read far too many of them in my life which have stopped me reading the book. It is nothing more than a strong recommendation from a man who is easily bored, and whose keen interest and attention was held by this story from start to finish. The author is good enough to say of me that, when I was serving as his Adjutant when he was in command of a Bomber Squadron during the last war, he had never known anyone from a political background who fitted so happily and so readily into Service life. It was nothing to the miraculous way in which he himself stepped from strenuous active service to the Civil Service in Whitehall, and finally to the Diplomatic Service in such disparate posts as Madras, Korea and New York; and made a resounding success of them all.

His war-time service in the Mediterranean and in Bomber Command at home was not unusual, but lengthy and intense. He does not attempt to plunge into the controversies which have since arisen about the bombing policies pursued by Harris, but contents himself with saying that they made a definite contribution to victory, which is incontrovertible; and with an occasional sigh of regret at the appalling wastage of war which has plagued humanity since the dawn of history, and which if it is not soon stopped will lead to the total destruction of the human race.

Undoubtedly the Berlin Air Lift of 1948-9 in the direction of which he played an important and indeed vital part was the apex of his career. Of this he writes: 'It had been a very long year for all of us, and for me it was perhaps the most rewarding of my whole life.' Well it may have been, for historians will almost certainly regard the Battle of Britain and the Berlin Air Lift as the two most important single events of the Twentieth Century. The first stopped Hitler's drive against Western Europe, which if it had succeeded would have put an end to Western civilisation. The second stopped Stalin from doing exactly the same thing. And the effective cooperation between the British and American Air Forces in time of declared peace led directly to the subsequent creation of the NATO Alliance which has since prevented World War.

The distinguished historian CRL Fletcher once wrote of a favourite pupil: 'Nihil tangit quod non omat'. He touches nothing that he does not adorn. This can truly be said of Turkey Rainsford. All I want to say in conclusion is that this is a marvellous story, very well told. And that we are indeed fortunate to be invited now to read it.

Boothby
1986

Introduction

It has been said that in everyone's life there is material for at least one book although it is perhaps a good thing we don't all try to write one. Certainly I have hesitated for a long time to attempt any record of my own although I have been privileged to live and serve both as an airman and diplomat in a good many parts of the world. Coming as I did from an Anglo-Irish family I had expected as a matter of course to serve in some part of the Empire which in those days seemed to be populated largely by my aunts and uncles and their many children. There was never room in Ireland for more than one or at most two of a large family to earn their living at home and so, in the days when our schoolroom maps were largely red we thought of going to live and work in Africa, Canada or Australia or perhaps one of the colonies but always in the Empire — the word Commonwealth not having entered our heads or our schoolroom vocabularies.

The world, my father used to say, is going to the dogs and I have no doubt it is still doing so, but the rate of change which when he died in 1942 was accelerating rapidly seems now to be faster than ever before in human history. Looking back over quite a long life the years of World War II stand out most clearly and in many ways my whole life was shaped by that conflict, as indeed it shaped and changed and so often destroyed the lives of countless thousands. To have commanded two Bomber squadrons in wartime and to have survived was largely a matter of luck but I shall remember always the extraordinarily high quality and humour of those young men whom I had the honour to command, who came from all over the world to support and sustain the long drawn-out and desperately costly bomber offensive over Europe. It was not always grim. We got very used to the blank spaces at table, to knowing that so-and-so had got the chop, and to welcoming a new crew in their place. Their spirit never faltered and I shall not forget either the cheerfulness of the whole ground crew's greeting on our return from a trip to the Ruhr, delighted that *their* aircraft had come back, even if it wasn't in quite as good condition as when it had left for Happy Valley five or six hours earlier! Perhaps that was not really surprising because even before the war we were a very happy carefree lot knowing well that one day we might have to pay the penalty of being part of the insurance policy for the safety of our country, but in the meanwhile intending to enjoy life to the full. After the war life and the RAF itself were very different for those of us who survived but I felt and still feel now that every year is a bonus year and every day a bonus day. It is enough just to be alive.

Years later after the war when I was serving in New York in the Diplomatic Service I asked John Lindsay, the retiring Mayor, what he felt he had achieved most during his long reign in that turbulent and exciting city and he replied very simply 'I survived'. Perhaps survival in every sense is what it is all about, but I think and dream always of those who didn't, of the young men I had flown with, drunk with, and holidayed with and who didn't come back. I like to think that one day I shall hear 'Joburg' Smith singing Sarie Marais in his clear tenor voice and Bazalgette, who got a posthumous Pathfinder VC afterwards, telling rude stories around the piano, and then a door opening and a broad Australian voice saying 'Hi, Turkey, you old bastard, I never thought to see you here'. It is worth having lived just to be able to remember that.

Fred Rainsford

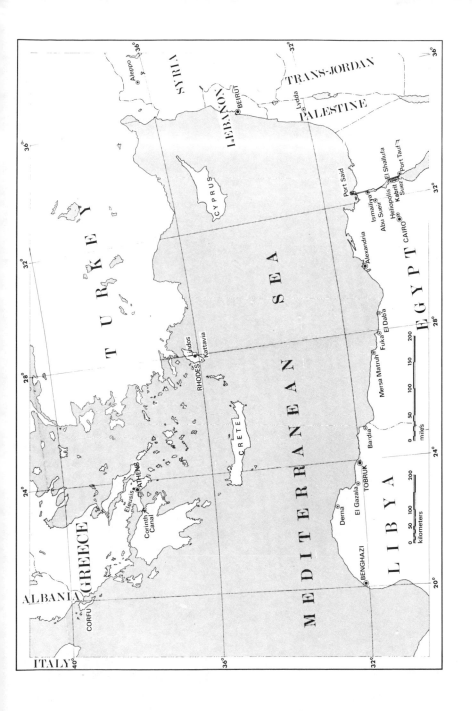

Chapter 1

Growing up in Ireland and Kenya

The first time I ever saw an aeroplane was as a young lad of about nine or ten. At that time, towards the end of World War I, we were living in County Leitrim where my father, a senior officer in the old Royal Irish Constabulary, was in charge of the local police force. We were then in a big rambling Georgian house and I remember vividly one morning when attracted by a strange irregular noise coming, it seemed, from everywhere at once I rushed out onto the lawn and just over the big chestnut tree in front of the house I saw this huge lumbering aircraft flying quite low and very slowly towards Leitrim village. The whole staff had turned out to watch it. The cook with a saucepan in one hand was jabbering wildly with excitement and the old coachman, rushing out from the harness room, was looking in astonishment at this entirely strange object diminishing to a tiny speck over the rambling bog road. I little thought then that I would ever have anything to do with aeroplanes or that they were going to play such a large part in my own life but then my involvement with flying and with the Royal Air Force were largely fortuitous. Indeed accidents and war have largely shaped my life, like those of so many others.

In those days for an Anglo-Irish child Ireland was a wonderful country in which to grow up. It was also a very peaceful place and although my father had no doubt been a little disturbed by the Dublin Easter Rising of 1916, in the West all was very peaceful during these last wartime days. Two incidents stand out clearly and a little in contrast. On one occasion, after Michael O'Leary, an Irish Guardsman, had received the Victoria Cross, I remember well sitting in a window at the top of the RIC Barracks in Carrick-on-Shannon watching him heading a victorious procession over the Shannon Bridge, the whole town in fête cheering him to the echo. A great many people, farmers in particular, were profiting from the war and I can recall being given a bell and being sent around the local farms and cottages to spread the good news which my father had just received from Dublin Castle that the war was over and we had won. My reception was by no means enthusiastic. We had assumed that everybody would be quite delighted but perhaps many foresaw that the price of farm produce which sold so readily in the British market then would decline rapidly and perhaps, too, the latent seed of nationalism was already beginning to stir. Certainly my tidings were not nearly as welcome as I had expected. On the whole though they were happy days, sitting on the haycocks helping, or impeding, the farm workers making hay, drinking buttermilk, listening at night to the corncrake in the fields and by day following the scythemen in the inaccessible corners, admiring their skill and wondering how on earth they avoided getting their feet cut off.

This rural idyll was to end soon. The Troubles were quickly upon us and the years from 1919 to 1922 are memorable. The change was abrupt. Life until then had been both peaceful and unhurried. My father used to read his official morning mail at home when he had finished shaving with a cut-throat razor, the bag having been brought out by a policeman on a bicycle two miles from Carrick-on-Shannon. While he was digesting this I would play with the courier, many of whom became great friends and some of them were killed soon afterwards. I remember a rhyme one of them, called Costello, told me about going to chapel. It went like this 'I go to church on Sunday, I sit behind the spout, I put a penny in the box and I take a shilling out'! Like all the RIC they did not serve in their own county. The Force being a national one anyone joining it was posted elsewhere and this was an accepted condition of service in what was really a gendarmerie. My father, who came from Dundalk, had served mostly in the West but never anywhere near his own home.

At the start of the Troubles I was sent to a preparatory school at Monkstown, near Dublin, and they soon began to affect our ordinary routine, restricting our visits to the Salthill beach and our occasional weekend outings. Sometimes the guerilla war (which is what it really was) moved quite close and we could hear sniping in Kingstown Harbour directed either at the occasional visiting warship or, more often, at the coastguard station. Our Maths master kept a gun in his desk and once I myself, in one of the playing fields, came across a very small revolver which I hastened to hand to our headmaster. He told me that it was a capital offence to carry arms and he took me with him to the police station walking hand in hand, I holding the small weapon pointed to the ground, and greatly excited by the whole adventure. I remember, too, very clearly the shelling of the Four Courts in Dublin in 1922. Although our school was five or six miles from the city we could hear the booming of the eighteen-pounders and we were allowed up the school tower to watch the smoke as the shells burst. It was a thrilling experience for a young boy. I heard afterwards that the eighteen-pounders had all been borrowed from the British by the Free State Army and that the gunners themselves were being instructed by the Royal Artillery in their use while the shelling was going on. Everything seemed to be changing so fast, stamps were being overprinted, pillar boxes repainted, and men with strange uniforms appeared in the streets. Dear, dirty, sleepy Dublin was in a state of turmoil but, whilst all this was very exciting to a school boy, it was immensely worrying for my mother in Leitrim, and I remember vividly one holiday hearing banging on the door and my mother's gentle voice saying very clearly in reply to the demand to open in the name of the IRA 'Promise you won't harm the children'. I hid under the sheets whilst men came in and searched the house and took away two of my father's shotguns. He himself was away and I don't think the men who came that night had any personal designs on him. But his life *was* very much in danger and at one of the gate lodges a man who worked for us arranged a code with a kettle outside his farmhouse which pointed one way if all was well and somewhere else if it was not. Another incident stands out very clearly. During the early days, before things got really bad, we were having a tennis party and my job had been to mark out the lines on the grass court and to act as occasional ball boy. On this particular day a number of army officers had come to play and they left their revolvers on the bench beside me while they played tennis. In the middle of a game two farm labourers, obviously the worse for drink, started fighting with pitchforks in the next field and the game was abandoned, whilst the players rushed off to separate the combatants, leaving me in charge of a whole armoury of weapons, which I longed to handle but didn't dare to touch.

All this had to end. Early in 1922 my father was compelled to retire having reached the age of sixty-two and we decided to move to the North which was peaceful then, Leitrim being no place for a retired senior RIC officer to live. We left in something of a hurry, leaving most of our belongings behind, but a crosscut saw, which had been stolen, was returned and left one night on the doorstep, it having been used in all probability to fell trees across roads for the ambush of security forces! This was a common practice at that time but we were rather touched to get the saw back although it was the last thing we needed to take to Belfast.

We were really sorry to be leaving Connaught. We had enjoyed a very pleasant life there until the last year or two and we knew almost nobody in the North, although my father had at one time served as a very young District Inspector at Ballymoney in County Antrim. Very few of my schoolmates in Monkstown had come from Ulster. One boy, I do remember, whose accent we found quite incomprehensible. After much interrogation we finally christened him 'Bread and Butter'! It turned out his name was Brendan Betty and his father was, I think, a Resident Magistrate in Enniskillen. I have often wondered what happened to him since.

The move to Belfast was a memorable one. We travelled on one of the old single track Irish light railways. It was probably the 'Slow, Late and Never Certain' which was our name for the Sligo, Leitrim and Northern Counties Railway. When we reached the Ulster border the train was stopped by a large number of the 'B' Special Constabulary, some of them sitting on top of haycocks with their rifles pointed at the train. We were there quite a while and wondered if life was going to be like this in Belfast, whilst they slowly examined our credentials. The rest of the journey was uneventful but we were very glad to reach a safe haven at last. We moved into an uncomfortable house on the south side of the city and I found myself going to a new school since it was not considered wise for me to return to Dublin much as I was enjoying my last year there. In retrospect we really had no choice, but the move to the North affected our whole way of life and I know my two sisters who were in Dublin, one at Trinity and one at school, and I myself felt that the world had almost come to an end when we had to go, almost as refugees, to what was then called the 'Black North', leaving behind all our friends in the South. But with the resilience of youth we children settled down quite soon in our new environment. We probably moved just in time although we missed the country greatly,

5

the warmth and the friendliness of the people, and the wide sky of the west of Ireland where we had put down – I think all of us – deeper roots than we ourselves knew.

I went then as a pupil to Campbell College. School days here were in no way memorable but we did have an extraordinarily good headmaster, Lieutenant-Colonel W D Gibbon, known universally as 'Duffy' and loved by everybody. He had had a splendid record in World War I, winning a DSO and a MC, and this naturally impressed us boys enormously. He was a bachelor and was reputed to be terrified both of women and of parents, but he was really a tremendous figure and he had written a book on Rugby when he was at Dulwich, so rugby and the Armed Services were the things that in those days seemed to matter most. I had had no great desire for a military career and the lst XV seemed to be managing rather well without me. Indeed I had vague ideas of becoming a journalist but, under the influence of Duffy and my contemporaries at Campbell, I was persuaded that perhaps a Service career *would* be a good thing and I soon imagined that I had a future in the Royal Navy. Indeed I had visions of myself on the quarterdeck with a telescope under my arm and the battlefleet all around. I joined the Army Class and at the age of about seventeen applied for Special Entry into the Royal Navy. In due course I found myself attending an interview with the Civil Service Commission in London. At this time I had only once been out of Ireland before on a very brief holiday in Scotland and it was with considerable trepidation that I faced my examiners, whom I assumed were all Admirals, in the Civil Service Commission building in Burlington Gardens. I shall remember that interview always. I suppose my alarm at the sight of my seemingly ancient inquisitors was very apparent because one of them hastened to put me at ease and, after inviting me to sit down, asked me if I had ever been abroad. 'Yes, sir,' I said, 'indeed I have, I've been to Scotland.' The laughter that followed echoed all around but, seeing my embarrassment, my questioner asked me very kindly if I had had any sport when I was over there. I said 'Yes indeed, I did a little fishing and I played a little golf.' He asked me where I had been and I told him at Dollar in Clackmannan. I felt my stock was rising rapidly. After a few more friendly questions someone else on the Board, who was obviously a keen fisherman, asked me what success I had had and I said that I had caught a few very fine trout. At this stage visions of the quarterdeck were becoming almost realities. Their Lordships were beaming until one of them said 'What flies did you use, young man?' I replied that I had caught them all on a worm. At this moment, I think quite unanimously, my examiners decided that the Royal Navy could, after all, get along without me! I myself sensing the quite remarkable change of atmosphere in the room realised that perhaps a service career was no longer the thing for me.

A year or so later, still being undecided as to how to earn a living I was persuaded by a distant cousin of mine to join him in Kenya as a pupil farmer on the Mau Escarpment. I had very clear and detailed instructions on what to wear, and also on what to do to prepare myself for this new adventure. I took riding lessons, bought some tropical clothes, including a double terai hat, which was then de rigueur, and in due course embarked on a German ship for Mombassa. The voyage out in mid 1929 was fairly uneventful but I was greatly impressed by the extraordinary industry of the German crew who seemed to spend their time painting the ship when they were not acting as stewards and who appeared to do entirely without sleep. One of them was buried on the voyage; I could not help feeling he had died from overwork. At Kilindini I was met by a friend of my cousin's and proceeded on the Kenya/Uganda railway to Mau Summit, where I was to spend another and most interesting year and a half.

The farm to which I went was on the edge of the Londiani Forest and my boss, who had lost a leg in the First World

7

War and tended to be a little irascible, had started by planting flax but the market had dropped out of that and, when I was there, we were growing wheat. The soil was almost virgin and the only fertilizer we ever used was guano. Unfortunately we got a great deal of black stem and yellow stem rust, and, as the price of wheat dropped dramatically by about 1930 the farmers were in a very parlous condition indeed. All this I was to find out later. In the meanwhile I thought the country quite delightful and Nairobi a small and friendly colonial town. From the capital at about 5500 feet the railway on its long journey to Lake Victoria Nyanza climbed tortuously up tree clad escarpments through forest and grassland, which only intensified the first impression of greenness. 'C'est magnifique mais ce n'est pas l'Afrique' was my first inward comment, qualified perhaps by the sight of herds of zebra and hartebeest or giraffe and vivid striped gazelle grazing contentedly by the railway line, and regarding with gentle boredom the smoke wagon which had been such a terror to their ancestors. The country was lovely but I came down to earth on alighting at Mau Summit, which at 8321 feet is one of the highest points of the railway, and was then the centre of a big wheat growing area. I found myself in the middle of a crowd of jabbering, gesticulating Africans; two of whom grasped my bag and directed me to the ancient Ford, a T-model, which was to convey me to my destination, addressing me the while in a torrent of voluble ki-Swahili, which seemed to have no relation at all to the language I had endeavoured to swat up amidst the distractions of the sea voyage. I soon discovered that the farm hands expected every man to know Swahili, though English would carry one as far as Nairobi. I had therefore to devote the first couple of weeks solely to becoming used to the farm staff and to the sound of their language, and, incidentally, to revising and crystallising my first impressions of this truly remarkable country. It is not easy to give an adequate impression of the wonderfully bracing feeling of exhilaration which comes from living at 8000 feet almost on the Equator – an exhilaration which tended to make me see life through very rose-tinted spectacles. The atmosphere was so rarified and so absolutely clear that one could see and hear for miles. An African could shout across a valley and obtain an answer from a boy a quarter of a mile away on the other side. In the early morning, going out to start the tractor, I could hear our neighbours starting up theirs three miles away. In fact it became quite a matter of rivalry amongst the boys (we called all natives 'boys' in those days) to see who could have their tractor ready first. It was pretty cold there in the early mornings, even though the latitude is equatorial. Everyone burned wood fires in the house at night and wore the thickest of overcoats when out motoring. Frost, indeed, was not entirely unknown, and I have seen thin films of ice on the water in the early morning. In the daytime it was warm with a dry cloudless heat – for the sun was nearly always shining – but it was scarcely ever hotter than it was in Britain on a real summer's day.

Sunrise was a never-to-be-forgotten sight. At six o'clock every morning – for on the Equator the sun rises at the same time all year round – at six o'clock the yellow glow that had been creeping up over the forest-clad hills suddenly burst into resplendent life. As the great rim came over the hills the whole world seemed to spring alive. What had been a long sleepy valley became a scintillating glory of fairy gold as the sunlight caught the dew on the grass and on the wheat, dispersed as with a wand the clinging mists, and moved on in a blaze of triumph to the waters of Lake Victoria Nyanza, sixty-five miles away.

It was then the world looked at its best. Never before had the forest with its dense green foliage – its myriad entanglements of cedar and white olive, of podo and micharagi and mweri, and a thousand other trees we knew only by the native names – looked so impressive. Never had the air seemed so full of song. The 'honk-honk' of an awakening

9

anvil-bird mingled with the raucous cries of parrots and the sweeter song of canaries in blissful and triumphant defiance of all the laws of harmony! It wanted only the glimpse of a couple of reed-buck – most timid of all animals – grazing the damp grass, to complete the impression that the sun had risen on a fairy paradise. And this was a sight which could be witnessed fully three hundred and sixty times in the year, for though the rainfall was heavy it most considerately took place almost entirely at night.

The first thing any newcomer had to learn was the common language. On an average farm of about fifteen hundred acres twenty or thirty boys were permanently employed, and double that number in harvest time. Fortunately the version of the ki-Swahili language spoken on the farms presented no terrors to the novice, and I found three or four weeks sufficed to give me a fair working knowledge of it. Unlike the pukka ki-Swahili of the Coast – which was perhaps the most adequate of all the Bantu languages – the version spoken inland and used all over East Africa as a means of inter-tribal communication had only a very limited vocabulary and was not capable of any of the more subtle shades of expression. However, it was quite sufficient for all ordinary purposes, and it did, moreover, serve as the medium for gaining some knowledge of the native tribal languages – a knowledge which was useful if one was to acquire any real insight into the African mind. This was not easy.

The jabbering crowd who paraded at six o'clock in the morning for the day's orders dressed in old sacks and blankets (and Mother Nature too!) looked like a party of primitive savages who had mislaid their war-paint. To see them a little later building roads and driving oxen, handling machinery and erecting stores with the minimum of supervision, was to realise something of the rate of rural development in Africa even then. On Sunday the same boys – or at any rate the younger ones – would come up to receive their pay dressed in immaculate khaki (which used, I'm afraid, very often put my own to shame!), wearing a fatuous sort of 'Who's going to walk with me?' expression on their shiny faces.

It was quite extraordinary how quickly the absolutely raw recruit would pick things up. I knew a boy straight out of the Native Reserve, who had never even seen a white man before, display such an aptitude for things mechanical that in fourteen days he could be safely left to drive a thirty-horse-power tractor. A boy's particular bent largely depended upon the tribe to which he belonged. The wa-Lumba and Nandi were particularly good with cattle, the wa-Kikuyu at machinery and building grass bandas or houses, and the Kavirondo – a very fine tribe physically – were useful at handling bags and manual labour generally. Of course individual aptitude varied enormously, and no boy ever knew nearly as much as he thought he did. On a wheat farm employing Harvester Threshers and other modern machinery things were apt to be a little bit complicated, and it would be futile to expect even the best labourers to understand how everything worked. But they all *thought* they knew and they were quite capable of taking a whole machine to bits if they got half a chance to locate a noise that had been caused by a single missing split-pin. After which they would call one of the bosses in, remarking blandly, 'Bwana, tinga tinga ne kuisha vunjika,' meaning 'the machine has broken down,' and leaving you to put it together again!

The African loved the impersonal. He would tell you calmly that the tractor had 'run' a big-end, or that two oxen were missing from the boma, as though it were a perfectly natural act of providence, never for a moment admitting or even conceding as possible that he himself forgot to change the oil in the tractor, or repair the wire around the stockade. This omnipotent Providence (the ki-Swahili word is Mungo) played a very large part in his philosophy and

11

governed largely his domestic code – which had scarcely changed since the advent of the white man. The acts of birth and of death, of famine or plenty, sickness or health, were all to him 'Shauri ya Mungo' – Acts of Providence – and if a boy's wife died he would have no hesitation in asking you for leave one day to bury her, and on the next to go and look for another! Always supposing that he had sufficient cows and goats to afford one, for wives (as some white men have discovered too) were expensive luxuries, and in Kenya then they cost five oxen and twenty-one goats each. Some of the wealthier chiefs had three or four wives, but two was a much more usual ration, and a great many boys, through purely financial reasons, were complelled to embrace monogamy.

One of the European settler's duties was to give any medical assistance within his power to the boys on his farm. This in the case of one like myself whose knowledge of medicine extended to no more than the elementary precepts of first-aid, was apt to give rise to difficult and occasionally amusing situations. On Monday mornings in particular there were generally two or three sufferers from a complaint which I could only diagnose as 'Monday morning sickness', that is, disinclination to work, plus the effects of drinking too much native wine the night before. However, a dose of castor oil, together with the red medicine, usually put them right. This red medicine, which had a wonderful reputation on the farm, was – be it whispered! – merely the tiniest fragment of potassium permanganate, which I used to put in everything from quinine to Epsom Salts, and which, because of its red colour and somewhat unpleasant taste, was considered by the native to be wonderful stuff. Sometimes, of course, there would be more serious cases, burns and ulcers, which I would bandage as best I could, knowing well that the patient would probably remove the bandages as soon as he was safely out of sight.

I remember a boy coming up one day and asking to borrow a pair of scissors. He said he had lost his own, though

I knew quite well he had never had any. However, I spared his pride and merely asked him what he wanted them for. 'Oh!' he said 'I want to cut my tonsils out.' It transpired his wife was intending to carry out the operation! Needless to say, he did not get the scissors.

It was not often that in the settled area of the Colony one could gain any real idea of native life as it was lived in the Reserves, where the witch-doctors were still all-powerful and the influence of the white man was scarcely felt at all. Just occasionally, though, the primitive instinct would find voice, and old half-forgotten tribal customs make themselves felt again. Then the most incredible things might happen and a gang of contented cheerful Africans became transformed into a crowd of howling savages.

I recollect one very hot afternoon in June. It was after three o'clock and all work on the farm had stopped save for a couple of tractors humming away in the distance seeding the late wheat until dusk. I had developed a splitting headache through working too much in the sun, and so made up my mind to go and have a rest. Scarcely had my head touched the pillow when I was roused by a series of ear-splitting yells, which seemed to suggest that at the very least a native rising was in progress. I grabbed a gun, thought better of it, and had just put it back again when my houseboy came rushing in to say that the wa-Kikuyu headman – one Njerogi by name – wanted to speak to me. I hurried out, to be met by the most amazing sight.

All the wa-Kikuyu on the farm were there with their wives and their relations, their grandparents and their babes in arms, a total of between forty and fifty all told, arrayed in a more weird medley of costume than can have ever graced a fancy-dress ball. Bright, vivid strips of americani were combined on the women with the traditional goat-skins and the horrible coiled bead ear-rings which were their peculiar pride. The men mostly affected blankets, secured loosely by a single knot on one shoulder, bright head-dresses of cock

13

feathers and little anklets of blue monkey-skin. And with both sexes every exposed part of the body was painted and striped with all the colours of the rainbow, so that the most timid looked absolutely ferocious, and I was tempted for a moment to think that the whole scene was simply a lingering nightmare.

It soon proved real enough, and I discovered the headman Njerogi in the middle of it, wearing a particularly fine head-dress and an even more elaborate colour scheme. He greeted me quite civilly, and then, being African, proceeded to discuss the weather, the harvest, and the price of maize. It was useless to ask him to come to the point, so I listened politely until at last he said casually 'You see this dog?' – indicating a very wretched-looking little mongrel terrier that he was leading on the end of a piece of string. I replied in the affirmative. 'Well' said Njerogi, 'he's mine. I just wanted to ask you if I could kill him.' I didn't understand this at all – but, not being in an inquisitive mood, I gave him the required permission, provided he killed the dog well away from my house. They all seemed greatly elated at this – though a boy in the rear disconcerted me rather by shouting as he was almost out of earshot, 'Remember, bwana, you said we could!'

I'd just got back to my room when my houseboy, who had vanished during my conversation with Njerogi, reappeared and informed me cheerfully that now I'd done it all right, that I had just authorised a kisani, which was strictly illegal, and that in the morning the police would come to shut me up. I cursed him in several languages, and without stopping to inquire what a kisani might be, sent him post-haste to fetch Njerogi back. In a few minutes he returned with Njerogi and several others – all looking crestfallen and sullen. I demanded explanations, and presently, with the aid of my own houseboy who, being of another tribe, hated the wa-Kikuyu like poison, I succeeded in grasping the story.

It seemed that some months before somebody had stolen

two of Njerogi's goats. According to Njerogi's own account they were two of the fattest and healthiest goats that had ever been known in the district, but opinions on this point seemed to differ. Anyway, he had lost two goats and all his efforts to discover them, or (as I suspected) get substitutes, had met with no success. Accordingly, Njerogi had decided to hold a kisani or revenge. The wretched little dog was to be solemnly killed, his blood mixed with wattlebark and native wine, and as it was drunk a great curse sworn against the thief who stole the goats. And within two weeks the thief would die. 'And', declared my boy, of whom I had expected better things, 'most certainly he will die'. It occurred to me afterwards that possibly the thief was suspect already and that it was intended to poison him under the cloak of an old custom.

There was nothing for it but to forbid the kisani and dismiss the revellers, who departed unwillingly enough with a rather ludicrous air of 'We're all dressed up and nowhere to go'. In the morning I sent a chit to the nearest police outpost, asking for information about this practice and some time afterwards received a reply to the effect that kisanis are strictly illegal and could be permitted in no circumstances whatever.

The average settler in those pre-war days was too much concerned with the ravages of wild animals and locusts – not to mention the then depression in agriculture – to be concerned with the political future of the Colony. His problems were more immediate. There was nothing new in the incessant warfare which waged all over Africa between man and the animal world. Indeed for Europeans it added a zest to life, for the buck which grazed our wheat at night might give an excellent run for the hounds in the morning, and the buffalo which knocked our stoutest fences about like heavy artillery could afford a thrilling chase some time later. But locusts were in a different category. In 1929 the Colony

15

suffered from an invasion which wrought incalculable damage and cost the Government £70,000 to fight. In 1931 it was repeated on an even larger scale. From Uganda and Abyssinia and the great spaces of French Equatorial Africa vast swarms came flying south-east, swarms so dense that for days on end they resembled a pink dust-cloud. When I left the country in May of that year millions of these great pink and yellow grasshoppers had settled on the land and were busy devouring green crops everywhere. Fortunately this invasion was of mature locusts, which die as soon as they have laid, and are not nearly as avaricious as the young hoppers, who soon begin to emerge from their eggs. In this hopper stage, locusts could be fairly well dealt with by poisoning them with bran salt, which was supplied free by the Government, and in open country by driving them into long ploughed trenches.

The Africans were very fond of the insect as an article of food, and would collect quantities in sacks and petrol tins. They cooked them with salt and water, and I was assured that locusts made excellent soup.

One hot day at Mau Summit sitting on the Harvester Thresher (not yet known as Combine Harvesters) looking up through the dust I saw three huge aeroplanes in perfect formation crawling over the escarpment and heading slowly south. They were the annual training flight of Victoria transport aircraft on their way from Cairo to the Cape. Some weeks later I saw them heading northwards on the return flight to Egypt and I remember wondering what it would be really like to be up there. I was to find out sooner than I knew.

16

Chapter 2

Learning to Fly — and then the War

Soon after returning from Kenya during the beginning of the great depression when prospects of a successful Colonial agricultural career were becoming increasingly bleak, I found myself an impecunious agricultural student in the Faculty of Agriculture in The Queen's University of Belfast. My long-suffering brother Cecil had been good enough to pay my fare home when everyone in Kenya seemed to be going broke, thereby saving me from the indignity of returning as a Distressed British Subject. He was good enough also to pay my University fees out of his small stipend as a junior doctor in the Colonial Medical Service in Uganda. I hoped, after taking my degree, to return to East Africa as an Agricultural Officer in the Colonial Service but I didn't mind if I ended up in Malaya or Hong Kong.

The less said about my academic achievements during the next four years the better, although I did manage to get a General Degree in Agriculture which I have hardly ever used. I think the only useful thing that I learnt at University was something of the art of public speaking. I joined the Literific, the University Debating Society, and the first time I attempted to speak I stood up and sat down again not having managed to utter a single word. The second time was only a little better but I managed to blurt out that I agreed with the motion. However some strain of Irish obstinacy induced me to persevere. In due course as President of the Literific I had great fun participating in various inter-university debates in England and Wales on a whole variety of subjects about which I knew remarkably little. Queen's gave me a gold medal (awarded in silver, money being short) for all that.

The first year agricultural students shared many lectures with the large Medical Faculty and I soon became friendly with two young medical students who were responsible, although they didn't intend it, for my very reluctant and entirely accidental entry into the ranks of the Royal Air Force. In 1932 my brother, who was due home on leave from Uganda, had sent me some money to buy a second-hand motor car for his use and with this I purchased an elderly Lea Francis and more or less learnt how to drive it. My two friends, having heard of this, told me one day that they wanted to learn to fly at Aldergrove, near Belfast, and were proposing to join the RAF Special Reserve Squadron based there and they wanted me to join with them, or at any rate drive them up to the airfield for a test. Being rather proud of my new driving ability, although I held only a very shaky Provisional Driving Licence, I readily agreed and in due course we set out from Belfast. Trying to avoid a bus I managed to crash the car which ended up in the ditch and went on fire, the only injury being to a dog belonging to one of the students. My brother, when he heard about this, not surprisingly was unamused.

We finally got a lift to Aldergrove and were each given a flight in an Avro 504 aircraft with an open cockpit. I didn't enjoy mine at all and decided that in no way did I want to make this my career. But my two friends were greatly impressed and decided that the RAF was the life for them. The next stage was a medical exam and with great reluctance I submitted to this also, only to be failed for lack of physical condition. Both the others passed with ease but were told afterwards that, in the event of war, they would be more use as medical officers than as pilots while I, as a mere student of agriculture, was just the sort of cannon fodder that was required! This alarmed me considerably and I had of course an excellent excuse to drop the whole thing having failed my medical exam. However the streak of Irish obstinacy to which I have already referred compelled me to persist and, having told my mother that I had failed for lack of physical condition and that she must double my rations I went back again about six months later and passed the medical exam easily, finding myself soon afterwards a reluctant and rather frightened Acting Pilot Officer on Probation in No 502 (Ulster) (Bomber) Squadron of the Royal Air Force with a commission from His Majesty King George V. It was now May 1933 and I realised that I must make a serious effort to learn to fly although by no means clear how I could manage to combine this with the study of Agricultural Science which I found very different indeed from lording it over the simple African of Kenya. Flying turned out to be even more difficult than I had expected but I had a splendid instructor in Flight-Lieutenant Jackie Sender, an ex-Merchant Service Officer, who claimed that he had never yet failed a pupil and so week after week, month after month, at weekends I made my way to Aldergrove and had dual instruction. Every time I got near to the fateful moment of going solo I seemed to have an exam and when I went back again I had forgotten what little I had learnt. Finally, after I had done about twenty-five hours of instruction (which was probably a record even for Jackie Sender) I was given a flying test by the Adjutant of the Squadron, an ex-member of the Rifle Brigade with a fine 1st World War record in the RFC and the RAF, of whom we were all greatly in awe. I took off all right and having attained a safe height he throttled back the engine. I was so terrified of the man that I did absolutely nothing until he let out a frightful oath, put the nose down, opened the engine up, landed and told Jackie that in no way would I ever make a pilot. I tended to agree. Somehow or other Jackie persuaded the Commanding Officer to give me another chance and some weeks later I was given my solo test by another instructor and passed all right. After doing one or two more circuits and landings I adjourned to the Officers' Mess where a tremendous party broke out. Those were leisurely days and no one minded very much if several of us took the afternoon off. I do remember though next morning having the very worst hangover of my life (and I claim to be an authority on this subject) having bought champagne, which I could in no way afford, for everyone in sight. So relieved were the permanent staff at having finally got me airborne alone and down again in one piece that I was gladly excused duties indefinitely even though it had taken me over twenty-seven hours to go solo and practically a year to do it, which probably constitute the only two records I shall ever hold in my whole life. I can still remember the horror of waking up in my small room in the Mess next morning with a splitting headache, watching the room going round and round and wondering why three coloured and decorated balloons shaped like an enormous penis were dangling over my head!

Flying got a little easier from then on until one day attempting to do a slow roll over Lough Neagh, which adjoins the airfield, I managed whilst inverted to knock both the switches off. Not surprisingly the engine ceased to function so, as I was at a fairly safe height, I decided to try to re-start it by diving towards the airfield. Nothing of course happened but the sound of this somewhat unorthodox manoeuvre alerted most of the staff, and my instructor was the first to greet me without great surprise when I managed to achieve a fast downwind landing with the aircraft still in one piece. Various rude pictures appeared after that on the instructional blackboard of a large thumb and a couple of even larger switches, but since no real damage had been done except to my own pride I was fairly readily forgiven.

502 Squadron was one of five Special Reserve Squadrons which were quite different from those in the pre-war Auxiliary Airforce. In the Special Reserve Squadrons there was one Regular Flight and one Special Reserve Flight. The Squadron was commanded by a Regular Wing Commander, in most of my time at Aldergrove by a distinguished 1st World War pilot John Russell with a DSO. The Regular Flight had a Squadron Leader as the Flight Commander and the Reserve Flight was commanded by a Flying Instructor with another Flying Instructor as his deputy. The pilot trainees were mostly local farmers, university students and businessmen. When in due course we graduated from Avros onto the much larger twin-engined Vickers Virginias our crews of four or five came from every walk of life. The aircraft itself was a development of the Vickers Victoria and like all its contemporaries did of course have an open cockpit. It cruised at about seventy-five knots and stalled at about fifty-five. Absolutely flat out with its two Napier Lion engines it would reach about eighty or eighty-five knots and even in those days this was considered pretty slow going.

Once a year the whole squadron, with the single engined Avros included, would take off from Aldergrove to fly down to Manston in Kent for the annual Practice Camp. The journey would take anything up to ten or eleven hours with a refuelling at Sealand in Cheshire, and a second one at Castle Bromwich near Birmingham. The whole Belfast Press would turn out to see us taking off and when we reached the Antrim coast we would send a signal saying 'crossing commenced' and another one later saying 'halfway across' and then finally, on reaching the Scottish coast, we would announce that the crossing was completed. It was rather like flying the Atlantic or so it seemed to us. Arrived finally at Manston we took part with other squadrons in the early Air Defence of Great Britain Exercises, the fighters of the day –

Harts and Hinds and Furies – practising interception, with the searchlights and anti-aircraft guns having useful training too. We were quite remarkably inexperienced but we worked hard and flew hard as well as savouring the night spots of Ramsgate and Margate. One summer night, having got lost through cloud over Coventry whilst flying as Captain, I force-landed at an Imperial Airways emergency landing ground at Penshurst in Kent which had fortunately illuminated its flare path for the duration of the annual Air Defence Exercises. Coming in to land I decided to ignite one of four magnesium flares which we carried on the wings but, overshooting a little, my starboard wing tip, on which the flare was burning brightly, hit a pyrotechnic shed and ignited the contents. The resulting Brock's benefit was memorable, Very lights and flares of all sorts going off in every direction. In due course the airfield caretaker emerged through the smoke and very kindly fixed accommodation for my crew and for myself. Next day one of the Regular Officers flew down with a fitter and rigger from Manston and the aircraft was quite readily repaired being much less damaged than we had feared. In the meantime we had passed the time drinking cider in the local pub.

In those days our Commanding Officer encouraged us to get airborne as much as possible and once we were considered reasonably competent there were very few restrictions placed on us. There was a certain tendency to treat the squadron like a flying club but the practice that we young pilots got did teach us something about navigation and meteorology, and perhaps most importantly, the considerable limitations of both ourselves and of our aircraft. Our Air Officer Commanding, Air Commodore MacNeece Foster (affectionately known as 'Snoos'), was very fond of 502. As he often stayed in Donegal on occasions when he was visiting Aldergrove we would sometimes fly our aircraft and land on the hard beach at Magilligan in County Londonderry while the AOC would come across

Lough Swilly by boat from the Free State. After a picnic we would fly him back to Aldergrove. Sometimes we would go to another beach at Tyrella in County Down but on at least one occasion the aircraft got stuck and we had the greatest difficulty in digging it out before the tide came in. Air Commodore Foster was a highly distinguished World War I pilot and he was a man of tremendous courage and enthusiasm. Although he was based in England he knew all our names and took a great interest in our careers. When any of us had gone solo he was apt suddenly to appear and, to the considerable alarm of our Flying Instructors, demand to be taken up by the new pilot. I remember one occasion very vividly when three of us had managed to qualify in what was called our passenger-carrying test, which meant that you persuaded some other equally junior officer to fly with you in return for a great deal of beer afterwards. Once you had carried one passenger you were considered competent to carry anyone else and the AOC, who knew all this, would demand to know if we had passed our passenger-carrying test so that he could fly with us. On this occasion at a Guest Night in the Mess he discovered that we three had passed our tests quite recently and demanded to fly with us next day. We were all immediately sent to bed by our Flight Commander. In the morning, since my own condition was palpably worse than that of both the other officers I was detailed to be the last one to get the great man airborne. I managed to achieve this and all went well until the Air Commodore asked me to fly him to various places in Northern Ireland, many of which I knew quite well but had the greatest difficulty finding on a map whilst at the same time endeavouring to control the aircraft and maintain a semblance of coherent conversation with the AOC through the very primitive inter-communication system that we had at that time. Finally, navigating with the aid of the railway and a fleeting glimpse of Lough Neagh through very broken cloud, I succeeded in returning to base and achieved a spectacular landing touching down in the middle of the grass airfield and ending up practically at the hangar doors! The AOC didn't look half as shaken as I felt and my ever patient instructor said to me kindly that perhaps it would have been better if I had landed a little further down!

The return journey from my last summer practice camp at Manston was uncomfortably eventful. On crossing the Solway Firth whilst flying as Second Pilot in a Virginia the starboard engine started banging loudly and the pilot, who fortunately was an experienced regular officer, decided that if we could get across the water we must force land immediately. This he did skilfully in a soft boggy field but of course the aircraft went up on its nose. Fortunately it didn't catch fire and from around Whauphill in Lanarkshire a number of small dark men approached, righted the aircraft, and plied us with what seemed to be a mixture of poteen and whisky and which did us a power of good. I never heard what happened to the aircraft.

In those days we were not only very young but also very gullible and we Reserve Officers held the Regulars in enormous respect and would believe almost anything they told us. There was a conspiracy amongst them to persuade us that lurking in the heavens there was a thing called a Sky Hook and that under certain rather rare conditions of weather, due to a temperature inversion or something of the kind, we could quite easily find ourselves stuck upstairs in an aeroplane with no possibility of coming down. I am not quite sure that we ever entirely believed this but we were always warned on take-off to be very careful because there could be sky-hooks around today!

Great advantage was taken of my too obvious credulity. At one squadron summer dance when the Commanding Officer, who had a bad stutter, was present I was solemnly told that on no account must I attempt to sit out any of the dances with my partner outside the Mess and that the CO took an exceedingly dim view of anyone who did so. I was

24

assured that during the evening at some time a whistle would be blown and that all officers were required immediately to report to the Commanding Officer. After a few dances since all seemed quiet I took my girl out for a stroll and when I returned a little later a Regular Officer at the door told me that the whistle had blown and that I was to report to the CO at once. Greatly alarmed I rushed up to the Wing Commander who was dancing at the time and stammered out that I was sorry that I had missed the whistle! He stopped in his tracks amidst gales of laughter from all around the room and asked me w-w-hat the-the h-hell I was talking about? . . . !

At one time we used to practise trying to land as near as possible to the hedge on the approach road which skirted the airfield but this was discouraged when, inevitably, somebody landed *on* the road. In spite of our somewhat lighthearted approach to aviation several of my contemporaries of those early happy days had most distinguished wartime careers in the Royal Air Force. An old school friend of mine who joined the squadron about the same time as I did, one Bill Gardner, ended up as an Air Commodore with a CB, an OBE, a DFC and bar, and an AFC and managed to survive the war.

Having gained my degree and having some little time to wait for the possibility of a Colonial Agricultural Scholarship which would have entailed a year studying at Cambridge and another one at the School of Tropical Agriculture in Trinidad, I took a temporary job on a pig farm in County Tyrone. This farm was in a large estate owned by a soap manufacturer who had somewhat unconventional ideas about pig rearing and in particular about developing a pedigree herd. He had engaged a good Farm Manager but as the boss, who was a great nature lover, believed in allowing his pedigree pigs the freedom of a large wooded estate it was extremely difficult for the manager to achieve results. At this time the owner decided that pig recording was the 'in' thing and as I had just come down from Queen's I was engaged to set up a full scale pig recording system with an enormous number of very complicated forms to fill up. This entailed considerable difficulties partly because the farm manager, who knew far more about pigs than I did was inclined to be pretty sceptical about the whole business and partly because it turned out to be almost impossible to capture the animals to weigh them, let alone feed them regularly, and after a while it became pretty apparent that there really was no useful job that I could do. Realising then that war was becoming increasingly likely and because by now I was beginning rather to enjoy flying I decided to apply for a Regular Commission in the Royal Air Force.

Having received my commission in March 1936 from Edward VIII 'In the first year of our Reign' I was posted to Upper Heyford in Oxfordshire. This was a permanent pre-war station and the discipline was strict. I was posted to No 215 Squadron which was still in the course of formation having been hived off from another unit at Worthy Down in Hampshire. Although I was qualified by day and night as a bomber pilot in the Special Reserve I was much annoyed at being tested all over again. Worse was to follow. At an early morning parade which the Station Commander always took, it was soon apparent that I was not very good at marching in step. The CO, who was a very smart military looking figure and a great martinet, ordered me to parade for a private drill session a quarter of an hour before anybody else, at the mercy of an elderly Flight Sergeant who I got the impression didn't care very much for officers in general and saw no special reason to make an exception for me. I had to admit that this private tuition did not come altogether as a surprise. Some years before when a very junior member of the Campbell College Officers' Training Corps I had had the same trouble and on one occasion whilst on a route march I tried to join in the singing of 'Tipperary'. A message came back from the leader of our very fine Pipe and Bugle Band, of which we were inordinately proud, saying 'For God's sake tell Rainsford to shut up, even the Band is now out of step!' I felt too that my own father would have approved since he himself on leaving Trinity had been trained as a young cadet on foot at the old RIC Depot in the Phoenix Park in Dublin and on horseback at The Curragh. All these indignities came to an end fairly soon as the Squadron, after six months, was moved to Driffield in the East Riding of Yorkshire. We greatly enjoyed the change. The local people were exceedingly friendly and especially the girls who used to say 'go North for a lass, go South for a man' and indeed we were welcomed absolutely everywhere. Our Station Commander, Group Captain Murlis Green, a Night Fighter Pilot of World War I, lived close to the airfield on a barge and when we young officers were invited to enjoy his quite lavish hospitality considerable restraint was required to ensure that we managed to step off on to dry land! We worked hard, flew a lot and were soon re-equipped with Ansons and the Handley Page Harrow, which was the first large modern twin-engined aircraft which any of us had flown. Thus re-equipped the Squadron went from strength to strength and we won the Minot Bombing Trophy against competition from many of the older squadrons in 1938 at Acklington in Northumberland. When we were not flying we visited the old castles at Alnwick and Warkworth and walked over the causeway to the Holy Isle of Lindisfarne. Life was good indeed.

Amongst my contemporaries at Driffield was a young Welshman, John Llewelyn Rhys. A good pilot and a keen party man, at night I would hear his typewriter banging away until I went to sleep. He wrote three books 'The Flying Shadow', 'England Is My Village' and 'The World Owes Me A Living', and he married a rising novelist Jane Oliver shortly before he was killed in a flying accident at Harwell early on in the war. His books had the real flavour of pre-war flying, the sheer fun of being airborne and the joy of being young and alive. These were the days of little flying clubs and air circuses, with pretty girls only too willing to fly with you and the knowledge that perhaps, if you waived the five shilling charge for a joy ride, they might show their appreciation afterwards ... !

One episode at Driffield revived memories of the difficulties I had experienced in learning to fly at Aldergrove. When I was on leave in Belfast a fire had broken out in the wooden hutted living quarters of the Officers' Mess which destroyed many officers' belongings, although not my own. On my return I was detailed to fly about a dozen of these unfortunates down to London to replenish their wardrobes. The airfield chosen was Hendon – a fairly narrow grass field with an approach over the railway line towards the hangars. On my first and second attempts to land I overshot badly and was aware as I went around once again of a certain rising interest amongst my passengers. This time I made it all right, coming to rest near the main hangar, to be greeted by the Group Captain Station Commander – one Harry K. Goode – who as a Flight Lieutenant had decided that I would never make a pilot. There was no need for him to say 'Rainsford, I presume' but I feel he felt his judgement had been vindicated!

After two years at Driffield, where the Yorkshire people had overwhelmed us with hospitality, the Squadron was posted to Honington near Bury St. Edmunds. Just before leaving Driffield some of us decided to pay a farewell visit to the pub in the town where we had been made very welcome by the landlord who, to the annoyance of his somewhat domineering wife, used to drink with us pint for pint often until after closing time. On this occasion we took him back to the Officers' Mess for a final glass or two but unfortunately almost as soon as we had decanted him from our ancient jalopy into the ante-room he fell fast asleep. Very considerately, as we thought, we carried him to bed in an empty room and forgot all about him until the next morning when all hell broke loose. The Station Commander, who knew our habits only too well, sent for several of us and told us that the landlord's wife had rung up to say that her husband who had last been seen with some young officers, presumably from his Station, was now missing. After a brief search, since we had all forgotten where we had deposited the corpse, we found the landlord fast asleep and very the little the worse for wear. Fortunately the Squadron's impending move to Suffolk saved us from more than a very severe ticking off.

At Honington No 215 Squadron, of which I was now the Adjutant, shared the airfield with No 9 Squadron which was then commanded by Wing Commander Hugh Pugh Lloyd, who was later to achieve fame as the Air Officer Commanding Malta during that Island's long drawn out siege. In the summer of 1939 we were re-equipped with Wellingtons – a fine aircraft and a great improvement on the Harrow.

The pace was quickening now; we felt the Brussels' Ball was coming to an end – that Waterloo must be coming soon. I don't think any of us particularly looked forward to war nor indeed feared it very much; our mood was one more of curiosity knowing well that some people were bound to get killed but being pretty sure that we ourselves would come through all right. War broke out on 3rd September and the Station Commander ordered a parade of all ranks. We lined up by squadrons in front of our aircraft and the Chaplain said a prayer. As air raids were expected immediately our aircraft were dispersed along the three mile tree-lined avenue leading up to Wimpole Hall, which meant taxi-ing them across a main road. Hard standings were to come later. We soon got used to the blackout and although crew training was stepped up life went on much as before. But not for long.

After two very expensive raids on the German fleet at Kiel and Wilhelmshaven, in which my own squadron was not involved, it was soon realised that training facilities for Bomber crews were really woefully inadequate. This was to have a profound effect on the future of 215 Squadron. After we had lost some of our very best crews on postings to replace casualties, it was decided that 215 should be given the task of carrying out bombing and gunnery training in safe areas over the Irish Sea. We had a fairly free hand to select our own airfield and after trying Squires' Gate, near Blackpool, and Newtownards in County Down (where the Commanding Officer and myself stayed in great comfort with the Londonderrys at Mount Stewart), we moved to Silloth in Cumberland, and then finally settled down at Jurby in the Isle of Man. This suited our CO, Wing Commander Lindsay Quine, who was a Manxman himself, very well indeed. We worked hard at Jurby and enjoyed the Isle of Man whose inhabitants got used to us very quickly indeed and, since there was a war, complained very little about the noise of our night flying. We had occasion quite frequently to drive from Ramsey at the north end of the island to Castletown at the south and whenever driving with my Commanding Officer in the Staff Car we crossed a little bridge the Wing Commander would order the driver to slow down whilst in full uniform he solemnly saluted the fairies, at the same time softly singing the little nursery rhyme 'In and out the mountain, Down the rushing glen, We daren't go a'hunting, For fear of little men'. I perforce had to follow suit feeling more foolish than I had ever done in my whole life! The driver's face in the mirror was a study to be remembered always.

After a few months at Jurby, 215 Squadron was disbanded and when some more air crew had been posted to other training units and operational squadrons the nucleus was moved to Bassingbourn, near Royston in Hertfordshire, where we formed No 11 Operational Training Unit to mate up and train bomber crews, all of whom were volunteers and had already received basic training in their respective skills as pilots, navigators, wireless operators, bomb aimers and air gunners. It was gruelling work but the spirit of these new entrants, many of whom came from Canada, Australia, New Zealand and the Colonies was quite superb. I served here for a year as Adjutant, Flight Commander and Chief Ground Instructor and in September 1940, together with others on the staff, was rewarded by being Mentioned in Dispatches.

At the end of 1940 there was a demand for Bomber crews to serve in the Middle East. Having attained the rank of Squadron Leader and anxious to see some active service, I volunteered and in February 1941 I flew a Wellington out to Malta, landing after an air raid, which had greatly damaged the airfield at Luqa, with less than half an hour's fuel in my tanks. The trip out had been an intersting one. Taking off from Stradishall, near Newmarket, at dusk on February 21st with overload tanks and very little personal kit we flew across France at about 15000 ft on a clear, starlit night. Keeping well to the west of Paris as we approached the Unoccupied Zone lights began to appear and when we reached the Mediterranean coast we could easily pick out Marseilles on one side and the bright twinkling lights of Catalonian cities on the other. They were cheerful sights after blacked out England as well as a useful position check. We flew then across the Mediterranean to the North African coast turning east just inside Tunis, and then down almost to sea level on the final leg hoping to avoid alerting the Italian fighters at Pantelleria.

A few days after arriving at Malta, there was a spectacular air raid in which most of our aircraft were damaged. My own received a direct hit through the cockpit, which fortunately I was not occupying at the time. By now I was living in Admiralty House in Valetta since the Officers' Mess at Luqa had been totally destroyed by enemy action. Admiralty House itself up till then had escaped almost unscathed. It was, of course, famous for its association with Lord Nelson and Lady Hamilton in another era and during another war. I shared a room with an Australian Wing Commander who had been there for some time and one night, being kept awake by intermittent anti-aircraft fire I asked him if the town itself was likely to be bombed. He assured me that this was extremely unlikely but almost immediately afterwards there was a most tremendous crash and dust and ashes flew everywhere. The Wing Commander and I both dived under our beds colliding in mid-air and in a little while the building was full of women and children, all of them very frightened but unfortunately none appearing to be injured at all. As the confusion began to subside a bedraggled figure crept in from the street wrapped in a blanket, accompanied by a weeping, scantily clad Maltese girl. It transpired presently that he was a young officer en route to the Middle East who had lost all his clothes through the half of the room in which they were placed being destroyed by the land mine. His lady friend had fared little better. I wondered idly if perhaps they put it all down to the fortunes of love and war . . . A few days later, the sirens once again sounding, I flew one of the few remaining Wellingtons out to El Adem and then on to Kabrit on the Suez Canal where almost at once, with the acting rank of Wing Commander, I found myself in command of No 148 Squadron. My war had really begun.

Chapter 3

Bombs on Benghazi

The airfield at Kabrit, on the west bank of the Suez Canal, was situated at the junction of the two Bitter Lakes – the end of our single runway being only a few yards from the bank of the canal. We lived in wooden huts and shared the station with an old and very distinguished bomber squadron, No 70, which had been in Egypt for some considerable time and their people were a very great assistance to newcomers like myself who knew nothing of the desert and its often treacherous ways. Kabrit was one of a number of wartime airfields built alongside the canal and was by no means an unpleasant place in which to serve. At Kabrit Point the Maltese keeper of the Suez Canal Station was well disposed and Group Captain Joe Fall, our Station Commander – a Canadian with a fine First World War record – lived there. Senior officers were allowed to use the Canal Station's little bathing beach and we were made welcome too at the French and United Services Clubs in Ismailia and Port Tewfik when transport was occasionally available. Close to Kabrit Point the Combined Training Centre practised amphibian landings across the canal in Sinai.

Morale was all important and although recreational facilities for other ranks, apart from occasional leave trips to Cairo and Alexandria, were almost non-existent it remained remarkably high. The NAAFI manager was a great help and

I was pleasantly surprised to see how resourceful the troops were in finding and making their own amusements. I think the novelty of living in the desert had a good deal to do with this and provided home mail arrived fairly regularly, which it did, I had little worry in the early days about the spirit of the squadron. There was a job to be done and we were all in it together and although discipline was not obviously relaxed, very few airmen were ever put on a charge. However, I soon had cause to realise how conservative the average Briton is about food. More often than not the Egyptian sweet potato, or yam, was sent up on the ration lorries and, although I personally preferred it to the home grown spud, it was most unpopular with the troops. For a short period even the sweet potato was unavailable and we had an issue of rice. Unfortunately this included weevils also and although our excellent cooks took great care to float them off I was greatly relieved when this issue ceased and we went back to the now much more acceptable yam.

Our job in the Heavy Bomber Force (as we then were) was to try to support the Army by cutting down the enemy's seaborne supplies and this involved bombing Benghazi Harbour almost every night. Two other Wellington Squadrons were based at Shallufa, a little way down the canal, and between us we ran what came to be known as the Mail Run. We would take off after lunch in the heat of the day with a full bomb load and fly to advanced landing grounds in the desert from where, after re-fuelling and a further briefing, we would take off again about dusk on the bombing run to Benghazi. We aimed to be over the enemy lines in darkness and to get back to our side about dawn and by the time we had landed, been de-briefed and had our breakfast, it would be almost twenty-four hours before we got back to base again.

My own squadron's main landing ground was known as LG60, although we used several others too, and was about thirty miles from the coast. We would fly up there from the

Suez Canal in khaki shorts but at night the temperature would drop very rapidly indeed and when not flying we would sleep in our tents under six blankets. At LG60 our aircraft used to land on a dried up salt lake on which at night we placed out own flare path and the enemy never found it. The terrain varied. Towards the coast it was pretty flat and at a pinch one could land almost anywhere. Here on the escarpment jagged brown rocks and huge boulders lay everywhere in a long line protecting the little Italian seaside settlements from the Libyan desert. Sandstorms — sudden, dangerous and almost unpredictable – arose without warning obscuring the flat coastal landscape in a yellow mist and clogging the air intakes on the ground and in the air. Fortunately they seldom blew far inland.

Back at Kabrit we had to be careful both on landing and taking off to look out for ships going down the Suez Canal, since our runway was pointed straight at the water's edge which, fully laden, we only just cleared. At this time the Germans were in the habit of dropping mines in the Canal at night hoping to block it by sinking some of the considerable traffic that was still passing between the Mediterranean and the Red Sea. To counter this we had at Kabrit, in a different unit, some Wellingtons with magnetic rings, which flew up and down the canal trying to detonate these mines which very often incorporated trip devices so that an aircraft could pass over them four or five times before the mine went off.

The war in the Spring of 1941 was not going too well. Benghazi, which we had taken in February, was lost again in April. We ourselves could see no end to the Mail Run and indeed there was a song which ended 'We will fly the Mail Run until we die'. Many did. My own first raid on Benghazi on June 3rd 1941 was fairly typical of others, although not without incident. We took off around dusk from our advanced landing ground, this time at Fuka, after the aircraft had been refuelled while the crew had a late supper and a last minute briefing. We were warned against being

35

shot down by our own AA at Tobruk which was still in our hands. Since surprise was impossible and even the tactical approach to Benghazi Harbour was limited by considerations of fuel and the need to get back to our side of the desert before dawn, we knew that the enemy would be waiting for us around midnight. German support for the Italians was not yet strong and we expected our reception to depend largely on whether or not anti-aircraft reinforcements had recently arrived. Night Fighter opposition was not expected. Flying on a clear night with a half moon and supported by a good New Zealand second pilot and a superb Canadian navigator, Bob Alexander from Toronto, I had no worries at all about getting lost.

We were one of the first on the target – a semi-sunken ship known as 'George' which the Italians were using as an off-loading point for ships berthed along the Cathedral Mole. The cathedral itself, from the shape of its two domes, was always known as Mae West and although our aiming points were usually very close it seems to have survived the war pretty well unscathed. As I started a steady run up to the target with only a little light multi-coloured flak coming our way, I heard the tail gunner, another New Zealander, shouting 'Break, break'. I was listening to the bomb aimer saying 'Right, right, left, left, steady' and was annoyed at the interruption until I heard the chattering of the tail Browning guns and a strong smell of cordite pervading the aircraft. We dropped our bombs somewhat hurriedly then, more or less on target, and as we turned for home the tail gunner, Sergeant Moore, announced that we had been attacked by a small formation of Italian CR 42 biplane fighters, the first of which he had shot down. I was determined that my own reactions would be a little quicker next time! We had suffered no damage ourselves but were more than a little excited and, what with this brief encounter and the coffee and caffeine tablets we consumed to keep awake on the return flight to our landing ground, I don't think any of my

36

crew got much sleep on what remained of the night.

Flying back to Kabrit next day in the early morning was a memorable experience. Taking off after a very short rest and a good breakfast we flew straight into the great red rising Egyptian sun. From about 10,000 ft one could see the curvature of the earth and after about an hour or so, as we got nearer, we glimpsed the rich green of the Nile delta. Crossing over this patchwork quilt and beginning our descent we could see fellaheen working in the fields and military convoys moving along the roads. Leaving this glimpse of an ancient civilisation behind, tired and happy, we knew that the short trip over the now familiar eastern desert strip to the canal zone would get us back in time for lunch. Dishevelled, unshaven and sand everywhere, we were debriefed quickly and headed for the Mess where, after a couple of the local Stella beers and a late lunch, we slept. This time all the other crews had come back safely; it had been quite a day.

From time to time I would fly up from base to spend a few days with our small advance party at the desert landing ground. The clear, fresh air and the blissfully cool nights were a welcome change from the sticky heat of the canal zone and many of the airmen preferred this to the semi-civilised life at Kabrit. Once or twice during slack periods we drove down to the coast for a swim. The long sandy beaches were superb and the sight of a dozen or more airmen stark naked, splashing happily like children in the warm sea, was good to witness. Although our landing ground was well inland, food and water came up regularly and sometimes Australians from around Tobruk would visit us and swap Swan beer for tinned Wall's sausages, of which we had a plentiful supply.

Although Benghazi Harbour was our principal target we were allocated other ones too. The Germans had conquered Greece in April after coming to the rescue of their Italian allies who were being rapidly defeated by the very gallant Greek army, and the RAF Heavy Bomber Force was given

37

the job of trying to disrupt supplies from Piraeus and other ports which were being shipped to Cyrenaica. It was believed that the Luftwaffe was operating from German bases in Rhodes on their occasional bombing and mine laying sorties along the Suez Canal, so we bombed these airfields too. On 12th May, flying direct from Kabrit, we attacked the small airfield of Katavia at the southern end of Rhodes. Flying at night this was not too easy to find with the chance of missing the Island altogether and ending up over Turkey. My navigator managed to locate our target all right although not everyone else was as fortunate, but although opposition was very slight we saw no effects of our bombing at all. However, some sixteen years later, when I was Air Attaché in Athens, I visited Katavia again and was surprised to find some of the tails of our 250 lb bombs being used by local villagers to grow geraniums! Swords into ploughshares indeed ...

About a week before this operation my Station Commander, Group Captain Joe Fall, told me that both the *Queen Mary* and the *Queen Elizabeth* had arrived at Suez carrying Australian and New Zealand reinforcements for the Western desert and that the commander of one of them (I have forgotten which) was a cousin of his and was also a captain in the Royal Naval Reserve. He invited him to lunch with us and afterwards I flew Captain Fall around both ships. Next day he was good enough to invite his cousin and myself on board. He told us that having disembarked the Australians and New Zealanders he was waiting to embark prisoners-of-war on the return journey, most of whom were Germans. Although these would have a strong escort he was quite determined that no chances should be taken with them as he felt that the Germans who had been captured on the Western desert were a pretty resourceful lot and were quite capable of trying to take over his ship. He said that his own crew would be very much on the alert for this and were carrying side arms also. This seemed quite a contrast from the docile Italian prisoners we had at Kabrit who performed useful tasks around the camp. Indeed, on one occasion in a minor sandstorm, I found some of them playing cards in the tent with their British guard, which was, of course, entirely against all regulations especially as the airman's rifle was lying on the ground!

Once, returning from a bombing raid, I got caught out with others by a quite unexpected and rather rare sea mist. Since visibility was very bad and I could find no sign of our landing ground, I flew along the coast towards Alexandria hoping to find somwhere to land. I could see nothing suitable and with fuel running low I turned back heading inland a little and just as my gauges showed almost zero we saw a flare path almost underneath. I put down quickly and was greeted by the Duty Officer who said that they had been getting a little worried by my being so long overdue. By sheer good luck I was back at my own landing ground!

Amongst the aircrew at Kabrit were two officers who in the course of time became great personal friends. Both were Scotsmen and although vastly different in character, they were quite fearless and their infectious enthusiasm did a lot to maintain morale when casualties were beginning to mount. 'Jock' Baird – or to give him his full title Flight Lieutenant The Honourable R A G Baird – was the son of Lord Stonehaven and had served for some years in the Gordon Highlanders before joining the RAF. A superb pilot, he came to 148 from South Africa where he had been serving as a flying instructor on the Empire Training Scheme.

Jock was a very unusual character with a strong, and sometimes excessively strong, sense of humour and an almost schoolboy liking for practical jokes. He hated pomp and ceremony, most staff officers, and anyone he thought was not genuinely trying to get on with the war. He had many stories to tell about India where he had been for a time the ADC to the Viceroy, Lord Willingdon, and had apparently tried pretty successfully to stir up the somewhat conventional social life of New Delhi in the days of the Raj. He told one about Lady Willingdon, whose preference for purple was carried to the extent of purple furnishings practically everywhere. Jock decided that to complete this pattern he would order purple lavatory paper too and had this placed in all the vice-regal conveniences. It seems that Lady Willingdon, who sent for him next day, was unamused. Another of his stories illustrated his boredom with the overheated and too orderly life of Vice-Regal Lodge. It seems that at a splendid Vice-Regal Ball Jock, who was in attendance in full uniform on His Excellency, decided to stir things up. Absenting himself briefly from the party he dressed himself as a woman and easily regained entrance. As no one recognised him or seemed at all interested, he placed cushions in the appropriate places and retired to the ladies' lavatory making loud groaning noises which soon caused help to be offered to the poor pregnant lady! Whether Jock's transfer to the RAF was in any way connected with all this I do not know but there was never a dull moment when he was around. Sometimes I had to tell him to cool it a bit as, on one occasion, when he goaded a senior army officer in Cairo telling him that it was time he saw the light and joined the RAF! But in spite of all this Jock was the most tremendous fun and his keenness for operational flying and his natural gift of leadership made him a most valued, if somewhat unconventional, member of the squadron. We were to serve together again.

The other Scot who was just beginning a remarkable career was George Mackie, a young farmer from Aberdeen who joined us from the UK as a navigator after carrying out a number of bombing raids over Europe. On the flight out to Malta his aircraft had been attacked by an enemy fighter which was duly shot down, and having completed some hair raising trips to Germany, he seemed already to have a charmed life. We flew together quite a lot – once on a long trip to bomb the oil tanks in Piraeus Harbour after the Germans had invaded Greece – and he was the life and soul of a Mess party knowing every verse of The Ball of Kerriemuir! He, too, joined me on a second tour.

In July I was confirmed in my war-time rank of Wing Commander and officially appointed in charge of 148 Squadron. Although I had assumed command of this unit in March a more senior officer, Wing Commander E C Lewis (known as 'Sparrow' Lewis) had been posted out from the UK to take over 148 soon afterwards. When he arrived I handed over to him and reverted to my basic rank of Squadron Leader and became a Flight Commander again. This had certain advantages in that I was able, relieved of much administrative responsibility, to do more operational flying and I was able to get to know my men better too. Amongst the aircrew at this time was a certain Sergeant R Todd who has since become well known as Bob Todd of the Benny Hill show. I met him again quite recently when I was invited by Thames Television to watch the *This Is Your Life* programme in which he was the surprised and delightful guest of Eammon Andrews. I was, of course, glad at last to have firm command of the squadron of which I had grown very fond, just five years since I had first received a regular commission in the Royal Air Force. Very much aware of my responsibilities I felt it was time now to take stock both of my own feelings and of the probable duration and course of the war.

I began to think about casualties. These to date in 148 had not been particularly heavy – certainly not on the scale of Bomber Command's long drawn out offensive over Germany – but they were not insignificant either. In a way I had grown used to losses. Many of my pre-war friends had been reported killed or missing already. During the summer of 1938 I had gone on a long golden holiday in the West Country with a South African, 'Joburg' Smith, who was later to become my best man, and a New Zealander, Bill

41

Williams. We had flown a lot together and were very close indeed. In 1940 Joburg was lost on a raid on Stavanger in Norway during the Nazi invasion of that country and Bill went missing later on over Germany. Their loss affected me deeply but since we were no longer in the same squadron, flying and living together as we had done for some years in Yorkshire and in Suffolk, and perhaps because of the time lag on each occasion before I heard of their loss, my grief was very private and, as it had to be, controlled. There was too much to do and too many good people dying to allow time for mourning. But I wondered why this had to happen to two such gentle happy people who had travelled from so far in a spirit of youthful adventure and whose whole lives of great promise lay ahead of them still.

As squadron commander I had to consider my responsibility to the relatives of my own crews who went missing and at the same time I could not help wondering when my own name would appear in a casualty list. At first when we lost a crew I made a practice of writing in my own handwriting to all the next-of-kin, usually five or six letters at a time. Once or twice when we lost two crews I had to write up to twelve separate letters. After a while I began to feel that my duty now must be primarily to look after the living and to ensure that the squadron operated as efficiently as possible with the maximum strength of serviceable aircraft and trained aircrew. I told my Adjutant, who knew my own style of writing very well indeed, to do all the letters for me and I would sign them. It was a hard decision to make but by this time replies were starting to come in from all over the world and I knew that I had done the right thing since there was no way I could carry on corresponding with the next-of-kin and still devote myself to the business of war.

In June we had been ordered to send a detachment of Wellingtons back to Malta to attack Italian and German airfields in Sicily and Crete as well as Axis shipping at sea. These aircraft stayed at Luqa for about three weeks completing some eighty-four sorties in nineteen days. Although these attacks were generally successful the losses of aircraft on the ground were considerable and in due course instructions were given for the detachment to be withdrawn. By this time the crews were very tired indeed.

The problem of aircrew fatigue was now beginning to worry me a lot and it was also coming to the attention of 257 Wing who were our superior authority. At this time no operational tour lengths or numbers of sorties required had ever been laid down in the Middle East. Several Egyptian based squadrons, notably No 70 at Kabrit and No 216 Bomber Transport Squadron at Heliopolis, had been in the desert for years. Flying personnel would expect to serve with them for three or four years and then, perhaps after home leave, to do another tour with the same squadron. The war, of course, altered all this but this question of aircrew fatigue had only now begun to become really important. Although no policy about this was laid down for some considerable time I and other Wellington squadron commanders were able to persuade higher authority to send some of our crews back to the UK, and this process continued very much on an ad hoc basis, largely depending upon when reinforcements were available, usually from the training schools in South Africa and Rhodesia. I began to wonder, too, how long I was likely to serve in the desert myself although I was still, by Middle East standards, almost a newcomer.

Above all I wondered about the progress of the war. The history of various Desert Campaigns in those early days has been written many times but we were hardly even spectators. Living as we did on the canal bank we were far from the army in action, although sometimes we would see the criss-cross of fire from tank battles or little spasmodic encounters flaring up and dying down against the black of the desert night. Sidi Rezegh and El Gazala are battles remembered by Eighth Army veterans but we hardly knew of these actions. We did, of course, meet soldiers on leave in

Cairo and occasionally we would take a visiting officer or a personal friend on a Mail Run trip with us. No one ever queried my authority to do this and once when I found that my first cousin, Lieutenant Colonel R B Rainsford of the 2/2nd Punjabs was doing an amphibious landing course at the Combined Training Centre at Kabrit Point, we took him twice in one night on a short raid on Derna. On another memorable occasion, a good deal later, we took Harold Denny of the *New York Times* on a Benghazi run, first making sure that although America was not at war, he knew how to handle a gun turret since I refused absolutely to carry passengers. In his report in the *New York Times* on the 9th October 1941 Harold Denny wrote, 'My airplane's captain was a typical well-bred young English and Public School and University man, member of a famous English airplane manufacturers'. This captain was Pilot Officer I D N Lawson who joined us from de Havilands and who was to survive the war and end up as an Air Marshal. We were all part, and we hoped a valuable part, of the desert campaigns of which, flying over them at night, we saw so very little but we began to wonder when the war in Libya would end. The fall of Benghazi in April had been a major shock and although Tobruk continued to resist stubbornly, from our point of view it was one more place to be avoided since, naturally enough, aircraft straying over it on the Mail Run was apt to get shot down by our own forces.

As the war spread the bomber force had another change of targets – in many ways a welcome relief from the long monotonous flights to Benghazi. In May a pro-German revolution broke out in Iraq under Rashid Ali who seized control of a great deal of that country. The small British garrison at Habbaniya, consisting mainly of airmen, put up a stout resistance but help was urgently required from the bomber force. Although my own squadron was not actually detailed to take part No 70, who were with us at Kabrit, sent a number of aircraft to bomb the Iraqis who were encircling the airfield. We in 148 lent them some aircrews and worked all night helping them to service their aircraft and, although from our squadron's point of view this was a fairly minor diversion, it was a great change for those who took part.

We were much more actively involved a month later in Syria. The German infiltration into that country, which was under control of the Vichy French, had become dangerous and Wavell, although his forces were already over-stretched, was forced to undertake an invasion of Syria which began on June 8th. The bomber squadrons, based as they were beside the Suez Canal, were well situated to give support. On July 2nd we bombed the railway station at Beirut. This was a comparatively easy trip since most of the route we were flying over the friendly territory of Palestine. Opposition over the target was minimal but my aircraft was shot at by a ship stationed a little way out from the harbour which, on reflection, we decided was probably British! On July 10th we bombed the airfield at Aleppo which was very near the Turkish border. This was a much longer trip and we were particularly anxious not to stray over Turkey which at that time was being woo-ed by both sides in the hope that she could be persuaded to join in. Our reception here was much more lively and my own aircraft was hit by anti-aircraft fire although not seriously damaged. Apart from this interlude and the earlier one in which we had been diverted to attack the Germans on the mainland of Greece and on the Island of Rhodes, the squadron continued to bomb targets in Libya. As a change from Benghazi it might be Derna or Agedabia, according to the fluctuations of war, but mostly it was the Mail Run as before.

In August we were given the task of trying to drop mines in the very narrow Corinth Canal and to bomb both the bridge across it and the sides of the canal in the hope that by blocking it we could prevent Axis ships from moving from the Aegean to the Adriatic. It was an exciting raid and on this occasion all four Wellington squadrons took part. I myself decided, since we had a moonlight night and I had a first class navigator (who was afterwards to be killed at Arnhem), that I would try a low-level approach placing the mines at the eastern entrance to the canal whilst other aircraft bombed the canal itself. We found the opening all right and, flying at about 50 ft as we started to lay our mines, coloured light flak came at us from the cliff tops, fortunately without our being hit. It was the first, and indeed the only, time that I have been shot at from above by anti-aircraft firing down at me! Our only casualty that night was a gunner in one of our other aircraft flying close behind me who was badly wounded and unfortunately died soon afterwards from gas gangrene.

As this had been one of our more successful raids and the bomber force had been receiving congratulations from Middle East Headquarters, I published the following notice in our own daily routine orders. 'The Commanding Officer wishes to place on record his appreciation of the outstandingly fine work performed by all personnel in connection with the operations on the night of the 8th/9th August. Whilst the work of all sections, without exception, was magnificent, that of the armourers in bombing up a large number of aircraft under most difficult conditions and at very short notice is particularly worthy of commendation'.

Years later in Athens some South African friends brought their yacht into Piraeus Harbour and offered my wife and me a trip to Corfu through the canal, stopping at the little port of Itea, quite near Delphi, on the way. I wished, when we set off, that I knew how long mines remained active as we must have passed very close to the spot where we had laid ours some sixteen years earlier.

In the meanwhile, although targets had changed little, quite a lot had been happening to our equipment. In the summer our Wellington Ic's with the Bristol air-cooled engines began to be changed for Wellington II's which had Rolls Royce Merlin X engines cooled by glycol. These aircraft were a good deal faster than the earlier version but occasionally would catch fire through a glycol leak. They also lacked any efficient flame damping and as night fighters began to become more active this was a serious problem which my engineer officer did his very best to solve. One of the advantages of the Wellington II was that it was a good deal faster than any of the other night bombers and we would sometimes do the Benghazi run in almost an hour less than the other Wellingtons of the bomber force. Once or twice with these new aircraft and working from a very advanced landing ground we carried out two raids on Benghazi in one night. In October and November we received four new Wellingtons specially modified to carry the first 4000 lb bombs which had just begun to arrive in the Middle East and they were promptly put to good use in attacks on Benghazi and Bardia in support of the major British offensive, Operation Crusader, which commenced on the 18th November 1941. One of the bombs which I dropped on Bardia shook my aircraft at 7000ft.

For a time the squadron was flat out and probably achieved a record amongst Middle East bomber crews by having, on one occasion, eighteen aircraft available for operations although we could only muster complete crews for seventeen. We flew then nightly supporting the British advance in Cyrenaica but although Benghazi fell to us on Christmas Eve it was to be re-taken again by Rommel about a month later. This time we concentrated on enemy supply lines and as a change from bombing targets in Benghazi town we tried placing mines in the harbour. We dropped supplies to the remnants of British forces in Greece and in Crete; we bombed Piraeus again and attempted attacks against Italian warships engaged on convoy escort in the Mediterranean. The adrenalin was flowing fast and our worries about the lack of home mail which had become irregular and the sheer boredom of living in the desert were soon forgotten.

Christmas came as a welcome break. It seemed that by mutual consent hostilities, in the air at least, were suspended for two days. We made the most if it, performing all the traditional service rites — the Officers waiting on the airmen at lunch time after Officers and NCOs had visited each others' Messes. We held a competition for the best decorated billet. Once again I marvelled at the resourcefulness of the airmen, although perhaps I shouldn't, as many of them were highly skilled technicians. I was used in the desert to good drinking mugs being made from beer bottles but here at the base, where more facilities were available, their ingenuity was quite extraordinary. After much deliberation the judges finally awarded the prize to Maintenance Flight who had decorated their billet to look like an old English pub complete with balloons, streamers, mock holly and a Christmas tree. For a while the war was forgotten.

The conduct of the various desert campaigns will be mulled over for years to come at Staff Colleges and by military historians. Many lessons needed to be learnt and perhaps they have been. It is no part of my purpose as an airman who was involved only peripherally in these ground battles to dwell on them now but the fall of Benghazi for the second time on the 26th January 1942 did have a profound effect on the morale of the squadron.

The war generally was going badly. We had lost the *Prince of Wales* and the *Repulse* in the South China Seas on the 10th December and Hong Kong fell on Christmas Day. Singapore was to follow on the 15th February and the outlook seemed pretty bleak, although we had been encouraged a little by the entry of the United States into the war after the Japanese attack on Pearl Harbour on the 7th December. American assistance up to then had, of course, been almost overt and a number of American airmen were serving with British forces. Indeed, for a while my own Adjutant in the desert had been a man from New Mexico at a time when officially the United States were not yet at war.

We were all beginning to get tired and for the first time a few applications for compassionate posting home were received although very seldom granted. Mail was arriving erratically and all ranks were beginning to be more openly concerned about their families at home, more particularly those in the squadron who had relatives living in the big cities in Britain likely to be bombed. I myself was worried about my own family which was widely dispersed. My wife was in England, my parents in Belfast, my brother separated from his children as Senior Medical Officer in the Seychelles probably for the duration of the war. I was particularly concerned about my sister, Primrose, who was married to a parson in Hong Kong and had only just escaped being captured by the Japanese through the accident of being on leave in Australia. Newly married, she lost all her possessions and until her husband eventually found a parish at Wanganui in New Zealand they had a pretty rough time, although I did not, of course, know any of this at the time. I felt that our little branch of what we liked to call the Imperial Irish was certainly living up to its name!

Although in our heart of hearts we all knew that we had a lot to be thankful for in that we were not already dead, wounded or prisoners-of-war, that didn't help a great deal. The general feeling seemed to be that we had been quite a while in the desert, had done our best but didn't seem to be getting anywhere. It was a mood, of course, that passed but there is a definite limit to anyone's courage and anyone's endurance and by January 1942 some of us felt that we were getting a little bit near it.

Looking back I think the thing that I missed most, apart from female company, was a decent library. I had brought a very few books with me from home, notably Macmillan's Golden Treasury of Irish Verse, given me by a college friend, and one or two others of the same kind. At school in Dublin, and later on in Belfast, I had been greatly influenced by the Celtic Renaissance and my appetite was insatiable for the poems of Yeats and A E Russell, the plays of Synge, O'Casey and Shaw and the gentle allegorical tales of James Stephens. How I would have loved to have been able to read The Charwoman's Daughter again! Like Wavell I longed to gather Other Men's Flowers although the gleanings in the desert were very thin indeed. Sometimes, to while away the long hours while waiting for our aircraft to return, I would try my hand at writing verse, mostly doggerel, but now and then I managed something that I thought might almost be called poetry. I found this very difficult and a weakness (if a weakness it was) that I could share with nobody for poetry to me was, and still is, a very private thing. But I still feel that to write one good poem is ample justification for our brief sojourn on earth.

In February things changed fast. A few American Liberators began to arrive in the Middle East and a squadron of them was being formed at Fayid, a little further up the Canal, under the command of a Squadron Leader Wells who had been a flight commander of mine for a while and had won a good DFC and Bar. When my own posting to the UK came through on the 3rd February, with a view to learning to fly Liberators and eventually coming back to the Middle East again, Wells was good enough to offer me a lift home on a Liberator which he was taking back to the UK with a number of senior tour expired aircrew. Rather than face the long journey by sea I accepted his offer gratefully.

Now that the die was cast and although I had no choice whatever in the matter, with the contrariness of human nature I began to wish not to go. I knew that I was tired and needed a long rest but I had grown very fond of 148 and knew its people pretty well. Apart from the officers and the NCO aircrew with whom I had flown a good deal I had managed to meet and talk to a great many of the airmen too.

I liked to wander at night into their cookhouse and see what was being prepared for the next meal, or perhaps to walk across the airfield to talk to the armourers who were bombing up aircraft and often changing their load for the umpteenth time. I had always tried to make it known, both as flight and squadron commander, that I was very happy to see anyone in any kind of trouble, and although in many cases there was very little I could do about their domestic affairs a good many of all ranks seemed to find some relief just in talking about their problems to someone else. I had begun to feel in a very real way that although I could not know even the names of all the several hundred in the squadron I was responsible for their well being and that they were, in a very special sense, my friends. I began to think of some of the good times we had had together.

In July a visiting Staff Officer from Cairo, after an excellent lunch, offered me the loan of a Lysander. It seemed that these slow flying aircraft, whose primary role had been air reconnaissance for the army, were now considered too vulnerable for use in the desert and there were quite a number of them in store. Suffering a little from my own hospitality and although my experience of flying single engine aircraft was very slight indeed, I accepted his offer gladly. When in due course this aircraft was flown down to Kabrit from the Maintenance Depot near Cairo, I was a little concerned to find that it did not have with it any instructional handbook or even a maintenance schedule. I hesitated for a while about trying to get it airborne but I reflected that I could hardly refuse to fly it now that it had been specially delivered for my use and so with the aid of a very good Flight Sergeant, a technician, I taxied it gingerly around the airfield and finally, when everything seemed in order, having disembarked my passenger, I took off only to discover what neither of us had realised that, when flying this aircraft solo, some adjustment of weight was required. I found that although the aircraft climbed very rapidly indeed it seemed to have a strong will of its own and wanted to continue to do so quite indefinitely. I had to press the stick hard forward and cut the engine before I managed to make a reasonable landing. However, when I had become a little more familiar with the Lysander it proved very useful indeed and sometimes I would fly it up to the advanced landing ground, or occasionally on short leave to Lydda in Palestine. On these latter occasions I would take someone else with me and we would collect quantities of Jaffa oranges which were lying in the untended orange groves and bring them back to base. We also managed to acquire quite a lot of decent local wine costing us about half-a-crown a bottle so when we got back to base my popularity was assured. Although the aircraft was taken away again a few months later it had done a lot to keep my own spirits up at a very busy time indeed.

There was a story going around Middle East Headquarters in that summer of 1941 which caused great amusement when it finally filtered down to the Canal Zone. It seems that a certain young officer was found naked and somewhat incoherent in a main street of Cairo early one morning. He was duly court martialled and charged with 'Conduct unbecoming to an Officer and Gentleman' and to this he pleaded 'Not Guilty' on the advice of his Defending Officer – a barrister in civil life. The accused admitted all the facts alleged by the prosecution but based his defence on a certain paragraph of King's Regulations and Air Council Instructions. It was the one which laid down that 'An Officer shall at all times be suitably attired for the sport upon which he is engaged!' If that story wasn't true it should have been.

There were happy days to remember but when a little later 'Kong' Wells phoned me to say that his aircraft was unserviceable and might be so for a while I was reminded that my fate was in other people's hands. A week later I was detailed to fly home with some two hundred other tour expired aircrew on what was known as the Takoradi Run – the four thousand mile flight across Africa by which reinforcements were arriving from the West Coast, and time expired aircrew like myself were being ferried for shipment to the UK, often by Pan American crews in Dakota aircraft. Things moved quickly then, and after two or three farewell parties in the various Messes at Kabrit I handed over the Squadron and was driven to Cairo to start the journey home. I had been away just a year; it was time now to go.

Chapter 4

Bob Boothby — Adjutant

Cairo at that time was a hive of activity but I had no time to linger amongst the flesh pots much as I would have liked to have done so. After a brief visit to Air Headquarters and a very little shopping in the local bazaar I found my way to Heliopolis to commence the journey home.

We took off in the cool of the early morning in a Pan-American Dakota with thirty or more very tired aircrew as passengers in what proved a very uncomfortable journey indeed and one that I shall remember always as one of the most tiring of my life. We sat on the sides of the aircraft on long bare metal benches and as the sun climbed into a cloudless sky it became almost unbearably hot. Since we were all already pretty weary after long tours of operations in the desert it was by no means a journey that any of us enjoyed. We flew down the Nile over ancient monuments, past Wadi Halfa and on to Khartoum in the Sudan. Next morning we were off again across Africa staging through Chad and the French equatorial territories of Central Africa until at last we reached Kano in Northern Nigeria. After night stopping there we flew on to Lagos, now feeling very weary indeed. At Apapa we waited a day or two but since no ships were available there we were ordered to fly up the coast to Freetown in Sierra Leone. We did this in a day passing over the thick tropical jungle of West Africa and landing briefly to

54

re-fuel at Monrovia, the Liberian capital. When we arrived at Freetown, and probably for security reasons, we were all embarked on a ship in the harbour which was being used as a collecting point for passengers in the still assembling convoy. Although we weren't allowed ashore it was a very welcome break.

After a few days I was detailed to sail in the *Matadian*, a small oil tanker carrying palm oil which was placed together with another tanker, the *British Hussar* which was carrying fuel oil, in the middle of the convoy. We sailed at 08.30 on February 21st and after all the ships had reached their rendez-vous we were some fifty-one vessels in all. Although a few large passenger vessels were included, the convoy consisted of mostly small, fairly elderly merchantmen mainly, though not entirely, of British origin. In this mixed company our cruising speed was down to about six knots but we soon got used to this. As I had always loved the sea I began to enjoy sailing with this great armada, protected as we were by a ring of Naval sloops and corvettes and by an occasional flying-boat from some base in West Africa. Since the ship was such a small one and I was the only passenger, I was given the one spare cabin (which also served as the ship's hospital although it showed no signs of ever having been used as such) and was made quite comfortable, although since all the crew were extremely busy I was left a great deal to my own devices. I tried to relax and to forget that an oil tanker would probably be the obvious target for a German submarine and there was no reason that I could think of why a U-boat commander should assume that we were not carrying highly inflammable fuel oil instead of our much less vulnerable cargo of palm oil, destined for Unilever in Manchester. Sometimes though, as the long journey got under way, I couldn't help wondering how many ships sailing at this slow speed were ever likely to reach home. My musings on this point were interrupted quite suddenly when I found that, after all, I had a job of work to do.

55

Within a very few days of leaving Freetown Captain Shorter and one of his officers became ill, probably with acute malaria, and for a time the Master was a very sick man indeed. In these circumstances and as there was no one else available he asked me to take my turn on the Bridge.

The watch I was given was the second dog watch from 18.00 hours to 20.00 hours. My instructions were very simple; all I had to do was to maintain station in the middle of the convoy and this was achieved by ringing down to the engine room for a couple of extra revolutions if we were falling behind and for a couple less if we were getting too close to the ship in front. The helmsman soon got used to the sight of the officer on the bridge wearing an RAF greatcoat and although we spoke very little, time, for me at any rate, passed very quickly. It was an odd experience, particularly after dark, sailing in the middle of this huge convoy on a starlit night through a phosphorescent sea. Forward we watched the glistening white wake of the tanker ahead and on either side we could just discern the outline of the other ships striving, on the whole pretty successfully, to keep station. The sea remained fairly calm though with a strong ocean swell and since the quartermaster seemed well used to sailing in close formation I had little to do and, knowing that the captain, sick as he was, would be instantly available in an emergency, there was not too much to worry about. In the RAF, on heavy bombers, we practised formation flying very little and I have to admit to always feeling very much happier if other aircraft kept well away from my own. At sea it seemed different; we had a feeling of being closely protected by all the ships around and had no wish at all to be alone. I was glad of the chance to do something useful and hoped not to disturb the captain who was struggling to get some feverish sleep in his cabin just above me on the bridge. After a few days both the Master and the sick Mate began to feel better and I was relieved of any responsibility, being rewarded from then on by a bottle of beer each day from what I suppose must have been some medical store since the ship itself was otherwise quite dry!

I had nothing more to do now but there was a great deal to think about as I watched this great convoy sailing slowly northwards and its attendant naval vessels scurrying around for their protection, sometimes to the far horizon and back again. With almost nothing to read there was a great deal of time on my hands. I knew, of course, that the captain would know where we were and would doubtless be receiving messages from the convoy's Commodore regarding what lay ahead, but I felt it was no business of mine to inquire and although I thought I heard him once saying that he had heard the Scharnhorst was about, I did not like to ask any questions, but it didn't exactly help me to sleep. By day we all wore lifejackets but I found these too uncomfortable to sleep in at night and I reckoned that in emergency, sitting as we were in the middle of the convoy, there would probably be time to put one on.

I began to think a great deal about this last year in the desert and to wonder where I could have done better although I knew I had done what I could. It was for me a unique and rewarding experience to have had wartime command of such men in an overseas theatre. I felt now that when I came back, as I expected to do with another squadron, I had learnt a good many lessons both about handling men and about the problems of desert warfare as waged at long distance from the air. I reproached myself bitterly for not having been more sensitive earlier to the very real problems of crew fatigue. One of our very best crews, whose captain had done over sixty operations, was shot down by our own ack-ack when they strayed inadvertently over Tobruk on a Mail Run trip and I felt that I should have withdrawn it from operations much earlier. The strain under which men were suffering was brought home to me vividly on another occasion when a commissioned air gunner, with a splendid flying record, demanded to go on a

57

night raid and when told by his Flight Commander that on this occasion he would not be required, manned the rear turret of a Wellington on the ground and refused to leave it although ordered to do so by his skipper, and then by the squadron adjutant. Realising that the man was on the verge of a breakdown I asked the Medical Officer to intervene but he, too, was unsuccessful. I decided then that the only thing left to do was for me to climb into the aircraft myself and try to coax him out. This proved exceedingly difficult as although he remained entirely respectful the officer refused absolutely to leave the turret, saying that it was his duty to take part in this particular operation. As he was in charge of two fully loaded Browning guns I was a little concerned about his future behaviour, but after quite a long time I managed to persuade him that he had important work to do on the ground. When he came out he was immediately taken into medical care and posted away for a very well earned rest. Perhaps because the war was still comparatively young, very little thought had been directed to this problem of crew fatigue under desert conditions – fatigue caused not only by flying strain but by separation from kith and kin. I realised that it would have to be studied much more carefully when I came back on another tour. Whilst showing every understanding of individuals who were almost cracking up, and knowing from my own experience how much people's physical and mental endurance varied, it was necessary always to remember that we were there to man the maximum number of aircraft possible with competent resolute crews for the purpose of carrying on the war and that an excessive display of sympathy could be bad both for morale and efficiency. It was a fine balance.

I knew that I myself had been extremely lucky to have emerged, physically at least, unscathed. Several incidents stood out in sharp focus. The one which perhaps was the most dramatic was an occasion when, taking off from Kabrit with a full bomb load, an overloaded lorry full of Egyptian workmen came careering across the runway in front of me just as I was about to attain flying speed and was totally committed to the take-off run with the Canal only a couple of hundred yards away. I did the only thing that seemed possible and as I saw the terrified look on the face of the lorry driver, who obviously thought that his last moment had come, I veered off the runway to starboard, much to the concern of my own crew who did not realise what was happening, and became airborne just over the canal banks. I knew that if I had carried on all the occupants of that lorry would have been killed and probably most of my own crew as well although, since it had all happened so quickly, I do not remember either at the time or immediately afterwards feeling particularly alarmed.

The other incident, which could have ended disastrously, occurred soon after taking off from base with a full bomb load en route to our advanced landing ground. On this occasion, after we had begun climbing, I noticed that the oil pressure on the starboard engine had dropped to zero. It was a hot afternoon and although we carried very little fuel, as for some reason this was plentiful at the desert landing grounds, the big bomb load meant that we were quite heavily laden. Both the oil temperature and the cylinder head pressure, which were the other critical indices, remained normal but I did not at all like the idea of flying up to the advanced landing ground with no oil pressure showing. My bomb aimer, George Mackie, who was standing beside me was quick to realise what had happened and it was obvious to both of us that I must turn back as quickly as possible to Kabrit.

As it happened in those days we had practised very little single engine flying and I had had a tragic example of this when an Australian pilot, who had lost one engine, made the mistake of turning into the feathered one and, losing control, had crashed almost in front of my office, killing all the crew. With this very much in my mind I climbed, with both engines still running, to about 4,000 feet and jettisoned all the bombs, hoping greatly that they would not go off, which I thought was quite likely with the hard rock below. Fortunately they did not and with the aircraft thus lightened I feathered the suspect engine and turned very gently to port, at the same time warning Flying Control that I was coming back on one engine a little urgently so that they would have the runway clear and the fire tender and ambulance standing by. Turning very carefully towards the airfield on one engine I managed to achieve a straight approach and landed without mishap although it was difficult on one motor to keep the Wellington on the runway.

There was nothing very special about this incident in many ways but it was good for my own confidence and, more importantly, that of my crew. I was reasonably happy by now about my own ability as a pilot, having been rated above average since July 1939 both as a pilot and a navigator by my Squadron Commander but I knew my own limitations and, since we had done so little asymmetric flying, and virtually none with a bomb load, I was relieved that the incident had ended as it had done without damage to the aircraft or anybody aboard. I was glad though when the instrument maker, whose job it was to look after that aircraft confirmed that in fact the oil pressure gauge was deficient and that there was nothing the matter with the engine itself. This had been my own opinion but I was happy to have it confirmed although I felt that in any case I had done the right thing in taking no chances and coming back to base.

As we chugged slowly northwards the weather began to cool a little and we seldom saw the welcome sight of flying boats escorting us although the ships of the Royal Navy were nearly always visible somewhere on the horizon, and now and then we would hear the explosion of their depth charges which might, of course, have been directed against submarines, or whales. We soon got used to this and were relieved that our escorts were so alert. It was an odd feeling

coming home so slowly by sea after having flown out to
Malta in one long night and I began to get awfully bored. I
read and re-read my Golden Treasury over and over again,
scribbled some more bad poetry and wondered if we were
ever going to get home. The mood of depression which had
begun to affect the whole squadron at Christmas time began
to return and I kept wondering what we had really achieved
during my year in the desert. How far had the Mail Run with
all its effort and substantial casualties really helped to win
the war? There was no way of knowing although afterwards
it was good to read the verdict of the historians who credited
us with achieving far more than we had realised at the time.
No doubt this lack of information was no one's fault because
it was impossible contemporaneously to judge the effect of
our bombing on enemy supplies and morale, and photo-
graphic reconnaissance and other intelligence sources
could only give us a very incomplete picture of what we had
in fact achieved. Years later it was possible to get a much
clearer and more objective assessment both of our strategic
objectives and of our successes and failures in this long
drawn out campaign.

In volume III of the official history of the Second World
War in the Mediterranean and Middle East, there is an
assessment of the continuous attacks on Benghazi and on the
Axis supplies across the Mediterranean to Cyrenaica and to
Egypt. The author states (on page 15), 'As regards the
enemy's supply system the principle was to attack it at vital
points from the ports of loading all the way to depots in the
forward area. The method was first to interfere mainly with
rearward points of the system and then deal with the stocks
that had been accumulated nearer to the front.... The
Wellington Squadrons of No 205 Group based in Egypt had
as their principal target the Port of Benghazi for the simple
reason that apart from a few small ports used by coastal
shipping all the enemy supplies had to be landed at either
Tripoli or Benghazi and the use of Benghazi saved a very

long haul by road from Tripoli. Accordingly the Wellingtons kept up a steadily increasing effort and during the first week of November 1941 dropped nearly two hundred tons of high explosive incendiaries in and around the harbour area. The night attacks were supplemented during the daytime by Marylands from the South African Airforce and the dislocation caused by these day and night attacks is reflected in the frequent references in enemy documents to the need for more anti-aircraft defence at Benghazi . . .

Gradually the main weight of the air attacks was shifted to points farther east, petrol stores and ammunition dumps, workshops and concentration of transport. To give some idea of the intensity from the 4th to the 13th November depots and workshops were attacked by a total of fifty-one Wellingtons and twenty-six Blenheims by night, and by eleven Marylands by day'.

The official history quotes evidence from the German side. It gives an account of a visit paid by General Von Paulus (who was afterwards captured with his whole army at Stalingrad) to the Axis forces in Cyrenaica. He is on record as having reported on the 12th May on leaving Rommel's headquarters in the desert that 'Supplies were most unsatisfactory and that the first essential is to provide for the proper defence of the sea routes to Tripoli and Benghazi and of the harbours themselves and that additional air and anti-aircraft units should be German'. It seems clear that even at this stage in the war the Germans' faith in their Italian allies was by no means unlimited! It is recorded that the Mail Run, until it ended with our third and final capture of Benghazi on the 20th November 1942, had involved some hundred and two attacks by night bombers and no less than five hundred and seventy-eight effective sorties which with our comparatively small resources meant, in the early days at least, that very little effort had really been available for anything else. With hindsight, and having regard to our available resources and our knowledge of the enemy dispositions at the time, it still seems to have been worthwhile.

Unknown to the sole passenger on the good ship *Matadian* the convoy had been having various problems of its own. It was interesting to read many years later the report of the voyage by the Commodore in charge, Vice-Admiral R A Marten, RNR, sailing in the motor vessel *Defoe*. A Greek ship, the *Rinos*, had difficulty in keeping up and then managed to get lost, finally rejoining the convoy in the middle of the night to the mixed alarm and relief of all concerned! Several of the Naval escorts, who numbered about twelve in all, were detached on various missions and soon after sailing on February 26th the two large passenger ships, the *Scythia* and the *Rangitata*, proceeded independently. The *British Hussar*, the only other tanker in the convoy, was unfortunate enough to lose a man overboard but later received great credit from the Admiral for refuelling one of the escorting ships at sea in rough weather. I knew none of these goings on at the time but perhaps the Master was aware of what was happening to the other ships around. By early March we had seen no enemy activity and although the seas still remained reasonably calm it began to get cold. It was obvious then that we were in Northern waters and I began to think that we all looked like making safe harbour after this long voyage. Sea birds were now becoming plentiful and by the middle of the month I sensed that we were off the North coast of Ireland. Our ship's original destination had been Liverpool, but just before reaching the Mersey we were ordered to proceed up the Ship Canal to Manchester to discharge our cargo of palm oil there. We arrived on St. Patrick's Day and I felt quite sorry now to be leaving *Matadian* whose Master and crew had made me so very welcome throughout the journey home. It was sad to learn many years later that in 1944 the *Matadian* had been sunk off the West Coast of Africa while sailing independently, although fortunately without any loss of life.

It was good to be home but shocks were awaiting me. I learnt that my father had died in Belfast a few days before we docked at Manchester and I had just missed his funeral. When I got to London to report to the Air Ministry I was told that the Liberator, captained by Wing Commander Wells in which I had nearly been a passenger, had flown into the Mourne Mountains towards the end of its long flight from Africa and that all on board had been killed. Air Ministry were not quite sure whether I was a passenger or not but fortunately they had not notified my next-of-kin that I was possibly missing. When I went home on leave to Belfast soon afterwards I was shown the scar near the top of Slieve Donard where the Liberator had crashed on the last leg of that tragic journey.

Long leave followed. I felt full of resentment against the war, although I never doubted that we were right to fight and that we would win in the end. It was more anger against the war itself – the awful stupid slaughter of young lives and the loss of so many of my own friends, and I hated being expected to wear uniform on leave and being hailed as a hero by well meaning friends and strangers, when I myself knew that it was only through sheer luck that I had managed to survive, and that those who hadn't would soon be forgotten.

I found it almost impossible to sleep and nightmares, from which I had often suffered as a child, began to return. I dreamt that I was lying in my little brass bound bed quite terrified of the house being blown up or burnt down by the IRA. I had read in the *Irish Times* about police stations being attacked through the gable end, and although I had no idea of what the word gable might mean, every time a board creaked or a window rattled in our old house, I knew that my last moment had come since I felt quite sure that I was sleeping in the gable end too. At that time loyalist houses were being burnt down frequently and although I knew my own family was well liked locally, that might not prevent our home being gutted 'on orders from above'.

A story I heard long afterwards was not untypical of Ireland at the time. It seems that an IRA gang arrived one evening at the Big House and announced quite politely that they had come to burn the place down. The owner, for whom this unwelcome visit was not entirely unexpected, replied that he was hunting next morning and would they please help him to save his horses? This they did willingly enough and when all the animals had been moved away he asked for help in moving his family and some of their more valuable possessions also. The night being quite young this assistance was readily given, and when everything movable had been placed on the front lawn petrol was sprayed everywhere and the house burnt down. One of the arsonists, probably with an eye to business and as the flames got a grip on the great Georgian mansion, is reported to have said to the owner, 'I suppose, sir, you'll be looking for a bed in the morning?'! That story could well be true.

Sometimes this nightmare merged into a happier dream. We were back as children covered with rugs and blankets in the well of a hired wagonette going to the annual Christmas party at Croaghan in Co. Roscommon. The older children and our parents sat outside, occasional sparks from my father's pipe causing my mother some alarm. It was a very special occasion – the great house with its classical pillars ablaze with electric light, which in those days was a rarity indeed, and a welcome change from the oil lamps and candles in our own home in Leitrim. Inside there was warmth from imported English coal (we used only turf and dreadful Leitrim coal from Arigna which consisted mainly of slates and stones) and for us it was a fairyland. Apart from good food, crackers and funny hats the great attraction was an HMV gramophone with a big horn blaring out, almost unintelligibly, music, Christmas carols, and Irish songs. We loved it and would creep away to put our noses down the

65

horn to see who was inside. Happy and tired now, driving down the long avenue to the pole road, with the carriage lamps shining on frosty bushes, we began to sleep. By the time the long moonlight shadows of the telegraph poles had begun to cross the road we were in the Land of Nod.

Perhaps these dreams – a mixture of anger and weariness, of bitter resentment and a desperate sub-conscious longing to be a boy again in Ireland – acted as a kind of catharsis. I would wake up, my face wet, utterly drained but already beginning to feel better.

I was staying then in an old timbered cottage in the heart of Kent and in the springtime it was a good place to be. My spirits began to revive as the weather improved and once again I was filled with admiration for the courage and uncomplaining fortitude and humour of ordinary British people who, because I was in uniform, insisted on trying to spoil me and share what few comforts they had. I realised again that there was no better country than Britain in which to live or people I could be more proud to serve. When my next posting came I felt ready to go to war again.

It was decided by some higher authority that after all I should not be converted on Liberators to return to the desert, possibly because I had already done a good deal of operational flying and the policy had now been adopted that time expired aircrew should be employed for a tour on instructor duties to help to convert to bombers the large reinforcements coming in from Flying Training Schools in North America and Africa. With this in mind I was sent on a course to learn to fly the Armstrong Whitworth Whitley – a twin engine bomber which had done yeoman service early on in the war, including dropping leaflets over Germany and mines in the North Sea, but now coming towards the end of its useful life in service. As soon as I had completed this course I was posted to command the RAF station at Molesworth, near Huntingdon, which is now, of course, an American Cruise Base. Although I was still only a Wing

Commander the responsibility of running a station, as opposed to a single squadron, was an interesting challenge and I had begun to enjoy it when once again, after only a few weeks in command, I was posted – this time as Chief Instructor – to a bomber Operational Training Unit at North Luffenham in Rutland equipped with Wellingtons.

This suited me well enough. I knew, and liked, the Wellington so flying was no great problem and in any case as Chief Instructor I was not expected to do much myself although we were under great pressure to turn out as many well trained bomber crews as quickly as possible. After a few months there, although we were still only a training unit, we were required to send some crews on the first of the big Thousand Bomber Raids on Cologne. This attack made history and was a tremendous success, and although we sent only a few aircraft, crewed by a mixture of instructors and senior pupils, it did a lot too for our own morale knowing that we really could hit the Germans hard where it most hurt. This raid gave many of us who took part their first real glimpse of war, and it impressed the whole station, living as we were in the depth of the English countryside, with the reality and the urgency of our task.

Soon after my arrival at North Luffenham, where I was in charge of the Training Wing of this big station, my new Training Wing Adjutant was posted from No 9 Squadron at Honington, where I had been when the war started. He was Flight Lieutenant Robert Boothby, MP, and in time we became very great friends. Some account of his RAF days is given in Lord Boothby's recently published autobiography – *Boothby, the Autobiography of a Rebel*. Like many of the administrative officers who joined in wartime from civil life, Bob Boothby was a breath of fresh air and his tales of parliamentary life and his ready sense of humour combined to make our association a very happy one indeed.

Bob was, and is, one of the kindest men I have ever met. On one occasion when things were a little slack he asked me if I would like to go and spend a weekend with him in Edinburgh. I agreed readily and since the Station Commander – another Irishman, Group Captain Rudolf Taafe – was willing to let us both go, Bob duly booked tickets for us on the main line to the North. When we got on the train it appeared that my Adjutant, as a Member of Parliament, had the privilege of having a sleeping berth, which was a luxury in those days, while I, as a mere Wing Commander, was, of course, expected to travel hard arsed. This did not please Bob at all and when we had got on the train he insisted that in no circumstances should I, as his senior officer, be allowed to sit up while he languished in a bed. We discussed this weighty matter at some length and when we had reached a complete impasse Bob from somewhere or other produced a bottle of superb malt whisky which was a very great treat in those somewhat spartan times. We had a long drink of that and wished each other excellent health, and then we had another one, and I have to confess that my memory of the rest of that night is a little hazy but to the best of my recollection we shared the parliamentary berth in turns until we reached our destination, and we managed to arrive in Edinburgh in remarkably good shape. During a really memorable weekend Bob's mother, Lady Boothby, made us very welcome indeed in their lovely home at Murrayfield near the rugby-football ground. One of the highlights of my visit was a lunch in the Edinburgh Golf Club on grilled Tay salmon. That meal in the middle of wartime was one of the best that I can ever remember. The whole weekend was typical of Bob's warmth and generosity and it made a very welcome break indeed.

I have another memory, too, of Bob as adjutant. Once, when we were working under considerable pressure and training reports were a little behind, I turned to him somewhat crossly and said, 'Bob, the trouble with you is that your home is in Edinburgh, your constituency is in

Aberdeen, and your heart is in the House of Commons'. Bob replied with that utterly disarming smile of his, 'Sir, I couldn't have put it better myself!' There was nothing more to be said and I wasn't at all surprised when a little later Bob decided that after all his real work in wartime lay in Parliament and I in no way disagreed, but we all missed him a great deal, and I have never known anyone from a political background who fitted so happily and so readily into Service life. Ours was a happy relationship and sometimes now when I call at his London flat he tells his delightful wife, Wanda, to pour his Commanding Officer a drink! During subsequent years it has been a joy to follow with admiration and respect Lord Boothby's quite remarkable and very individualistic career as a parliamentarian for sixty consecutive years, and as a broadcaster and journalist.

My own time at North Luffenham ended most unfortunately. On August 25th our Maintenance Wing Commander (an ex-General Duties Officer who had been a pilot before transferring to the Technical Branch) asked me to teach him to fly a Wellington. I assured him that this would give me great pleasure and we did a few circuits and landings together. Just before changing seats to let him fly the aeroplane himself, I decided to demonstrate a really perfect landing. Unfortunately I forgot to lower the undercarriage and in the final approach ignored the warning signals in the cockpit. Just as I was about to touch down Flying Control called up rather urgently but as I was concentrating on the landing I switched off the microphone and only realised what had happened when there was a slight crunching sound underneath the aircraft and the fire tender drew up on one side and the ambulance on the other. The landing itself on grass, sine undercarriage, had been a good one and the aircraft was very little damaged, but as I was the Chief Instructor and an experienced Wellington pilot, it was more than a little embarrassing, particularly as at that time we were under great pressure from Bomber Command to reduce the number of flying accidents which were having serious effects both on the supply of aircraft to the front line and on the availability of crews. When I went to tell my Station Commander, he realised at once that I was pretty ashamed and was good enough to say that since his two senior officers had been involved in the accident, he rather wished he had been in the aircraft himself! Although I should have had a red endorsement in my log book for gross carelessness, I was saved from this by the Group Captain saying that I was still under considerable strain and had done a pretty good job. The fact that eminent test pilots had been known to do the same thing was little consolation and shortly afterwards I was posted as a student to the wartime Staff College at Bulstrode near Gerrards Cross. I was by now a very chastened officer indeed.

Chapter 5

Happy Valley by Night

The peace time courses at the RAF Staff College at Andover, which had lasted a full year, were discontinued soon after the outbreak of war but by now had been reinstated in a big country house in the Chilterns. The students lived mostly in huts in the grounds of the estate although a few married ones who elected to live out managed to find accommodation locally.

The Staff College in wartime seemed a bit like being in the last term of school or in the final year at university, working frantically for exams and hoping to get a decent degree despite missed lectures and much academic neglect. We were all pupils again, very keen to get our Staff College qualification and extremely aware of the pressures of life and war since we were expected to complete most of a year's course in three months. Our Commandant at the time was Air Marshal Sir Roderick Hill, a very eminent airman indeed who was both an engineer and a pilot and would have made an excellent Oxford don. He had a fine academic mind but some of his thoughts on higher strategy, expressed in a language that few of us understood, were far above our heads. The Assistant Commandant Air Commodore Aubrey Ellwood (who later became Commander in Chief of Bomber Command) was extremely fond of music. Living in this somewhat cloistered and rarified atmosphere some of us were convinced that if we didn't attend recitals by some group we misnamed The Gorilla Quartet on Sunday afternoons we were unlikely to pass. We had other things in mind.

The course itself was an interesting and intensive one aimed at making us competent staff officers. Amongst the students was Wing Commander Peter Townsend who, after a tour in Fighter Command, received his DSO soon after the course started and threw a considerable party accordingly. Another eminent fighter pilot was a New Zealander, Squadron Leader Alan Deere, who had made a great name for himself in the Battle of Britain and after retiring as an Air Commodore headed the RAF Sports Board. He was to do me a very good turn in years to come.

As a change from the heavy load of paperwork we found many of the lectures extremely interesting. One of these was given by General Ira C Eaker whose growing US Eighth Air Force was now beginning to operate over occupied France to gain experience before joining in the bomber offensive against Germany. He paid a warm tribute to Air Marshal Sir Arthur Harris with whom he was now on terms of personal friendship and expressed particular appreciation of the help being given by the RAF in the supply of ground equipment which was often in very short supply. This was a much appreciated gesture that at many times and in many theatres the Americans were more than happy to reciprocate. Another most distinguished visitor was Air Chief Marshal Sir Charles Portal who was then Chief of the Air Staff. He gave us a brief and rather stern lecture on the importance of staff work and told us that if some of us felt that as staff officers we had little chance to die gloriously for our country in battle he assured us that he was quite prepared, on his own staff, to work us to death and replace us with students from the next course, and he seemed to mean every word of it.

After three gruelling months at Bulstrode I was posted in

January to the staff of No 3 Bomber Group near Newmarket with the mystic symbol ws (wartime staff) after my name.

No 3 Group headquarters in 1943 was situated in a country house at Exning which belonged to a peer who, it was said, having moved to the West country during the war, had been unlucky enough to have been killed by a bomb soon after he got there. In beautiful surroundings and with a lovely garden it was in all respects a very comfortable and pleasant place in which to work. For a little while many of the staff were able to return to the domestic life which had been interrupted already so often during the war and I was lucky enough to find a billet in Newmarket itself. Our work at 3 Group was mainly helping to process orders from Bomber Command for the nightly operations which had been agreed in the morning conference on the secret scrambler telephone between the different Group Headquarters and Bomber Harris and his staff at High Wycombe. We did of course make a point of visiting the operational stations very frequently but were not expected to take part in bombing raids ourselves.

The expansion of the Bomber Force was now well under way and targets were becoming more varied and further afield. On the night of February 3rd in 1943 over 250 aircraft attacked Hamburg and on the next night, although No 3 Group was not involved, about 200 made the long flight to attack industrial centres at Turin – the Fiat works being badly damaged. Some 243 aircraft, including many from 3 Group, were involved in an attack on Cologne on the 28th February and 409 bombers took part in a very successful raid on the U-boat base at Saint Nazaire on February 28th. In March, Berlin was attacked twice and Munich and Nuremberg also, this latter town suffering very heavy damage to the big Siemens Factory in which engines were being manufactured for both submarines and tanks. By April raids by about 500 aircraft had become commonplace and on the night of the 14th of that month 462 bombers did heavy damage to the ball bearing and precision instrument factories in Stuttgart. The pattern continued with ever bigger attacks and on the 28th of April no less than 593 mines were laid in the biggest mine laying operation of the war so far around Belgian ports and Danish islands. As usual losses on this type of operation were quite small. By May, as the nights were getting shorter, the main effort of Bomber Command was devoted to attacking the Ruhr and what has become known as the Battle of the Ruhr was launched with a raid by some 572 aircraft on the big industrial city of Duisburg. This attack in good weather succeeded in inflicting extensive damage on marshalling yards and factories, but the German night fighters too were very active and we lost some 34 aircraft missing and another three destroyed.

No 3 Group at that time was equipped with the Stirling Bomber, a large heavy four engined aircraft built by Shorts at Rochester and in Belfast, and in many ways a very sturdy machine indeed. Being built by ex-carriage makers it was an exceptionally comfortable and well laid out aircraft but unfortunately it rapidly became too heavy for its engines as more equipment, and in particular armour plating was added, and after a while it had difficulty in climbing above 12,000 or 13,000 feet with a full bomb load, whereas the other newer aircraft, the Lancasters and the Halifaxes which were all coming on stream then, were able to reach some 7000 feet or so higher. As a result of this the Stirlings being on their own suffered extremely heavy casualties and were due to be replaced as soon as possible. Our one Lancaster squadron in the Group at that time was equipped with the Lancaster II which had Hercules air cooled engines made by Bristol's, as opposed to the standard Lancaster with the Rolls Royce Merlins. They were being built as a precaution in case the Rolls Royce factory should be destroyed, and on the whole the versatile Lancaster performed very well with this alternative engine.

At the end of April 1943, after about four months on the staff, I was asked if I would like to take command of this Lancaster squadron. There wasn't too much choice as I knew my time had about come around to do another tour of operations. The last few months had been a welcome change and I was beginning to feel rested. My first daughter Josephine had been born in February and as I prepared to go to war again I wondered if she was ever likely to be able to get to know her father. But, as always, when I was posted to learn to fly the Lancaster at East Wretham – a grass airfield near Thetford in Norfolk – such gloomy thoughts disappeared. There was much to learn and much to do, and such good people to do it with.

Our base at East Wretham was on the edge of a wood and would have been a difficult place for the enemy to find. Perhaps because the Lancaster II had a particularly good take-off we operated from a grass airfield and were quite possibly the only Lancaster squadron ever to have done this. The aircraft itself was a delight to fly and in many ways it reminded me of the Avro Anson which I had flown a good deal at Driffield, but perhaps as they were both built by the same company this was not very surprising. The Lancaster could maintain height easily on three engines and without a bomb load readily enough on two, especially if they were on opposite wings. It was easy enough to fly although being used to only two throttles on take-off, and being somewhat clumsy, I found handling four at a time was a little more difficult, but I soon got the knack of it and with a bigger crew and a Flight Engineer to hold the throttles open and to raise and lower flaps as necessary it was not a difficult machine to handle. It was not easy however with a full bomb load to climb above about 19,000 ft, whereas the standard Lancaster with the Rolls Royce Merlins would usually get to 21,000 ft without much trouble, and height over the enemy searchlight zone was of great importance. It took me only a week or two to be reasonably competent on this new type which was well on the way to becoming the standard, as well as by far the best heavy bomber of the allies in the European theatre of war, although the Handley Page Halifax was a clear runner-up in the night bombing role.

At East Wretham the Officers' Mess was in a big red brick house, East Wretham Hall, quite close to the airfield and we made ourselves very comfortable there. Before 115 Squadron had arrived on the scene the station had been occupied by a Czech bomber squadron and it was said that, popular as the Czechs were, some local people objected rather strongly to their habits of making love to the local girls on warm nights in the graveyard, and sometimes indeed on the tombstones themselves. I confess I thought that this was not altogether inappropriate – the alpha and the omega, the beginning and the end – although I suppose that some oriental religion with its regard for ancestor worship would have considered this rather more suitable than our local Thetford parson!

Although I was not due to take over formal command of the squadron for at least another week or two the Station Commander, Group Captain Sims, who had just vacated the command of 115, agreed to let me carry out a mining trip in the North Sea before I took over. These sorties were very useful for training new crews and when the weather was unsuitable over Germany, Bomber Command would often send a few aircraft to drop mines off the Dutch and Belgian coasts. The seas in these areas were given arboreal or horticultural names such as Deodars or Cucumbers, I can only assume because some Intelligence Officer was a keen countryman. We would be instructed to lay our mines in one of these somewhat oddly named sections of the North Sea and the area chosen for any particular night would be selected by Bomber Command, no doubt in consultation with the Navy. These sorties were fairly straightforward although flying quite low over the water at night required a good deal of concentration. Enemy fighter opposition over the sea at that time was pretty rare, but occasionally areas which had been fairly heavily mined, or in which Axis shipping had suffered considerable losses, would be protected by flak ships and these of course could be deadly. Our intelligence staff at briefing would do their best to keep us up to date but if these vessels had been moved into an area which we were mining our reception could be pretty unfriendly, as well as unexpected.

On the 21st of May, just before taking over the squadron officially, I borrowed the crew of a New Zealander, Flight Lieutenant Jim Starky, who as a Sergeant Pilot had been with me in the desert and had done a really excellent tour of operations there including, on one occasion, a long walk back to base after his aircraft had crashed many miles away with two of his crew being killed. Jim had, as I expected, a first class crew and after doing a brief air test with them I felt they were happy enough to let me skipper them on this comparatively simple trip. We set off at dusk on a fine summer evening and as we crossed the Norfolk coast a fishing boat started flashing a morse message to us. The tail gunner, who was very alert, read back to me the signal from one of the fleet of little ships saying simply 'Good Luck'! It was a heart warming message at that time and I told him to send back our thanks, although I expect we were well out of range by the time he was able to do that. I felt it was a good omen and as we flew over the North Sea towards the Frisians, where we were due to drop our mines, it seemed to augur well for my second tour. Coming down to 100 ft or so we laid our mines in the allotted area and returned without mishap, and although it had given me no real idea of the reception to be expected over the Ruhr it was at any rate a start.

A few days later I took over command of 115 and was glad that during my short conversion course on Lancaster II's at East Wretham I had already had the chance to meet a great many of their personnel. It was time once again to take stock.

I realised at once that commanding a four-engined bomber squadron at home was going to be very different indeed from my time with Wellingtons in the Western desert. For one thing the aircraft were not the same and required a larger crew and carried a much bigger bomb load. This was no great problem but I was a little surprised to find how constricted my own role of squadron commander was to be, and how relatively little independence I had as a commanding officer compared to the Middle East a couple of years earlier. The squadron itself was a much bigger one too. Instead of two flights of Wellingtons with about ten aircraft each and a few in reserve we had three flights of ten Lancasters, each commanded by a Squadron Leader, and we were expected to operate twenty or more aircraft a night. My station commander, who had been the previous CO of 115, took a very keen and rather detailed interest in the running of the unit but when he was satisfied that I could cope on my own we got on very well together. At that time the big bomber offensive was really beginning to build up and the new four-engined night bombers with their heavy bomb loads were making a great impact on German industry and morale. Although historians will argue forever about the part Bomber Command played in winning the war I have no doubt at all that it was a pretty important one, and certainly many enemy sources have since confirmed this. We ourselves in 115 had only a small part to play but it was a well defined one, and as Bomber Command developed its strength control from Headquarters tended to become much tighter.

At squadron level we received our operational orders daily from No 3 Group Headquarters at which I had been briefly a staff officer, and they in turn answered to Bomber Command at High Wycombe. Targets were laid down from above and transmitted through the various Group Headquarters to the stations, and very detailed instructions were given about the heights of bombing, routes to be followed and times on the target. This was of course done to coordinate the efforts of the various Bomber Groups concerned operating from all over East Anglia and as far north as Yorkshire. An attempt was always made both to saturate the German defences, particularly over the target, and by various diversionary tactics to mislead the rapidly growing German fighter force as to our final objectives. Very close coordination and planning was required for all this and it meant of course that we had to take-off within a very short period indeed, perhaps fifteen or twenty minutes, and we were expected to be on the target, which might be as far away as Berlin, on a time scale of under half an hour. We knew that if we got there early we would have the search lights, anti-aircraft and fighter defences largely to ourselves, and if we arrived too late and the raid was practically over we would be flying into an absolute hornets' nest. All this required very accurate planning, careful flying, and good navigation and this latter was particularly difficult on cloudy and overcast nights.

As the war went on various navigational and target finding aids were developed by the research people (whom we called the 'boffins') and some of these aids were very effective indeed, more particularly at fairly short range and on coastal targets. It was altogether a different ball game from Egypt where we simply had to bomb Benghazi, or an occasional other target, during the hours of darkness, finding our own way there and our own way back with absolute tactical freedom as to our method of attack. In the desert there was very little risk of colliding with our own aircraft, or even with enemy ones, but flying with four or five hundred, and sometimes almost a thousand, other aircraft over a target in a raid that was concentrated in perhaps an hour meant that the risk of collision whilst flying in pitch darkness without navigation or any other lights was very real. Apart from looking out for enemy fighters we all had to keep our eyes skinned for anything else in the sky that looked like crossing our path. It was all a tremendous change, and although I knew from working at Group Headquarters how different things were likely to be I had not fully realised how little independence of action a squadron commander now had in this long drawn out offensive which required the most detailed and meticulous planning. There was no scope for lone rangers here.

I knew of course that I had been fortunate in having been given command of a really good unit, the one Lancaster squadron in a Stirling group. Once again very many of my aircrew were from overseas, and we had particularly large Canadian and New Zealand elements although we had men from almost every corner of the globe including at least one American pilot who seemed to bear a charmed life because he nearly always returned with his aircraft very much the worse for wear. It was with a Canadian captain, one Squadron Leader Avent, DFC, that I undertook my first bombing raid over Germany on the 23rd of May 1943. I flew as Second Pilot to this very experienced officer, the target being Dortmund in the heart of the Ruhr Valley. We took off at about midnight with a mixed bomb load of high explosives and incendiaries and climbed as rapidly as possible, hoping to be at or near our maximum height by the time we crossed the enemy coast over Holland. The crew were well trained and, knowing each other of old, the atmosphere in the aircraft was quite relaxed although I knew that they were all thoroughly alert. As we began to get near the enemy coast the tension began to rise.

Ahead we could see great banks of searchlights probing the sky moving back and forth, and now and then lighting up little cottonwool patches of floating cloud. Getting closer I saw another aircraft looking like a tiny moth illuminated briefly by searchlights and then, as we got nearer, another bomber, this time a lot bigger, coned in brilliant light. We watched it moving and weaving and the shells bursting around it and we prayed that somehow or other it would be able to escape that malevolent light. Our own briefing had been very clear. If a searchlight moved towards your aircraft, you turned straight into it so that it passed quite quickly and, when one strayed our way on reaching the coast, Avant did just that, and after hesitating for a second the light passed on. We knew that if we had turned away from a following beam a whole clutch of others would have fastened on us at once. This was a lesson often heard in the briefing room which I now realised was based on sound experience. As we passed the searchlight zone the pilot began to weave, moving back, forth, up and down, in a gentle undulating motion. This was to give our gunners, and particularly the tail gunner, a better chance of seeing any enemy fighters who might be following us, and it gave the crew some confidence, although we all knew that the advantage was very much with the enemy if he happened to spot us since he could choose the dark side of the sky and we, being a much bigger target and illuminated by whatever light there might be, could be attacked from underneath before we even knew an enemy was about. The Luftwaffe were well aware that our wing tanks were the weak spot and if they attacked us from below with cannon fire and incendiaries they could set a Lancaster on fire with a single burst.

After about an hour over enemy territory we could see great activity ahead and as we got closer other aircraft seemed to be all around us, above and below, everywhere, and Avent had to be very alert indeed to avoid collision. Now and then a German fighter would pass across in front of us but with so much action around it was hard to see, let alone identify, all the aircraft. As we approached Dortmund the coloured flares of the Pathfinder Force were dropping around the target and we could see bombs bursting and fires beginning to take hold. In one or two areas there were already great clouds of smoke and the activity of the German defences was very apparent. Two or three burning aircraft looking rather like giant fireflies, could be seen in the sky

81

some way ahead and then, quite suddenly, a Halifax with one wing on fire passed very close to us indeed. Over to starboard we saw a single airman floating down, his white parachute illuminated intermittently by searchlights and bursting shells.

There was no question here of having to search for the target and after dropping our bombs we flew straight on over the city on which the flames had now taken hold with a huge pall of smoke rising to over 10,000 ft. Turning to port as the navigator gave us our course for home we saw fires burning almost until we reached the Dutch coast.

On our way back other aircraft were still around and our vigilance could not be relaxed although as we began to descend over the North Sea towards our base with our nose well down weaving no longer seemed necessary, but as occasional enemy intruders were known to operate over our own bomber airfields at night the air gunners had to be alert until we had actually touched down. This we did some four hours after taking off, feeling excited and relieved to be home and ready to face a very comprehensive de-briefing inquiring about the probable success of the attack, the number of enemy fighters seen, the strength of the anti-aircraft and searchlight defences and so on. We were greeted by hot coffee in the crew room served by a pretty WAAF officer, and sometimes, if the night was cold, the doctor would prescribe a little rum to go in it. Back at the mess we would have an early breakfast of bacon and eggs, a rare luxury indeed and one of the things we looked forward to on the journey home. During the flight itself we had carried, in addition to a hot drink, a tin of fruit juice each (which again was a wartime luxury) and I used to write the name of the target on each tin and kept them for a long time until some batwoman years later threw them away.

We ourselves in 115 lost no aircraft that night and for me as a passenger it had been an exciting trip and one which made me realise more than ever how important it was that every member of a crew was not only fully trained but fully alert, since we all depended on each other for the success of our mission and for our own survival. I felt that my second tour had now really begun and I knew that I had a great deal to learn. Tomorrow was a new day and looking back now I don't think any of us thought of what was happening in the embers of the burning city we had left behind, any more than the German aircrews in 1940/41 thought of the Londoners at the receiving end of the blitz. We had a job of work to do and to the best of our ability we did it. A few days later we heard the result of the raid which had been by no less than 826 aircraft, one of the biggest number employed so far. Reconnaissance reports confirmed that the main steel works had been largely destroyed, and although we lost 38 aircraft that night the attack on this major industrial city was deemed a great success.

In the spring of 1943 the strength of Bomber Command was increasing rapidly as new aircraft arrived from the factories and trained crews from Operational Training Units. The Battle of the Ruhr was reaching its height. Although we were well briefed on the great importance of destroying the armament industry of the Reich we thought little beyond tomorrow. Many of our overseas crews, and perhaps some of our own, had never heard of the Ruhr. Living in Adelaide or Saskatoon they had not thought that for a few months, or perhaps for only a few days, their lives would be changed or extinguished in the tumult of the Happy Valley skies. When that time came they were not afraid of dying because they expected it, and they would be going where their friends had already gone. A E Housman had written: 'Life to be sure is nothing much to lose, But young men think it is, and we were young' but perhaps because of the intensity of the campaign we thought only of tomorrow night. Was it to be Essen or Dusseldorf, Aachen or Wuppertal? Or did we have a night off to sleep, or drink, or make love to some generous local girl lying in the warm summer grass who was apt to let slip that her last airman friend had gone missing just two weeks ago?

The war being now well advanced the question of crew fatigue, which had worried me a good deal in the desert, had already been sorted out (at least to some degree) by Bomber Command. It was decided that aircrew on their first tour should do a maximum of thirty operations, and if they survived that they would normally do another spell instructing new crews at advanced training schools throughout the country, and sometimes overseas. A second tour might come later and would require no more than twenty sorties, making a grand total of fifty in all. As the 'chop' rate rose from three to four to five percent a night on average the prospects of surviving fifty trips for any crew were very limited indeed, but a few of those who did, with courage and optimism unbounded, volunteered for the Pathfinder Force. Two of my own friends who did that were lost on this their third tour – one with a VC.

Soon after joining 115 a very experienced crew commanded by one of my Flight Commanders went missing on the penultimate trip of its second tour and I think this made us all extremely aware of how the dice were loaded and what the odds were. None of this seemed to affect morale and even, if as sometimes happened, we lost two or three crews a night there was never any hesitation about manning the aircraft for the next operation – only the individual longing to get the whole business over as soon as possible. There was always the chance of being among the few who might get through.

I wanted to have my own crew but this posed certain problems. Squadron Commanders were not expected to have their own, partly because of their other administrative responsibilities and partly because the loss rate amongst senior officers had already been pretty high. This meant in effect that we had to either make up a scratch crew or take somebody else's and naturally enough this was not very popular with the crews concerned. They knew their own captain and his ways and they had probably survived quite a few operations together and they didn't greatly relish having a new skipper for one night. It was of course a common problem amongst the commanders of bomber squadrons and some of us resolved it one way and some another – probably most often by flying with an established crew and taking their captain as a second pilot. Although this was a little wasteful, in that all the other aircraft on a raid would carry one pilot only, it was often the best compromise.

On 29th May, feeling now thoroughly at home with the Lancaster, I felt it was time to take part as captain on a raid, the target this night being Wuppertal. I chose a good crew and took the precaution of doing a pretty full air test with them in the morning so that we were all moderately happy together before operating that night. The attack on Wuppertal, on the edge of the Ruhr, on a clear starry night proved to be very much like many other ones afterwards, and although I had some difficulty to get to operational height by the time we reached the enemy coast it went well enough, and the fires on the ground and the automatic photographs we took when we released our bombs seemed to prove that the attack had been a success. From then on I felt, having carried out three operational trips within the first few weeks of my command, that I was accepted by the squadron and I could reconcile myself more willingly to the fact that Commanding Officers by now were neither expected, nor encouraged, to carry out more than one raid themselves each month.

The results of this attack on Wuppertal by some 611 aircraft came through in a day or two from photo reconnaissance pictures and intelligence sources and it was considered to have been a success. The Pathfinder Force, which was now getting into its stride, had marked the target very accurately indeed and a large part of the city had been destroyed by fire at a cost to ourselves of some 33 aircraft missing.

For a while as the war went on we continued to bomb the Ruhr losing perhaps one or two aircraft on most nights. In June to my surprise and joy I had a telephone call from a senior officer in the Bomber Group in Yorkshire saying that Squadron Leader Jock Baird, who had been posted to a Halifax squadron, had had a row with his Squadron Commander and would like immediate posting to me at East Wretham. Knowing Jock of old from the desert days, and having a vacancy for a Flight Commander, I accepted him gladly, and being an exceptional pilot he qualified on Lancasters in a few days and carried out some very good operations over the Ruhr.

On June 21st I took another crew to Krefeld, a medium sized industrial town on the west bank of the Rhine. We had our usual bomb load of one 4000 lb 'cookie' and a lot of 30 lb and 4 lb incendiaries. The target was well marked and the attack seemed a success but after the bomb aimer had called out 'Bombs gone!' my aircraft seemed very little lighter and I could not climb to the usual safer height of about 21,000 ft, as was our normal practice whilst returning over enemy territory. I thought little of this until the bomb aimer called up again to say that the 4000 lb bomb had hung up and couldn't be released! This posed something of a problem and flying back over the North Sea I discussed it with my crew.

It seemed that no one had heard of this happening before so I got the crew in turn to try to chop it off with the emergency axe we carried. Having no success and as I was quite unsure both of the security and the present position of this very large bomb I gave everyone the option of baling out over England or staying with me whilst I tried a gentle landing on our grass airfield. They all elected to stay in. When overhead at East Wretham I told Flying Control what was happening and, as the 'cookie' if it had gone off would have done the Control Tower no good at all, I thought they took it rather well. As I started on the final approach, well aware of some tension amongst my loyal and trusting crew, the Duty Controller called out on the RT 'Don't open the bomb doors, Sir.' I replied 'You're telling *me*; I'm sitting on it!' That conversation went down in the Squadron Line Book in the morning. Once again my luck had held and the armourers confirmed next day that the seizure of the solenoid that had caused the hang up was unique in their experience.

Various sources confirmed that about half of this town had been destroyed, largely by fire, during this attack. Our losses had been some 42 aircraft largely through enemy fighters intercepting the Bomber Force in moonlight on the return journey. Six of our aircraft were damaged by our own incendiary bombs raining on them from above, and this was of course a hazard which we had grown accustomed to but it was unwelcome nevertheless and not one which could be avoided easily.

On the night of July 12th the target was Aachen and on the face of it, it was not a difficult one being well this side of the heavy enemy defences in Happy Valley. As, after the usual briefing, I was going around the aircraft to see the crews before they took off Jock asked me if I would like to fly with him that night. We were old and good friends and I was very tempted to do so, but since the rules were pretty strict that senior officers no longer took the air together unless absolutely necessary I declined and said I looked forward to seeing him in the morning.

I think that must have been one of the longest nights of my life. The trip to Aachen was quite a short one and as the aircraft returned one by one, on the whole undamaged, there was only one missing and that was the one captained by Squadron Leader R A G Baird. I thought he had probably force-landed at one of our emergency airfields on the south coast or perhaps ditched in the sea, but as hour after hour went by without news I forced myself to realise that he was missing. For a little while hope lingered on, perhaps he or some of his crew were prisoners, but hearing nothing I realised that Jock, the wild, lovely, irrepressible Scotsman, was someone I should probably see no more. I thought by now I was immune to personal sorrow and could take losses as they came but I was wrong. Jock's death shook me greatly. Years afterwards I learnt that one member of his crew, Flight Sergeant Odendaal, a South African, who was a flight engineer and about whom Jock used to make rather ribald jokes had survived as a prisoner but no one else. I felt for a while a very deep sense of bitterness and sorrow and although I had been with the squadron only for a couple of months I wondered, briefly and ashamedly, if I was going to be able to carry on. The feeling soon passed. I was proud, and I hope showed it, to be commanding such a body of men but in my heart something had died. I knew only that I must go on.

As always there was too much to do to brood. Targets were now beginning to change and for a while we gave Happy Valley a rest. On the short summer nights with darkness our main, indeed almost only, protection from the rapidly growing German fighter force, careful timing was needed in attacking Germany. It was almost daylight now when after a raid we crossed our own coast again.

On July 24th the target was Hamburg and for the first time we dropped bundles of little metal strips (code named Window) to confuse the enemy's radar. The attack was a great success and our losses that first night were quite small. It was followed up night after night by further large scale raids, and by day the United States Airforce joined in. A great fire storm was started which largely destroyed the port and the city. Trees burnt like matches, water mains and sewers were wrecked and the fire service almost totally obliterated. It was by far the most destructive attack to date by Bomber Command and word of the burning of Hamburg spread all over the Reich. Coming back from that first attack the sky was bright behind us until we were far over the North Sea. In England wisps of snow white clouds hung over valleys and sleepy Norfolk villages, and church steeples rose out of the mists of an early summer morning. I have not seen a sight more welcome and more beautiful.

On August 12th we had another change of target; this time it was Milan, the centre of the Italian armament and aircraft manufacturing industries. It was a long trip from Norfolk and near to the maximum range of the Lancaster with a full bomb load but at least it was a change. Exercising the Commanding Officer's privilege I decided to go with Jim Starky, and, although I had flown with his crew before, this time I decided to take their skipper too. I managed to persuade myself that for this long flight the luxury of having another pilot was justified. We took off earlier than usual and flew straight towards our objective without any attempt at deceiving the enemy's defences as to our intentions by our usual diversionary tactics. Crossing the French coast we flew down eastern France seeing only a few scattered searchlights to remind us that we were at war. The air was clear with only a little high cirrus cloud diffusing an almost full moon's light. At about 19,000 ft we crossed the toe of Switzerland – a country, which being neutral, we should really have avoided altogether. The Alps, snow covered and glistening in silver moonlight, lay only a few thousand feet below with Mont Blanc, a little to our right towering above them all. For a little while we forgot about the war, the whole crew taking it in turns to gaze spellbound at this quite breathtaking sight. The attack itself was almost an anti-climax although we started fires, hopefully in the right quarter of that great city. Coming back we flew a little more to the west avoiding Swiss territory but seeing Mont Blanc now from the other side, majestic and indifferent to the flickering pink and white flames over Lombardy and the waywardness of man. For me it was a relaxed and memorable trip and it was to be my last in command of 115. Perhaps on the way back we all relaxed a little too much because somewhere half way across France I remember saying to Jim Starky, who was flying the aircraft at the time, 'That Halifax is getting awfully close!' Somehow in that peaceful sky we had forgotten for the moment that hundreds of other aircraft were all around us.

Many of us knew Italians and some had Italian friends and although I had bombed their supplies often in Libya, their prisoners, who were plentiful in Egypt, seemed a decent and unwarlike lot, willing and useful doing routine tasks about the camp. I wondered for a moment if we had made any of them homeless that night. Perhaps I was not as hardened as I had tried to believe.

The raid itself was deemed by the analyzing boffins in Bomber Command to have been only moderately successful. Some damage had been done to industrial areas and residential districts had been hit over a wide area. Out of some 500 aircraft that took part we lost only 3 that night.

The war went on. On the 17th August we were briefed in very great secrecy about a raid that was going to have a tremendous effect on the future of the war. We were told that our intelligence services, both air and ground, with a great deal of help from Scandanavian underground sources, had discovered that the Germans were planning attacks by unmanned aircraft and rockets on Britain and that these were being designed and tested at a remote airfield at Peenemunde. The name was that of a small fishing village on the right bank of the river Peene and the big top secret research station was situated nearby. It was at the seaward end of a long peninsula varying in width from 15 miles to about 500 yards and being on the east coast of the peninsula it looked out over an uninterrupted stretch of Baltic completely under German control. The great expanse of water provided a safe firing range for testing missiles being secretly developed at Peenemunde which at this time had not been attacked before.

The raid that night was a big one involving a great many squadrons and it was a change from other better known, well defended, German targets. We wondered if there would be any difficulty in finding Peenemunde and hoped that, although no doubt the Pathfinders would manage to locate it all right, the whole force might achieve complete surprise. In the event, because of a brilliant diversionary raid by a small force, most of the German fighters in the neighbourhood went elsewhere although they returned towards the end of the attack and inflicted heavy losses on the last wave of bombers, who were mostly from the Canadian group based in Yorkshire. The attack was, on the whole, a success and is fully described in Martin Middlebrook's carefully researched account *The Peenemunde Raid*. By destroying much of the research station and killing many of the workmen and a few of the senior scientists it probably delayed introduction of the V2 rockets by a few months and thereby saved many British lives. The good crew that we in 115 lost that night was part of the price we paid.

Just before the raid on Milan on the 12th August the whole squadron had moved the short distance to another airfield in North Norfolk beside the delightfully named village of Little Snoring. This time we operated from a proper runway and with winter in mind it was probably a good thing to get away from the grass. As always we found local people extremely friendly and on our rare trips to the small town of Fakenham we were most cordially received. Although petrol was severely rationed the garage there always seemed to be able to find a few extra gallons for aircrew who had run out of coupons, and very often the local publican would forget to ask for money for your drink. Their closeness was very real and, whilst no one ever thought of asking where we had been or where we were attacking next, they did somehow or other seem to know about our losses and their silent sympathy, expressed in little ways, was heartening and sincere. This kind of support was a very real factor in keeping our spirits up when things got rough. During the remainder of August, and in September, I was much concerned in settling the squadron down at its new location and I was becoming increasingly aware that my time as CO was beginning to run out. On the 3rd October the following telegram was placed on my desk:

P253 3 Oct His Majesty The King On The Recommendation Of The Air Officer Commanding In Chief Has Approved The Immediate Award Of The Distinguished Flying Cross To Wing Commander Frederick Fitzpatrick Rainsford (37507).

This was followed almost immediately by some congratulatory telegrams and several phone calls, and although I was not altogether surprised I admit to feeling pleased and proud. I knew, of course, that my survival was due to the efforts of many other people, to the splendid crews I had flown with, and to the maintenance engineers and all the ground crew who had looked after our aircraft so well. I knew, too, that it was largely a matter of luck.

About this time I had begun to suffer from a severe throat infection which refused to clear up and although I stayed on commanding the squadron for a little longer and moved it once again, this time to Witchford in Cambridgeshire near Ely on the 26th November, I knew that it was almost time I handed over to someone else. The move to Witchford from Little Snoring was not without incident. We were briefed to attack Berlin that night, and as a maximum effort was required, we were told to take off from Little Snoring and after bombing Berlin to land back at our new airfield. I did, of course, send an advance party on to Witchford, and after briefing the crews on the German capital I drove down to join them at our new base. Unfortunately a patchy fog came down and although we lost no crews that night we had the greatest difficulty in getting them all down. When finally they landed at Witchford the fog became so thick that some crews were unable to find their new billets and slept wherever they could. Not many squadrons could have moved quite like that!

In December I handed over the squadron and was admitted to the RAF Hospital at Ely with acute tonsillitis. I was fortunate in that the hospital was only a few miles from Witchford and many of my friends, including George Mackie (now Lord Mackie of Benshie) who had joined me in November, came to visit me there. George kept me up to date with the news of the squadron and went on himself as a Squadron Leader to have a quite brilliant tour as a Flight Commander in a Lancaster squadron which was a very unusual thing for a navigator to do. The DSO and DFC which he duly received were well earned indeed, and I have never known a braver man.

One day in Ely Hospital whilst I was recovering from my tonsillectomy, gargling with aspirin, not able to each much, and feeling very sorry for myself, sacks of mail started arriving in the ward. It turned out that these were congratulatory messages for a young Scot, Jock Reid, who had just been awarded the Victoria Cross for a remarkable sortie with another Lancaster squadron in which, although quite badly wounded, he managed to bring the remains of his aircraft home.

Lying in bed with little to do I began to ponder again the anatomy of courage. I had seen a very few aircrew who were unable to go on any longer and had to be taken off flying because they would have endangered the whole of their crew. Of all ranks, from Squadron Leader to Sergeant and of all the different aircrew trades, they were only a tiny handful. I remembered, too, the extraordinary courage of others who, after the most fearful experiences, had carried on either to their death or to the end of their operational tours.

I thought of a Sergeant Jolly who, when we were at East Wretham, had been attacked during a raid on Cologne on the 28th of July by an enemy fighter and had the tail of his aircraft set on fire. Since the blaze could not be extinguished this had fallen off complete with the air gunner who was presumably already dead. Several members of his crew were quite badly wounded. In spite of this and with the assistance of the survivors, who in addition to attending the wounded continued to help to man the aircraft, Jolly got back to East Wretham. I was standing on the tarmac watching the aircraft coming and I noticed this Lancaster approaching and touching down very nose heavy and running almost the whole length of the airfield before the tail came down. It was an extraordinary sight with the whole of the tail turret missing and the badly wounded lying quietly inside. In spite of all this Jolly was flying with a new crew a few days later, and although he got a well earned DFM for this attack and one of his air gunners, Sergeant Hall, got a Conspicuous Gallantry Medal I felt they deserved even more.

A few days after this Jim Starky, on a raid on Mannheim, was attacked near the target by a Ju.88 which raked his aircraft with cannon fire both fore and aft. The Lancaster was badly damaged and although Jim tried hard to maintain control, feeling this was hopeless, he instructed his crew to bale out. After both his navigator and wireless operator had abandoned the aircraft Jim managed somehow or other to regain control and set course for home. A superb pilot he coaxed the crippled aircraft back to an emergency landing ground at Ford on the South coast. Jim ended the war with a DSO and a DFC and became a test pilot afterwards.

I marvelled often at the spirit of these men – volunteers to a man – who had come from all over the world to fight this seemingly endless war. I felt no share in their glory. Although I had joined the Royal Air Force entirely by accident I had stayed on gladly and willingly knowing well that war was coming but accepting that as part of the bargain and of the privilege of belonging to a service in which I was so happy and so proud. I could not claim with Yeats' Irish airman, 'A lonely impulse of delight drove to this tumult in the clouds'. I had stayed in by deliberate intent.

Christmas of 1943 was not like any other Christmas I had ever known. The squadron went on flying; George Mackie and many others continued to bring me beer and goodwill messages. Life and the war went on. Although I was longer in hospital than had been expected I knew, as the New Year dawned, that I was lucky indeed to have such friends and to have survived two operational tours.

Chapter 6

The Berlin Airlift

The worst was over. I was posted after leaving hospital to an Air Staff job again, this time to a Base Headquarters at Waterbeach, near Cambridge, which controlled three large bomber stations. One of these was Witchford where my old squadron, 115, continued to operate, and although their aircrew personnel were changing very rapidly many of my friends were still there. The appointment was not an arduous one and, being something of a night-owl by now, it was no great hardship being up at all hours checking the results of the different bomber squadrons and reporting the results back to Group Headquarters. No longer had I to wrestle with the problems of whether to put my name down for an attack on Berlin, or to try to persuade myself that the Commanding Officer was quite indispensable and that I was too valuable to lose. As a Squadron Commander I was never detailed during the whole of the war to take part in any operation and sometimes I thought it would have been better if I had.

After a year at Waterbeach on the staff of a very pleasant Air Commodore, with whom I got on excellently, I was posted to command a station in Southern Italy. Unfortunately, as I was preparing to go, I slipped and broke an ankle and found myself back again at Ely Hospital. After a week or two there I was sent to the rehabilitation centre at Loughborough and whilst there was fortunate enough to be approached by the Senior Air Staff Officer of a new Bomber Training Group, Air Commodore J L Kirby, who had been my Flight Commander before the war, with the offer of the command of a Training Station at Gamston in Nottinghamshire, with the acting rank of Group Captain. I accepted gladly and the prospect of immediate promotion and a station of my own accelerated my recovery marvellously. Complete with Brass Hat I set off in November for my new unit. Gamston turned out to be an advanced training unit for aircrew, mostly Australians, who although already basically trained were waiting to join operational squadrons. They were part of the output of the various Empire Training Schools and were a most enthusiastic lot. Once again we were back on Wellingtons, but the war was beginning to wind down.

Life at Gamston was pleasant enough and I managed to find an old rectory close to Sherwood Forest in which to live at a rent of about a pound a week, and after selling the fruit on the trees of the huge orchard for fifty pounds, I lived fairly inexpensively. My second daughter, Clodagh, was to be born there in 1946.

One early Spring morning the telephone by my bed rang and I was told that there was an immediate air raid alert. This surprised me considerably since the war was patently coming to an end and no enemy bombers had been as far north to my knowledge for quite a long time. However, as there was no doubt about the urgency of the message we blew the station siren and scrambled into our air raid shelters. In a little while I heard the unmistakable sound of a doodlebug coming over and, shortly afterwards, the All Clear was given. It turned out that the Germans were making what was probably their final raid with the V1 on Britain and were launching these from Heinkel 111 aircraft over the North Sea. They were probably aimed at industrial targets in Northern England and the very few which came down in Yorkshire inflicted only minor damage.

When the war in Europe came to an end on May 8th, I paraded the whole station. Fearing that celebrations might well get out of hand, and knowing that we might be there for quite a few months yet, I was particularly anxious to avoid any trouble, and especially having any part of the camp burnt down in a fit of uninhibited rejoicing. I told everyone that whilst essential services would be maintained anyone who wanted to disappear for the next forty-eight hours might do so without a pass or any further authority but after two days I expected them back. They took it extremely well and although quite a number elected to stay on the camp the majority disappeared quite quickly – I knew not whither. I felt that this was the right thing to do and a few days later I told the station on our morning parade that I would do my very best to accelerate the return of overseas aircrew and try to speed up consideration of any compassionate cases for early demobilisation. As the Japanese war was still continuing there was, of course, no question of a complete stand down. For a little while we continued flying as usual and life went on much as before.

A month after the war in Europe ended I was posted again, this time to Bramcote, near Nuneaton, to command another Operational Training Unit. After some five months there I was moved on to Desborough, near Market Harborough, in charge of a Transport Conversion Unit equipped with American Dakota aircraft. With VJ Day behind us now, the emphasis was on repatriating our prisoners-of-war from the Far East but after about six months at Desborough I was assigned to the staff of Headquarters Transport Command at Bushey Park near London, reverting to the rank of Wing Commander. At this time I had not yet received a Permanent Commission in the RAF so, after a little while, with the future so uncertain, I succeeded in obtaining an appointment on the training staff of the Ministry of Civil Aviation, resigning at my own request from the RAF.

I became a Civil Servant, for the first time, in October 1946. In this capacity I was sent out as one of the British representatives to set up the Provisional International Civil Aviation Organisation in Montreal, which afterwards became ICAO. The flight out by Constellation took nearly four days owing to bad weather, with a long and uninhibited stop at Shannon Airport where we all got to know each other very well, but we were pretty late in reaching Montreal.

To my surprise when I got there I was appointed Secretary of a Medical Committee which was discussing the standards to be laid down for the different categories of civil aircrew in the post-war era. It was a rewarding experience as the Committee, most of whom were specialists of one sort or another, discussed at length problems such as how far long experience should compensate for a pilot having monocular vision, or what degree of deafness could be accepted by the different members of a flight crew when in all other respects they were fully fit. Not surprisingly these eminent and learned doctors, of many different nationalities, did not always agree, but I rather enjoyed listening to their various views and, just occasionally, being asked as a simple pilot to give my own opinion on some non-technical aspect of what was essentially a medical matter. It was very noticeable that the Americans, who already had a large civil aviation industry, tended to dominate all the discussions, and when on some occasions the European representatives were more or less unanimous on a particular point and the Americans didn't like it they would invariably reserve their position. They seemed to have no wish to compromise, but perhaps this was because their delegation did not appear to have the authority to make decisions that others had.

Back in London again, as the RAF began to take its post-war shape, I found myself offered a Permanent Commission almost at the same time as the Ministry of Civil Aviation, who had engaged me only temporarily, offered me established employment. I had no difficulty in making up my mind and was appointed to a Permanent Commission in the rather lowly rank of Squadron Leader on the 12th May 1947.

Before I got back into uniform I had been upgraded to Wing Commander and in that rank started an unexpectedly busy and demanding tour as Deputy Director of Air Support and Transport Operations (DDASTO) at the Air Ministry in King Charles Street. My Director was Air Commodore David Atcherley who, with his twin brother 'Batchy' Atcherley was well known throughout the whole of the Royal Air Force. Our immediate superior was Air Vice-Marshal Donald Hardman, who was afterwards to become Commandant of the Royal Air Force Staff College. At that time Lord Tedder was the Chief of the Air Staff and the Air Minister was Mr Arthur Henderson.

The Air Transport Department in the Air Ministry in 1947 was concerned not only with the routine operations of Transport Command but also with air support for the army in the tactical role. This included supply dropping by parachute and airborne landings by gliders. On this aspect we worked very closely with the War Office and were supported on our staff by an Army Colonel and a Major. My own responsibility here was to advise and, quite often, to deputise for David Atcherley at meetings with the Army's Director of Land Air Warfare who, at that time, was General Jim Cassels, famous afterwards as the Commander of the Commonwealth Division in the Korean War. Although this work was important, the primary role of our Department was to formulate policy for the operation of our limited but rapidly growing transport force, and in particular to help to maintain what was known as the Trunk Route to Singapore. This was flown in those days by York and later on by Hastings aircraft and took five days, staging through Malta or Idris in Libya, Habbaniya in Iraq, Maruripur in Pakistan, Colombo in Ceylon, and finally on to Changi in Singapore. This route was used to carry passengers, mail

100

and, in emergency, reinforcements and its operation was the main task of Transport Command. Apart from the Trunk Route we in the Air Ministry were concerned with other small operations on behalf of the Foreign Office involving regular flights to, amongst other cities, Warsaw and Vienna. In those days British Civil Aviation was just beginning to recover from the war and we always knew that most of these tasks in future could, and should, be carried out by civil aircraft and not by the RAF, but in the meanwhile we were committed in many instances to a semi-civil role.

We were concerned also in the Air Ministry, in conjunction with Transport Command at Bushey Park, in preparing routine plans for reinforcing or evacuating British garrisons in various parts of the world, and as the major exercise of bringing home British prisoners-of-war had long been completed these seemed to present no particular difficulty. Amongst these plans was one to supply, in emergency, the British garrison in Berlin, which in those days was quite small, and it seemed to be well within the capability of Transport Command although something else might have to suffer. None of us working on the Air Staff in that summer of 1947 could have had any idea that in our discussions with Transport Command we were in fact beginning the preparation of an operation that may well have saved the outbreak of yet another World War. The Berlin Airlift began in a very modest way but, like Topsy, it grew and grew and grew.

The origins of this remarkable operation are worth restating. Four Power co-operation for the government of the divided city of Berlin which had been in operation since the war, in 1948 had become very strained and by mid-June Russian co-operation had ground completely to a halt. The Russians withdrew from the joint governing body and increased their restrictions on traffic into West Berlin which had, of course, to come through the Russian zone, and by June 24th the city was, for all intents and purposes, blockaded. The Russian intention was fairly clear; they wished to take control of the whole of the former German capital and since this lay so deeply inside the Soviet occupied sector they seemed likely to succeed. They had cut off access to Berlin by road, rail, and canal by various excuses and in consequence the Western Powers were left only with the three air corridors which had been agreed earlier for communication with the Allied Occupation Forces and their ancillary staffs. There was no thought at all of feeding or supplying the German citizens of Berlin itself. This was a task that the planners had never envisaged and on the face of it it looked quite hopeless – indeed so hopeless that there was at least one American plan to drive a protected convoy by road straight through the Russian Zone to the city, come what may, even though this risked an eyeball to eyeball confrontation with the Russians and quite possibly another war. Fortunately wiser counsels prevailed but no one, certainly no one in the Air Ministry at that time, envisaged that there was any possibility of feeding and clothing the inhabitants, and supplying the industry of a great city by air for any great length of time.

The outline plans which had already been drawn up between Transport Command and the Air Ministry, in co-operation with the staff of the Air Officer Commanding in Chief of the British Air Forces of Occupation in Germany, were hastily brought up to date. We were still thinking in those early days primarily of supplying the British Garrison and the few British civilians in Berlin, numbering perhaps five thousand or so in all. As it happened the first steps in the airlift had been taken a little earlier. An excellent history of these preliminaries is given in Dudley Barker's account of the Berlin Airlift in the Official History which was published by the Air Ministry and the Central Office of Information a year later. I have drawn on this greatly in refreshing my own memory of these events nearly forty years ago. To quote this account 'Improvisation began as early as April 1948 when

Russian restrictions upon surface travel between Berlin and the Western Zones of Germany began to be felt. Until then the RAF had been flying a communication service between Buckeburg and Berlin. A small Anson made this flight three times a week. In April the Anson aircraft was replaced by Dakotas and the frequency of the service increased to three times a day. The only problem this service was intended to alleviate was the supply of the British Occupying Forces in Berlin'. Towards the end of June it was decided to put into effect our plans for supplying the British Garrison which had been code-named Knicker and sixteen Dakota aircraft were sent to Wunstorf Airfield near Hanover. The crews took with them kit for ten days and on June 28th the first aircraft carrying flour flew to Gatow in Berlin.

It was realised almost at once that as the Russians showed no signs of re-opening landward access to the city a much more ambitious operation was required. This new plan, which was named Carter Paterson, involved practically the whole operational strength of Transport Command. This name was later changed to Plainfare since Russian propaganda kept reminding Berliners that Carter Paterson was a big British removal firm and that it followed that our intention was only to take things out of Berlin and not to supply its inhabitants.

From July on the Airlift began to get really under way, the British target being raised from 400 tons per day on the 3rd July to 750 tons a day by the 7th, and this, of course, involved an enormous amount of reorganisation of the disposition of our air forces in Germany to make room for the newcomers from Transport Command and the massive supplies which were pouring into our airfields there. The Americans by now were already carrying out their share of the airlift under the code name Vittles, from the US Zone, using the Tempelhof Airfield in Berlin which was much closer to the heart of the capital than Gatow. Since they tended to use larger aircraft such as the Skymaster they could carry considerably bigger loads but in those early days we were not greatly concerned with their operations, although later on the whole airlift became very much an integrated British and American affair, with some limited assistance from the French who were very short of transport aircraft of their own. The airfield at Tegel in the French sector of Berlin was brought into operation towards the end of the airlift and this additional terminal would have been most useful if the operation had continued any longer.

By the late summer of 1948 it was beginning to be realised at Whitehall, at Bushey Park, and in Germany that its duration was quite indefinite. Many other agencies were now involved. The Army had a major role to play in supplying the British bases in Germany, in loading the aircraft at RAF airfields and unloading them in Berlin. Many thousands of German civilians were working enthusiastically at both ends and the RAF everywhere were absolutely flat out. The problem of flying aircraft down a narrow twenty mile corridor in and out of our one terminal airfield from different British bases in Germany had been largely solved. This was done basically by flying into Berlin by the southern and northern corridors and back to base by the central corridor. Any aircraft missing its turn to land went back again to its starting point with its full load. Within each corridor aircraft were vertically separated according to their cruising speeds and airfields of origin. After a very short time except in really bad weather there was a movement of aircraft at Gatow every ninety seconds, day and night. This was no mean achievement both by the hard-worked, and often overworked, aircrew and by all concerned, particularly at the receiving end in Berlin. Many different cargoes were now being carried including, in addition to food (which included dehydrated potatoes later on), supplies of coal and liquid fuel to keep the city's industry still turning over although at a rather lower capacity. Collision risks on the narrow corridors were a

104

continual hazard and their avoidance was a tribute to meticulous planning and the good training of transport crews. Whilst all this was going on in Germany many problems which could only be solved in Britain, either at Air Ministry or at Transport Command, were beginning to arise.

In our Directorate in London we were sorry indeed when David Atcherley was posted to command the Central Fighter Establishment soon after the airlift started, and as he was not replaced I moved into his office with the Acting Rank of Group Captain. I was now effectively the senior staff officer in the Air Ministry responsible for the day to day implementation of Government policy for maintaining the British supplies to Berlin. Fresh problems continued to arise but we took them in our stride. As week succeeded week and the Russians still remained intransigent it became plain that the airlift might go on for a long time. The outcome is a matter of history.

One of the things that worried us most in those early days was the maintenance of the Trunk Route to Singapore on which our essential communications by air with the Far East seemed to depend. As the York aircraft, which were soon to be succeeded by the Hastings, were responsible for flying that route and had to be used in their entirety on the airlift the Trunk Route was patently likely to collapse. This could be serious and not only because of the inconvenience caused to passengers, many of whom were from other Services, or were members of the Diplomatic Corps proceeding to or returning from overseas tours or visits. There seemed to be a real danger, too, of the staging posts which had been set up with great care beginning to atrophy. At each of these there was a small specialist detachment for looking after aircraft in transit, including Flying Control and maintenance personnel together with a limited range of spares and accommodation for tired aircrew and passengers. In the event this problem turned out to be not as serious as we thought, and although quite a number of staging post personnel worldwide were withdrawn during the airlift the Trunk Route was re-established a year or so later without too much difficulty.

There were many other problems arising from the uniqueness of this operation. When the British contribution to the airlift started with the first flight of Dakotas to Wunstorf, control came under the RAF Air Headquarters in Germany and this continued for a while as the airlift built up. However, it soon became necessary for a whole Transport Group to move over from Southern England to Germany and a little later on, as the Americans were by now carrying the major share of supplies to Berlin, an integrated Headquarters was formed with an American General in charge and the Air Officer Commanding No 46 Group, Air Commodore J W H Merer, as his Second in Command. Although this was the eventual solution to problems of Command the fact that a substantial portion of Transport Command was operating in an overseas theatre and under the day to day control of another Headquarters naturally caused difficulties, particularly in the initial stages. The aircrew still owed their allegiance to their home units and major maintenance did, of course, have to be done there where the necessary spares and equipment were available.

Many of these problems arose from the fact that aircrew had been sent to Germany at short notice and were not as well equipped, physically or mentally, for a long stay overseas as they would have been if they had been posted in the normal way for a tour of duty abroad. Some were married and they could not readily bring their families with them, partly because there were no married quarters available and partly because no one knew how long they were likely to be in Germany, and after a while the indefinite separation from kith and kin began to produce problems at both ends. Although much thought was devoted to it both by Transport Command at Bushey Park and by my own staff in London the solution was not an easy one. I began to remember my worries about aircrew fatigue in the Western Desert although the problem here was not so much operational fatigue (in the sense that crews were in danger of being shot down by enemy action) but worry about separation from their families. This concern was allied with physical tiredness from the heavy strain of flying day and night, sortie after sortie, in all weathers between their base airfield in the British sector and the one receiving station for their cargo in Berlin. In the end this problem was partially solved by allowing crews to take leave at home at regular intervals after ferrying aircraft back for major maintenance in the United Kingdom, and towards the end of the airlift it was even possible to fly a very occasional York, or one of the new Hastings, along the Trunk Route to Singapore by way of keeping it exercised. With hindsight this seems a fairly obvious solution to a not too difficult problem but it was a new one and since we were under great pressure from the Secretary of State for Air (who in turn was being pressed by the Cabinet for a maximum effort at all times), withdrawing aircraft from Germany had to be handled with considerable care.

Mr Arthur Henderson had on his desk each morning a report of the tonnage that the RAF had carried into Berlin the day before. As the Yorks were withdrawn from their long distance role to supplement the short range Dakotas the RAF target was increased to 840 tons daily. By fortunate chance the new Handley Page Hastings were just coming into service and with its greater carrying capacity was immediately used to support and increase the tonnage carried on the airlift. In July a careful assessment was made by our scientific advisers – 'the boffins' – of the amount of freight which would be needed to maintain a reasonable Berlin economy during the next twelve months and the figure arrived at was for the supply of some 4,000 tons of imports daily. This amount, it was calculated, would support the West Berliners, some light industry, and the needs of the Allied troops themselves. It became obvious that an absolutely maximum effort was going to be required both from the Americans and ourselves quite indefinitely.

Since the daily supply in summer and winter and in all weathers of this amount of cargo by air seemed almost impossible, precise calculations were made in Germany about how the load could be reduced. Dehydrated potatoes were one answer and although it had been suggested that loaves should be flown in to save fuel in baking bread it was decided that, since a loaf of bread contains about thirty percent of water, it was cheaper in the end to fly in fuel. Salt and coal were very short and for a while Sunderland Flying Boats were used to ferry supplies, landing on the Berliners' beloved Havel Lake, but this was essentially a short term measure suitable for summer time only and coal was an unpopular cargo with the crews since coal dust got everywhere. Realising in the Air Ministry that it was going to be extremely difficult to maintain these and other categories of supply, we in London began to give thought to the employment of Civil Aviation and this became one of my major concerns throughout the remainder of the airlift.

Once the Government had agreed in principle that civil aircraft should be used to the maximum extent possible in supplying Berlin, the problem of employing them was handed to the Air Staff. This proved extremely complicated since although many of the small charter companies which were beginning to be set up after the war were keen to take part, their equipment varied enormously. Some companies had only two or three useful aircraft to offer, some had only one, others had quite a lot more. Not only did the types of aircraft vary a good deal but their equipment was very often quite incompatible with that being used by the RAF, and in particular the approach and landing aids which were standardised in Transport Command were seldom available

108

on the civil aircraft which we wanted to hire. Another difficulty was that although many of the companies could produce two or three crews per aircraft some could not, and one or two were obviously quite incapable of maintaining regular and disciplined flying patterns under RAF control.

We took these problems as they arose and it was soon agreed that the whole of the civil element should be sent to Fassberg Airfield to operate from there under the overall control of the airlift Headquarters in Germany. Transport Command made a major effort to assist, loaning essential landing aids and training civil crews to use them and since a co-ordinated effort was required from this rather motley assortment of aircraft and crews, Mr Whitfield, a senior member of British European Airways who were themselves participating in the airlift, took charge of all the chartered civil aircraft. Additionally, since liquid fuel was in great demand we hired the whole of Sir Alan Cobham's Flight Refuelling fleet for the duration of the airlift and they performed yeoman service ferrying supplies into Berlin.

Sitting at my desk in King Charles Street, I was anxious not only to keep in close touch with the Headquarters of Transport Command in Bushey Park, where I had worked for a few months a year before, but also to see for myself what was happening in Germany. Sometimes, accompanying Air Marshal Sir Hugh Walmsley, who at that time was the Deputy Chief of the Air Staff, I flew at weekends to one or other of our stations in Germany. Gatow was a remarkable sight with dozens of aircraft on the ground either being unloaded or lining up to take off, with a movement every ninety seconds and a tremendous air of cheerful purpose about the whole operation. It was a real inspiration coming from a desk in Whitehall to see the enthusiasm with which everybody from the Station Commander to the German workmen unloading the aircraft went about their tasks without fuss or confusion, all knowing exactly what they had to do and really enjoying doing it. The appreciation of the citizens of Berlin was already very evident and in many little ways they tried to express their thanks.

Back in Whitehall other problems began to arise. The Treasury, not unnaturally, began to worry about the cost of hiring this large miscellaneous fleet of civil aircraft and were continuously pressing me to state what would be a reasonable cost to pay per hour for the use of eg a Bristol Freighter or a Halton. I refused absolutely to get involved, taking the attitude that although my staff could and would, in conjunction with Transport Command, assess the fitness of particular companies and their crews to take part in the operation there was no way we could participate in any sort of cost control exercise. We knew that if the airlift failed – and there were times when for various reasons our daily tonnage dropped considerably – we would be on the brink of war. I felt that the cost would have to be sorted out afterwards by better qualified people, but the urgent requirement to sustain the citizens of Berlin and our own forces there could not be assessed now in pounds and pence. No doubt many charter companies made a great deal of money out of the airlift but I do not see how, in all the circumstances, it could have been otherwise, and I have lost no sleep worrying over that.

It was hard sometimes to persuade the Air Minister, Arthur Henderson, that we could do no more. The demand for supplies was insatiable and although tremendous efforts, and on the whole very successful efforts, were being made to reduce requirements and to make Berlin more self sufficient we never seemed to be able to do quite enough. When the Air Minister realised that my Directorate was handling the day to day affairs of the airlift in London he began to make a habit of sending for me personally, instead of one of the far more senior officers who would normally have answered his call. On one occasion when our deliveries had dropped a good deal he told me that all training must now cease and that the situation was so critical that all training aircraft were to be immediately employed on the airlift. Although I well understood the reasons for his anxiety it was obviously quite impossible on an operation like this of quite indefinite duration to cease aircrew training altogether, but I thought it better not to tell him that. In the end by arrangement with Transport Command we kept aircraft at home for a short time after they had finished their major inspections in England to help to meet minimum training requirements, and this was an absolutely essential measure if we were going to look ahead more than a month or two.

In spite of all these problems and the difficulty of forecasting the future by the end of the year the Berlin Airlift had settled down, and as we got through an unusually mild winter without a too great diminution of supplies we began to feel that it could continue quite indefinitely. The Hastings aircraft were doing valiant service and although they had only just become operational they enabled a great increase in our daily tonnage to be ferried to Gatow. To quote Dudley Barker again, 'No one could tell whether the blockade of Berlin would be raised suddenly or would continue for two years or more. Only one thing was certain. The airbridge stood firm, and in the spring of 1949 the Western Powers were laying plans for more aircraft, more equipment, a vastly heavier haul across the bridge of air, on the assumption that it might continue for a considerable time to come'. By early summer the Russians had had enough and without warning the blockade was lifted quickly and as suddenly as it had begun. Although the airlift continued a little longer it had achieved its purpose and it will not be easily forgotten by the good people of Berlin. Their gratitude was shown soon afterwards through the fund they established to help the relatives of the seventeen British and Commonwealth crews who had died during the airlift to preserve their freedom. I felt it was a strange comment on the inconstancy of human affairs that, having commanded a bomber squadron six years earlier intent on the destruction of the German capital I, and so many others who took part then, should have worked so hard now to keep that city alive. It had been a very long affair for all of us, and for me it was perhaps the most rewarding of my whole life.

The City of London, as always, was quick to show the appreciation of the British people. I was fortunate enough to be invited to a celebration lunch in Guildhall attended by the Prime Minister, Mr Attlee, senior RAF Officers from Air Ministry, Transport Command, and Germany, Army Generals, and the American General Tunner who assumed command of the whole airlift when it got under way. In the Birthday Honours List of June 1949 I was awarded the CBE as the head of an exceptionally hard working and devoted staff with whom it had been a privilege and joy to work. As normal life began to return and the routine operations of Transport Command got under way again I was reminded of the saying of the RAF Engineering branch, 'The impossible we achieve instantly: the miraculous takes a little longer!'

The importance of the Berlin airlift in the story of our times is a matter for assessment by future historians but some four decades later it does not seem to have lost any of its significance. If it had failed – and for many months its success was in no way assured – the alternatives would have been to surrender the whole city to the Russians . . . or to go to war. To a world still recovering from World War II, with the capabilities of the atom bomb already demonstrated at Hiroshima, war, particularly war with a recent and very brave ally, seemed unthinkable but nevertheless a real possibility. To have surrendered the city would have been contrary to all that we had fought for and so dearly won.

There were many lessons to be learnt about the operation of Transport Forces. The primary importance of training, which had been emphasised by two successive Commanders-in-Chief of Transport Command, Air Marshal Sir Ralph

Cochrane and Air Marshal Sir Brian Baker, was again demonstrated. Some problems which had arisen from the operation of a large Transport Force in an overseas theatre and had been dealt with very much on an ad hoc basis needed further study. The role of civil aircraft and its ability to provide rapid support for Transport Command in emergency was one to which we in Air Ministry devoted immediate attention. We began to evolve a plan to form one or two RAF Transport Command Reserve Squadrons based on well established charter companies like Airwork whose crews would do some limited RAF training and whose aircraft would be readily capable of fitting navigational and landing aids. This study was well under way when I left on my next posting.

Some months later when I was summoned to attend an Investiture at Buckingham Palace I took with me my wife Audrey and my eldest daughter. As Josephine, who was then aged six, had her arm in a sling following a playing field accident she attracted some attention from the reporters and photographers who were hovering about the Palace. My ego was a little deflated when in due course I was sent an early edition of one of the Sunday papers (intended I think for distribution in the Outer Hebrides) in which a photograph appeared – the caption showing the child as the centre of attention! It was perhaps a fitting end to my own part in the airlift story and a reminder that tomorrow was a new day, and there were new tasks to be done.

Chapter 7

The Far East

With the airlift over I soon became due for posting again. Air Marshal Sir Thomas Williams, who was the RAF Commander-in-Chief in Germany and whom I got to know well during the Airlift, was good enough to offer me command of Wunstorf which had just become vacant. I was very tempted to accept this appointment. Wunstorf airfield is situated quite near to the town of Hanover and to be in charge of this station looked like being a most pleasant assignment. It had been designed originally for use by the light bomber pilots of the Luftwaffe and was well built and beautifully laid out. Living quarters were scattered among pine trees and the Officers' Mess looked out onto a tree-lined lawn. In many ways it seemed to me to be a Station Commander's dream. However, at about the same time Air Vice-Marshal Donald Hardman, for whom I had worked closely on the Air Staff during the Berlin Airlift and who had now become Commandant of the RAF Staff College at Bracknell, asked me to join him there and after some thought I decided that, having had experience of commanding stations before, another spell at Staff College would be more useful. I was well aware of how little I knew about other RAF Commands and other Services although I felt pretty up to date on both Transport and Bomber operations. So, having very regretfully turned down the opportunity of a two or three year posting to Germany, I was appointed to the Directing Staff at Bracknell in September 1949, ten years after the outbreak of war.

In those days the importance of staff work, which had never been altogether neglected in the RAF, was beginning to be more strongly emphasised. The wartime course which had been for three months only at Bulstrode had been lengthened to six months, and by the time I got to Bracknell we were on the first nine month course which was soon to be extended to the pre-war duration of a full year. At Bracknell we had some 96 students including a number from British Commonwealth countries and a handful of Americans, including always an American Officer on the Directing Staff. The pre-war Staff College, which was still at its old location of Andover, now did a similar course to Bracknell, but with many foreign students it had a slightly lower security classification.

At this time Bracknell, which is now the permanent Staff College of the RAF, was just beginning to settle down and since few married quarters were available nearly all the Directing staff and married students who chose to do so lived in the neighbourhood in such accommodation as could be found. It was the first time since the war that I had been able to resume normal married life for any length of time knowing that I was unlikely to be disturbed for another two or three years. The course itself was an interesting one and since the students were usually of fairly senior rank it was always made plain that we on the Directing Staff were not to regard ourselves as teachers although we planned programmes, gave a few lectures, and generally assessed the students who worked in syndicates of six. We were fortunate enough to have the service of very high-class lecturers – many from civil life – and in discussion afterwards on subjects as varied as submarine hunting or East-West relations many of the students who were experienced in some particular expertise often contributed as much as the lecturer himself. It was work that I greatly enjoyed and since the role of the Directing Staff was primarily tutorial we were not concerned in any way with the day-to-day running of RAF affairs. We had a fine library and there was time to think, read, and relax in an almost university atmosphere.

Academic studies were much relieved by frequent visits to Navy, Army and RAF establishments all over the country, including a few to Northern Ireland. On these occasions and after our return to base we had many lighter moments. On one memorable morning we were surprised to find an ancient gun drawn up outside the main College building and a label on it which said that it had been taken by Clive at Plassey in 1757 and re-taken by the RAF Staff College in 1950! It turned out that a team – which I think was led by an American – had acquired a tractor, taken the gun all the way from the Army Staff College at Camberley to Bracknell, and duly erected it on our Staff College lawn. I gather it was very speedily missed and that there was a certain exchange of telephone calls between our respective Commandants before the circumstances came to light. We all wondered greatly how this ancient artillery piece had managed to hold together during its quite considerable midnight journey but I never heard the full details of the escapade.

When my two and a half happy years at Bracknell had ended, during which my third daughter, Kathleen, had been born in Windsor, I was moved on again, this time to command the RAF station at Lichfield. At that time, because of the Korean war in which both the other Services were already involved, some limited expansion of the RAF was taking place. At Lichfield we opened a new Air Navigation School. Many of the students were reservists who had been recalled from civil life as also were some of the pilots who flew the Wellingtons and Valettas we used for training, or re-training, navigators. It was a thoroughly bad airfield with a canal at one end of the runway and a road at the other but the friendliness of the Staffordshire people (who insisted on calling the airfield by the local name of Fradley) made our time there pass very pleasantly.

Being a new station we were very busy with all the usual chores of organisation and arranging a proper training programme, but with the Korean war always likely to involve the RAF in a much bigger way we went to work with a will and very few of the reservists objected to being back in uniform. Most of them seemed to enjoy it and I remember one or two who rather wished that they had never left the congenial atmosphere of Service life. There were, of course, no married quarters available but I was fortunate enough to obtain a billet with a master of the Local Cathedral Choir School, and we soon made many friends.

It was the first time I had ever lived near a small Cathedral town and the reception we all received was heart warming. Lichfield has always been proud of its old traditions and as Station Commander I was invited to take part in many ancient ceremonies. On Doctor Johnson's birthday we would all stand outside his house in the centre of town where he had lived for many years and would sing his favourite hymns, and afterwards we would adjourn to the Town Hall where we drank quantities of excellent Burton beer and ate Simnel cake. I had never heard of this confection before but was informed that it was a very old recipe and was something to do with a romance between a man called Simon and his girlfriend Nell. There were many other old customs and once a year we were invited to beat the city bounds on horseback, calling at various hostelries on the way. As I didn't possess either a horse or riding kit I was excused any equestrian adventures but would join the cavalcade at suitable inns around the outskirts and wish the riders well on their journey. This too always concluded with beer, Simnel cake and speeches in the Town Hall.

In Lichfield the Assizes were taken by a Recorder from Birmingham and when I got to know him he was good enough to ask me to sit beside him in Court and although I

117

could not, of course, take any part in administering justice this was a much appreciated courtesy. When the time came to adjourn and after a sherry or two, we would discuss the various cases and I found this a most interesting change from the day to day routine of running an RAF station. I was never quite sure whether Higher Authority would have approved of my willing, and indeed enthusiastic, participation in all these local activities, but I felt from the broader point of view it certainly did no harm and my wife and I greatly enjoyed the friendship and hospitality we received so bountifully in that ancient city.

In October 1952, with the Korean war beginning to run down and after only some fourteen months at Lichfield, I was posted to the Headquarters Staff of the Far East Air Force in Singapore. This was my first overseas posting since the war and although it meant yet another move with my growing family we all looked forward to seeing something of the East. I had been in Singapore once before when Air Marshal Sir Ralph Cochrane, who had commanded Transport Command prior to moving to the Air Ministry, had let me accompany him on a Staff visit to the Far East Air Force Headquarters at Changi. This short visit gave me a chance to meet again my sister, Primrose and her husband who, after many adventures during the war including a narrow escape from the Japanese in Hong Kong, had moved to Singapore. Her husband David was now the resident Archdeacon under the famous Bishop Wilson who, when captured, had earned enormous respect everywhere by his fortitude in Japanese prisoner-of-war camps. On that brief visit I had been invited one morning to witness the execution of Japanese prisoners-of-war in Changi Gaol and had declined to do this unless I was ordered to be there. I had not in any way been involved in the Far East campaign and although feelings against the Japanese were running very high I did not feel any desire at all to witness the death, however well deserved, of men I had not fought against.

The Author, 1971. *Photo: Black-stone-Shelburne, New York.*

In Kenya the cattle were more reliable than the machinery.

Farm labourers at Mau Summ

My room-mate Geoffrey Perrin with T-Model Ford.

The 1930 Combine Harvester was noisy and dusty.

Pupil farmers lived in grass hu

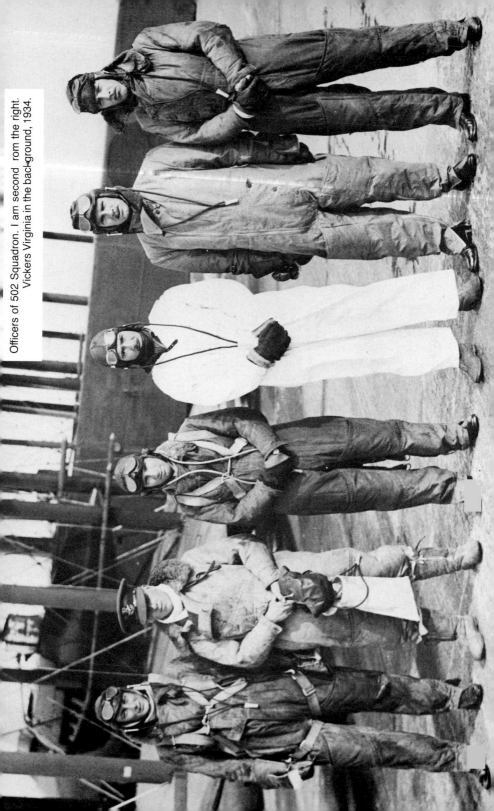

Officers of 502 Squadron. I am second from the right.
Vickers Virginia in the background, 1934.

Libya, 1941. 'Mae West' escaped our bombing. The burning merchant ship in Benghazi harbour did not.

Arming up Wellingtons in the desert.

The 'mail' had got through.

Benghazi waterfront damaged by bombing with a broken-backed Italian flying boat in the foreground. *Photos: Imperial War Museum.*

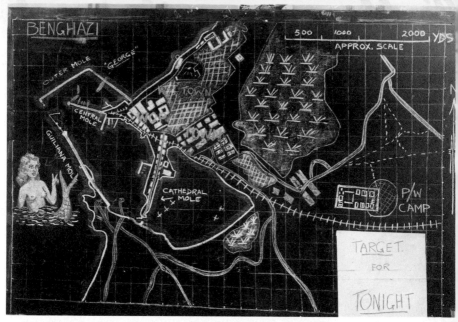

The standard briefing chart for the almost nightly bombing of enemy sea-borne supplies into Benghazi 1941/42.

My crew in 148 Squadron. The navigator, Bob Alexander, is second from the left in the back-row, and my second pilot, Ned Cowan from New Zealand, is on Bob's left.

L'alleanza militare

GIUGNO 1940

Il tedesco se la gode di aver fatto entrare l'Italia in guerra.

We dropped these leaflets in North Africa to induce our Italian foes to break away from their German masters.

Germany forgotten, it could be quite lovely up there. *Photo: Charles E Brown.*

This Lancaster—tail turret and gunner missing. Sgt Jolly DFM
flew this Lancaster back from Cologne. He was soon flying again!

The Berlin Airlift went on night and day.

Airmen and airwomen helped with the German harvest.

We even used Sunderlands until the Havel Lake froze over.

A typical morning at Gatow. Yorks line up. *Photos: Ministry of Defence.*

The author and Major Norman West, on parade. Athens in the summer of 1958.

John Freeman meeting Mary Clubwallah, an Indian fount of charity. My wife in the background.

John Freeman, the new High Commissioner, pays his inaugural visit to Madras.

Ambassador's residence in Seoul.

International 'hunting' competition at Cheju Island, South Korea.

I was always meeting visiting VIPs. This time it was the United Kingdom Minister of Housing, 9th November 1969. *Photo: The Port of New York Authority.*

The American Legion on parade in New Jersey, May 1970.

Leaving my wife to pack up our accommodation in Lichfield, sell the car and generally make the arrangements for joining me later, I sailed in the troop ship *Empire Fowey* for Singapore. The journey out – for officers at any rate – was not uncomfortable. The troopships of those days were operated by shipping lines plying regularly to the Far East and in our case by P & O. The *Empire Fowey* turned out to have been the ex-German *Potsdam* – a Strength through Joy vessel which had been converted post war for trooping purposes. Passengers were from all three Services with the Army usually predominating, and the officers in charge of the troops on these voyages and their staffs were usually drawn from the Army too, but several troopships were staffed by the RAF.

The trip out was an enjoyable one. We stopped briefly, without disembarking, at Gibraltar and again at Port Said where my mind went back to the journey out in a German ship some twenty-three years earlier on my way as a pupil farmer to Kenya. At Port Said the usual selection of bum boats came alongside and we were treated to the familiar spiel of the gully-gully men producing chickens from practically everywhere and, when the women weren't looking, displaying 'feelthy' postcards for our enjoyment. On this occasion we did not go ashore to Simon Artz to buy tropical clothing since all this would be available in Singapore, and there was no time to enjoy the night spots of Port Said but the journey through the Suez Canal brought back many memories.

We passed through the Bitter Lakes close by the airfield at Kabrit, now obviously disused, and I hoped that all the mines the Germans had dropped during the war had long since been cleared up or become inoperative. I recalled one day having seen the aircraft carrier *Illustrious*, battered by enemy bombing in Malta, sailing slowly southwards for extensive repairs in early 1942 and the cheers we gave that gallant ship to speed her on her way. As we reached Suez I remembered another night when a German raid along the canal had bombed and nearly sunk the White Star liner *Georgic* incurring heavy casualties. We could see something of this action from Kabrit and hear bombers flying down the canal, wondering if we ourselves were going to be one of their next targets that night.

After the long, hot passage through the Red Sea we stopped briefly at Aden and were allowed ashore for a welcome swim and to disembark some passengers, and we had another short stop at Colombo where we parted company with a number of Naval and RAF personnel posted for a tour of duty in Ceylon. About three weeks after leaving England we arrived in Singapore.

All on board our ship were looking forward greatly to a tour of duty in the Far East and the Island had been billed as a tropical paradise. In many ways it lived up to our expectations and after England, still recovering from wartime, the well-filled shops and plentiful supplies of food, drink, and, especially, tropical fruit were a very welcome change. The climate, when we got used to the rather sticky heat, proved very agreeable and there was abundant opportunity for exercise in swimming pools, on the tennis and in squash courts at Changi itself, and in the various clubs in Singapore City. Married quarters were very scarce and as I knew I was unlikely to be offered one for some considerable time my first priority was to obtain somewhere for my family to live. With much help from the headquarters' staff at Changi I obtained comfortable accommodation for them in the Grand Hotel which was about half way between Changi Camp and urban Singapore. My wife and family arrived on another troopship about a month later by which time, whilst living in the Officers' Mess at Changi, I had been able to explore the Island a little and to meet quite a few of its inhabitants, both European and Chinese, and it did not take us long to feel at home, particularly as some other newly arrived Service families were also living in the Grand Hotel.

At Changi, my appointment as Group Captain in charge of Organisation on the Headquarters Staff, gave me the opportunity for quite extensive travel. Being largely concerned, together with the Chief Engineer, with works services and establishment matters I welcomed the opportunity to get around the RAF stations and units in our very widely dispersed area as soon as possible. At that time the Far East Air Force (FEAF) area of responsibility extended from Ceylon in the west to Hongkong in the east. Additionally, as the Korean war had not yet quite come to an end, we had a very small detachment at an airstrip north of Seoul servicing the Auster aircraft of the observation unit – an AOP Squadron – which was stationed near the fluctuating front line and very close to what is now the border between North and South Korea. Although I had no wish whatever to get involved in the Korean war itself I had read a good deal about that country and found its history quite fascinating, and since hostilities were obviously coming to an end I took the opportunity to pay a Staff visit to this detachment.

The first stage of the long journey from Singapore was made in a Hastings aircraft of the Far East Communication Squadron staging through the American Air Base at Clark Field, near Manila, and refuelling at another American airfield at Naha in Okinawa, an island which had been the scene of some of the fiercest fighting between American Marines and the Japanese Army during the Pacific campaign. At both places we were well looked after, and night stopping at Clark Field I was much impressed by the extreme comfort with which the US Air Force was surrounded in a well established station which at one time had been a US Army Cavalry base. The small RAF detachment there, looking after transit passengers and air crew, obviously enjoyed their lot and it was good to see how well they had settled in at this major American Air Base.

From Okinawa we flew to an airfield at Iwakuni on the Japanese Inland Sea which had been built for the Japanese Air Force and which was now in charge of the Royal Australian Air Force and commanded by an RAAF Group Captain who made us extremely welcome. Iwakuni, on the southern tip of Honshu, at that time was a hive of activity being the taking-off point for Korea and dealing with a constant stream of visitors, reinforcements, wounded, and all the varied problems of a big transport staging post in wartime. Since I had to wait a few days for a passage to Korea I took the opportunity to see something of the neighbourhood and to learn about the history of the airfield itself. At one corner I was shown a small shrine where the Japanese kamikaze pilots had made their final prayers and committed their souls to heaven before carrying out suicide attacks on American warships. It was a touching sight and although it emphasised again the futility of war I wondered about the beliefs and motivation of men who were prepared, quite deliberately, to sacrifice their lives on behalf of the Emperor, believing that by so doing they would be at eternal peace.

A crowded boat trip around the Inland Sea gave a glimpse of Hiroshima, although from the water we could see little of the destruction of that great city; and a sight too, of Kure where the big Japanese aircraft carriers which had been sunk by the Americans at the Battle of Midway had been built. We were pointed out many shrines and temples along the shore and a very well fed horse grazing by the waterside which apparently was the Emperor's own and was now living in comfortable retirement.

The short flight to the Korean capital Seoul gave a first glimpse of a country that I was to get to know better in years to come. The city itself seemed a dreary place with ruined buildings and beggar children running around. Little boys, half clad and bright eyed with hunger, seemed to be everywhere and many had attached themselves to allied units, almost as mascots, often moving with the troops, and in return for food and cast-off clothing carrying out odd jobs to the limit of their considerable capacities. The few women around, even in those wartime days, wore brightly coloured clothes but were little in evidence apart from the inevitable camp followers prepared to give their services in return for American food and tobacco which they could sell easily, and almost openly, to support their numerous relations. Home life had obviously been completely disrupted and there were few families that had not suffered separation or loss already in that cruel fratricidal war.

After a day or two in Seoul I flew up to join the little RAF detachment on a bend in the Imjin River. The AOP base at Fort George was beside a big Army camp and on reporting to the Brigadier, who received me most kindly, I interested myself in the details of the fighting which, to judge from the noise of artillery fire, was taking place only a few miles away. Unfortunately I interested myself rather too much and after a very full briefing on the military situation I was asked if I would care to see something of the front line for myself. Although I began to wish fervently that I had remained in Singapore I could find no really creditable excuse for not accepting this offer but I made a firm resolution, not for the first time, that I really must learn to keep my big mouth shut.

A few hours later, flown by a young Army Sergeant, I found myself over the Imjin River heading into North Korea. Below little white puffs of smoke merged in some places into small dirty yellowish clouds and I was assured by the pilot that this was just the Marines having their daily battle. However, when little white dots began to appear in the sky rather close at hand I realised that our presence had not passed altogether unobserved. I felt then that my interest in the progress of the Korean war was evaporating rapidly and was being succeeded by a rather more personal interest in returning as quickly as possible, and preferably in

123

one piece, to the base we had just left. I considered – a little subjectively I must admit – that my early decease, which seemed increasingly likely, would serve no useful purpose and on this self invited mission would be entirely void of glory. In as steady a voice as I could muster I told the pilot that I had now seen enough and was quite happy to go home and I sensed that he was in entire agreement. On landing I had recovered sufficiently to thank the Brigadier for a most interesting – although I could hardly say enjoyable – experience but from then on I was extremely careful to limit my comments on the war to the widest of generalities.

Life in Singapore in 1953, according to many long term residents, had changed remarkably little since pre-war days. Although it was the twilight of the Raj and the wind of change had started to blow, here it was hardly a gentle zephyr. It was for Service folk a very welcome change from home and having settled my family, at least temporarily, in a comfortable apartment, a little nearer the airfield, owned by a remarkable Chinaman who had helped British prisoners-of-war in Changi Gaol I felt free to go on my travels again – this time to Ceylon.

Here at Negombo the RAF had a major transport staging post some fifteen miles from the capital and, since there were regular Trunk Route flights there from Changi airfield, transport presented no difficulty. Many new works services were being planned and, inter alia, we were concerned with building a new church, many married quarters, a recreational swimming pool and an extension of the main runway. This last named presented certain difficulties in that it involved cutting down a number of the surrounding coconut trees which, according to the Singhalese owner, were by far the best in his extensive plantation and produced regularly quite phenomenal crops. He suggested compensation should be assessed accordingly. I took the opportunity while in Ceylon to make a quick trip to the Temple of the Tooth at Kandy and to visit the Rest Camp at

Diyatalawa which had been used by the Navy and was now becoming an RAF responsibility. Colombo itself seemed thriving and the famous Galle Face Hotel had been affected little by the war.

Other visits followed, to Kuala Lumpur where we had a small active Air Headquarters and to the big airfield at Butterworth, opposite Penang Island. Both of these stations were heavily involved in supporting the Army waging the long drawn out guerilla war in the Malayan Jungle against Communist terrorists who, in 1951, had murdered Sir Henry Gurney the High Commissioner of Malaya on his way to the Rest Camp at Fraser's Hill.

The main effort of the Far East Air Force at that time was becoming increasingly devoted to this continuing and costly campaign. When the Japanese war ended the large Malayan People's Anti Japanese Army (MPAJA), which had been established originally with British officers, was disbanded, but a hard core of the Malayan Communist Party refused to hand in their arms and they set up camps in the jungle. Their object was to establish a Communist State and they hoped to do this by terrorist tactics, initially in rural areas and afterwards in the cities in a time scale of about two years. Their campaign of murder and intimidation was set in hand soon after the newly created Federation Government had been formed, and in January 1948 a State of Emergency was declared and military help was requested. Terrorist attacks had already begun to take a considerable toll of civilian life in isolated plantations and also of police and government officials. The campaign thus launched lasted for almost twelve years and increasingly involved all three armed services, government agencies, and the Malay police. Communist outrages reached their height with the murder of the High Commissioner in 1951, and in that year more that five hundred members of the Security Forces and five hundred civilians were killed. There was no easy or quick way to victory in an undeclared war of this kind but the seeds of success were laid in 1950 when Lieutenant-General Sir Harold Briggs was appointed Director of Operations and set in train what became known as the Briggs Plan. This aimed basically to win the support of the people by dominating certain designated 'Occupied Areas' and moving up to half a million Chinese from isolated rural communities into them. The intention here was to try to cut off the terrorists from the jungle squatters on whom they depended largely for their food. Local Chinese Home Guards were recruited to defend these settlements and schools and social amenities were provided. It was an enormous task and involved issuing Identity Cards to all adults and the dropping of many millions of explanatory letters by the RAF.

Although the immediate effects of the Briggs Plan were salutary, in 1951, heartened by Communist success in Korea and Indo-China, the Malayan Communist Party (who had now changed their name to the Malayan Races Liberation Army) began a new offensive and received some support from members of the Chinese community who were uncertain about their future. Although most of the guerilla attacks were against small police posts or other soft targets they became for a while more aggressive and in one attack eleven members of the Queen's Own Royal West Kent Regiment were killed.

By the time I reached Singapore the RAF was becoming steadily more involved and Field Marshal Sir Gerald Templer had taken over both as High Commissioner and Director of Operations. Sir Gerald's dynamic leadership was soon felt and the importance he placed on training and improving the efficiency of the police and intelligence services soon began to produce results. Full support was readily afforded to a leader universally liked, respected, and admired – a man who had that rare gift of leadership, the ability to understand the needs and feelings of his men. His grasp of detail seemed quite omniscient and he could talk with equal ease and authority to a reserve policeman, a harrassed planter, or a soldier in the field making them feel that his whole desire was to help them in every way possible. The campaign he led was very much a combined operation, and the RAF had already had great experience in Burma of supporting troops many miles behind the Japanese lines by supply dropping and casualty evacuation. These techniques were now put to good use and reinforcements arrived both from the UK, including an entire Lincoln Bomber Squadron, and from Australia and New Zealand who were becoming increasingly worried about Communist expansion in Asia. Bombing terrorists in the jungle was not usually effective, partly because of the difficulty of locating small groups in tiny jungle clearings, but much was done by spraying chemicals to destroy small plantations which supplied them with food. Helicopters were increasingly used to evacuate wounded but this involved extremely skilled flying since alighting areas were often very small and trees grew up to a height of two hundred feet. Some parachuting was done, particularly in Northern Malaya, by the SAS and because of the danger of being hung up in trees an abseil technique was evolved at the Changi Parachute School. Long patrols were carried out by Sunderland Flying Boats, in close co-operation with the Royal Navy, to prevent supplies coming in by sea from the North. The RAF Regiment, too, was heavily involved, fighting as soldiers in the matted jungle and ambushing terrorists fleeing from attacks from the air.

However, the chief role of the RAF during this long campaign continued to be supporting the army through reconnaissance, supply dropping and providing mobility for the various service and civilian forces engaged. It is not too much to say that the morale of all of these, and indeed the success of the whole operation, depended upon this air support and the knowledge that if the worst happened the wounded would be evacuated from the most inhospitable terrain to base hospitals in Kuala Lumpur and in Singapore.

Our role at Headquarters in the Organisation Branch was concerned largely with providing the necessary ground facilities for these operations, including the rapid building of temporary air strips and the provision of accommodation. With a view to the future we made plans to develop three more mainland airfields – one on the west coast of Alor Star, another one in the heart of the jungle at Gong Kedah and the third one on the east coast at Kuantan. Of these three Gong Kedah, which had been used as an airstrip by the Japanese, was largely overgrown but both the other small airfields were serviceable although needing much attention for regular military use. When the Air Staff had laid down their final requirements and the Chief Engineer had drawn up his plans it was my job to obtain the necessary money from the Treasury, and once a year I flew home to London armed with the Far East Air Force Defence Estimates which I had to justify in detail. But it was not all work and like most Service families at the Headquarters we found time to enjoy ourselves and to undertake an occasional recreational visit away from Pleasure Island.

One of the most popular rest camps was at Frasers Hill, some forty miles inland from the Malayan capital at a height of about 4,000 ft. To get there we flew to Kuala Lumpur and then drove quickly up the road on which Sir Henry Gurney had been murdered. At that altitude the nights were cool and every bungalow had provision for a log fire. The clear air reminded me of Kenya and a morning round of golf on the little local course, with Malayan girl caddies eager to earn a dollar or two, gave one an enormous appetite for lunch. The change did us great good. There were other opportunities also. Now and then a troopship coming into Singapore en route to Hong Kong or Japan would have room for 'Indulgence' passengers travelling almost free for a few days holiday and shopping in Hong Kong. On one of these trips with my family we sailed on the White Star Line *Georgic* – the same ship that I had remembered bombed and burning

128

in Suez Harbour in 1941. Her Chief Engineer pointed out the still buckled plates but I could see no sign of any other damage. The Runnymede Hotel on Penang Island was another popular place for local leave and was readily accessible by air through Butterworth (where I later learnt to fly Vampire jets) which was then beginning to be taken over by the Royal Australian Air Force. The Island's spectacular funicular railway, like the one on Hong Kong Island, took a little getting used to but apparently all its life had been accident free.

An interesting place to visit for a weekend away from Singapore was the old town of Malacca about one hundred and fifty miles north on the west coast of the peninsula. Malacca had been one of the very earliest Portugese settlements in the Far East having been a colony of theirs from 1511 until 1641 when it was taken by the Dutch. They in turn were superseded by the British in 1825. All three colonial powers had left their mark on the town and the narrow streets and early European architecture made a welcome change from the modern city of Singapore. In an old graveyard in the town I saw a huge stone slab marking the interrment of a Portugese mayor which had been overprinted with the name of the Dutch burgomaster!

From time to time we on the staff had opportunities to travel outside the quite extensive FEAF area. In November 1953 Group Captain Struthers, the then Chief Engineer, and I together with several other senior staff officers were invited by Sir Clifford Sanderson, our Commander-in-Chief, to join him on a visit with his wife to Australia and New Zealand. We took off one Saturday morning from Tengah on Singapore Island and landed at Djakarta in Java in time for lunch where we stayed a night with the Ambassador. Next morning we were off again for Darwin in north-west Australia where we were the guests of Quantas. Just before taking off from Darwin Sir Clifford said that he had recently been reading a book by Neville Shute *A Town*

Like Alice and if there was an airfield there he would like to drop in on the way to Adelaide. The crew organised a hasty change of the flight plan and we stopped for a few hours at this desert town which now, thanks to air travel and a new road, was becoming rather less of a backwater. We had time to buy some remarkable pictures by an aboriginal artist, Albert Namojira, and to visit the famous red Eyre Rock. Unfortunately the Royal Australian Air Force at Adelaide, which was our next stop, had not received the signal to say that our arrival would be delayed. The Guard of Honour when we turned up two or three hours after our expected time of arrival showed little sign of strain but I think our hosts were somewhat relieved at not having to start looking for us. After a few days in Adelaide, during which some of us took the opportunity to visit the vineyards at the Barossa Valley, we flew on to Melbourne and a day or two later to Sydney. The C in C's party were then moving on to New Zealand but I took the opportunity to go and stay with a cousin of mine, Brooke Moore, a practising surgeon at Bathurst over the Blue Mountains in New South Wales.

My cousin Brooke had a very strong sense of humour and after I had been there a couple of days he asked me if I would like to see the County Gaol. I agreed readily enough and when we got there he pointed out that the road leading into the prison was called Dr Brooke Moore Avenue after his father who had also been a surgeon. He introduced me to the governor and after touring the gaol Brooke asked me if I would like to see the disused Hangman's Drop. I had no particular wish to look at this somewhat macabre relic but felt it would be impolite to say so and after a few steps the governor said, 'I think you said, Group Captain, that you would like to see the Hangman's Drop.' Brooke added gleefully that it had last been used for the execution of two Irishmen in 1916 and the governor, at an obviously pre-arranged signal, told me that I was now standing on it and the execution cell was right beside me. I had not moved so quickly for a long time.

The trip back to Singapore was made via Brisbane and Darwin again. Although I had spent most of my month away in the very contrasting cities of Adelaide, Melbourne, Sydney and Brisbane and had enjoyed only the briefest glimpse of Australian rural life, I resolved to visit this huge country with its delightful climate and friendly people as soon as possible again.

A few months later Group Captain Struthers and I were back again in Darwin. This time, in conjunction with the Royal Australian Air Force, visiting a small airstrip in Portugese Timor which we were considering for possible joint development in emergency. With the real and growing Communist threat in South East Asia at this time, both our governments considered that planning for the rapid deployment of our air forces should be put in hand. From Darwin we flew in a RAAF Dakota to the little landing strip at Dilli where we were cordially received by the local Portugese Governor. We learnt that the RAAF flew regular flights there on which they conveyed films and sporting ammunition for the Governor's personal use and it became obvious when he invited our whole party to stay at his very comfortable residence that he was on the best of terms with the Australian Air Force. Group Captain Struthers and I spent a very pleasant twenty-four hours there and after lunch I thanked our host, perhaps a little too effusively, for the excellent wine and brandy he had been serving. Next morning, much to my surprise, I found that both were provided for breakfast but at that hour of the morning none of us was able to do the Governor's cellar full justice!

Shortly after returning from Timor I attended a conference at Kuching in Sarawak, presided over by the Commissioner-General for South East Asia, Mr Malcolm MacDonald. One of the items to be discussed was the development of civil airfields in South East Asia and, in particular, in Singapore and Hong Kong, and my general brief was not to commit the Air Ministry to any expenditure that we could possibly avoid since the requirement for these airfields was so urgent that there seemed no need for a contribution from the RAF vote. In wartime we would, of course, be able to use them anyway. Mr Malcolm MacDonald made an excellent chairman and he seemed to have a real understanding of the varied problems that came up. He had been much in the news because of comments that had been made in one of the London papers about his visits to Borneo and his bathing on one occasion with the Sea Dyak women who seldom bothered to wear more than a sarong tied around their waists. It had been suggested that Her Britannic Majesty's Commissioner-General should not be seen disporting himself with semi-naked women, to which Mr Malcolm MacDonald replied mildly that he saw no reason for anyone to dress up just for him!

After the conference was over we were paddled across the river for an official reception at the Astana – the residence of the Governor Sir Anthony Abel. The flotilla of little boats made a colourful scene and a happy prelude to a relaxed and friendly party on the Governor's waterside lawn.

One of my last staff visits before coming home in mid-summer 1955 (again on the *Empire Fowey*) was made to Hong Kong with the Chief Engineer. We had been there a number of times before on duty but this time were determined, on my farewell trip, to combine it with pleasure also. We travelled on an RAF Valetta to the little staging post at Labuan in Borneo. As usual when we began the long approach to the airfield the crew directed our attention to the bright orange flares burning in the small rectangular clearings in the jungle over Brunei, marking the oil fields which had made this tiny State one of the richest in all Asia. After staging through Clark Field next day and doing our business in Hong Kong we decided to pay a trip to the Portuguese colony of Macao which is only a few hours away by steamer. It was well worth a visit.

A monument on the quayside near where we disembarked showed where the Boston Tea Party schooner had loaded before sailing to the New World. In the graveyard of the ruined cathedral lay many of the old British East India Merchant Ship Masters, most of who had died very young, and we saw the tomb there of a Captain Winston Churchill. We stayed a night or two in the Hotel Centrale, which consisted of six or seven storeys. One or two or these were devoted exclusively to gambling and another one was a dance floor. Hostesses were plentiful and some of them apparently lived in the hotel. After dinner, and feeling in a somewhat end-of-term lighthearted mood, we danced with several of these girls who seemed to be a mixture of Portuguese and Chinese, all speaking quite good English. I asked one of my partners to be sure to call in on my friend at 2.00 o'clock in the morning and gave her his room number. A little later in the evening I asked another one to knock on his door at 5.00 o'clock, explaining that Rob Struthers had great difficulty in sleeping and was apt to get very lonely in the early morning. When I met the Chief Engineer at breakfast time and asked him if he had slept well he gave me a very odd look indeed, and to this day I am not quite sure whether or not he blames me for his somewhat disturbed and no doubt entirely memorable night!

One evening towards the end of my tour in FEAF at the suggestion of Group Captain 'Bosun' Morris, our Senior Personnel Staff Officer (a man who had played for the RAF and thought that rugby and flying were the only things that mattered) I accompanied the RAF Provost Marshal, Group Captain Jones, on a tour of the red light district of Singapore. These visits were directed primarily at reducing veneral disease and very occasional drug taking amongst servicemen and their purpose was well understood by the proprietors of the various places we visited. Accompanied by two burly Service Policemen we set off in plain clothes first to visit the

New World and the Happy World, both of which were considered to be fairly high class establishments of their kind. At the first one the Provost Marshal was immediately recognised and we were all at once offered drinks on the house. Everything here seemed to be entirely in order and we got the impression that quite good food as well as sex and expensive drinks were all to hand.

At the next stop, as the Chinese manager was not immediately available, we found friendly hostesses crowding around and obviously hoping to spend the evening in our company. However, when the boss duly appeared they were hastily dismissed and once again the smiling proprietor begged us to have drinks on the house and said how absolutely delighted he was that we had been kind enough to once again honour his humble establishment! These were the better places and from then on the establishments we visited, clubs, sex parlours and drinking houses grew shabbier and shabbier and tawdrier and tawdrier. I felt sorry for men who found their bodily relief and perhaps their sole entertainment in places of this sort and by the time our visit was over I had had more than enough. That evening taught me a lot and although I realised that in the surroundings I had seen, blackmail and the possibility of a major security breach of defence secrets were most unlikely, I felt that some supervision was necessary to protect the health of young men, many of who were serving overseas for the first time. Visits of this sort were required but it was important though that they be conducted with a sense of humour and of proportion, and in this respect I thought that the Provost Marshal and his men could not be readily faulted.

Chapter 8

Attaché in Athens

On the 26th September 1955, home based again, I was posted to command No 3 Recruit Training School at Padgate, some few miles from Warrington in Lancashire. This was one of five recruit training schools dealing with National Servicemen who came in every week to carry out their basic training on an eight weeks course. It was not a posting that at first I greatly welcomed but, like all my others, it was a change from the previous one, and in the end it turned out to be both demanding and rewarding.

Our job at Padgate was to look after some hundreds of young men from all walks of life who, although they had been kitted out before they arrived, were otherwise in all respects completely raw recruits. They lived in barrack huts containing about twenty or more new entrants, each hut in the charge of a corporal drill instructor. These corporals were very carefully selected and indeed on them depended very much the efficiency, morale and general well-being of all these young men who passed through our hands. Having done their eight weeks basic training here they all went on to other RAF stations throughout the UK to be given specialist training. The programme for all this in 1955 was already well established and indeed, although the final decision had yet to be taken, National Service was coming to its close. The mixture of new entrants from varied backgrounds included some from Public Schools and others from the equivalent of Borstal but regardless of background mostly they were somewhat apprehensive youngsters who on the whole were reconciled to the idea of two years compulsory National Service but, naturally enough, were wondering what it involved for them. When I got to Padgate I was told that in earlier days recruits had been weighed at regular intervals to make sure that the good and varied food they were given was keeping them in good shape but after a while the gain of weight was so regular and so entirely predictable that this practice was discontinued.

In our training programmes we needed always to be aware of the problems of young men at an impressionable and emotional age away from home and I was to some extent familiar with these from my own university days. Sheer loneliness, and the inability to adapt quickly to a completely new life could sometimes lead to real tragedy, and even a very occasional suicide was experienced in all the five recruit training schools. Every case was, of course, exhaustively investigated and I can only recall one during my time at Padgate.

Each week we passed out recruits who in their eight weeks had done a great deal of square bashing and been pre-selected for further technical or semi-technical training. This selection process was complicated and important. We on the permanent staff tried hard to persuade recruits to sign on for regular service and anyone who did so received the higher regular rates of pay. The minimum length for which further enrolment was required varied enormously according to the different trades and those that were somewhat unpopular, such as medical orderlies and assistant cooks, could do as little as one further year while receiving full pay. On the other hand popular trades like MT drivers had to sign on for a considerably longer period and there was a graduated scale which varied continually according to the needs of the Service. A tiny handful of

National Servicemen went on to become aircrew but the cost of training them on essentially short service engagements was so high that very few were taken from this source.

In the defence estimates of 1956 it was proposed that the National Service system would begin to be faded out, and that the reserve training commitments of most National Servicemen would be greatly reduced except for some specialists who might be needed in emergency.

There is no doubt that National Service did a great deal to train young men as citizens. For two years they were living a disciplined and communal life and if they showed aptitude were taught a skilled trade. Sometimes they served overseas also, mostly in Germany. Nevertheless from the point of view of the Royal Air Force, and no doubt other Services too, National Service was a very expensive commitment indeed. A very large amount of money and effort was spent in training young men who remained basically and essentially civilians and a great deal of Service manpower was involved in this commitment. Very few National Servicemen in the end volunteered to enlist on regular engagements for even very short periods, although it was found that at the pre-entry stage, when initially called up, quite a substantial number of young men, who had not already decided on their careers, did elect to become, for a time at least, regular members of the Royal Air Force. No doubt National Service did serve a useful purpose at a time when the post-war world had by no means settled down and its contribution to citizen training was inestimable but the Services were glad to see it go and I was not surprised, therefore, when in December 1956, after the rundown of Padgate was well under way, I was posted again, this time to Wilmslow some fifteen miles from Manchester, to run a mixed RAF and WRAF training station. For our final Guest Night at Padgate I invited all the previous Station Commanders I could contact to come along and they included a very distinguished First World War veteran, one

Group Captain Gilbert Insull VC, MC. It was an evening to remember.

Wilmslow turned out to be a much more comfortable and well established Recruit Training Station than Padgate and was well equipped to handle and accommodate both RAF and WRAF personnel. The course for the young men we trained was similar to that at Padgate (which for a while I continued to command also) but the women did six weeks only, Wilmslow being their sole recruit training station at that time.

The WRAF section was commanded by a Wing Officer, Betty Parker, and although I had served on other stations with WRAF personnel this was my first experience of dealing with young women just joining the Service. The problem was not as intimidating as I had feared, although I remember asking Betty when I first took a mixed parade how I should inspect a line of WRAF. She looked at me in some surprise so I said, 'Do I start at the top or at the bottom?' and she gave me one or two hints such as the permitted length of hair, but I felt that checking up on the appearance of young women – much as I enjoyed their company out of uniform – was not a thing that came to me very readily, even on parade. We had few problems with these girls and since their course was of such short duration we saw rather less of them than of the male recruits. Whenever possible we borrowed a band and persuaded some local dignitary, or a senior officer from one of the RAF Commands, to take the weekly passing-out parade since it gave me a break and was good from every point of view.

On one occasion the Lord Mayor of Manchester took the salute and another time the well-known Lancashire MP, Dr Edith Summerskill, inspected the parade. I was particularly impressed by her astuteness in recognising people, as when she spoke briefly to one recruit with a slightly pock-marked face and ended up by identifying him as a miner from a particular area which she knew well. I asked her afterwards how on earth she had done this and she said that his accent was obvious and that from the little marks on his face she knew that he had been working down a mine. One noticeable thing about these parades, when the WRAF were passing out, was that the airmen were always much smarter and since parents were nearly always present to see their boys and girls on parade it was a joy to see how the different squadrons vied with each other to produce the best turn-out.

One morning I received a telephone call from the office of the Commander-in-Chief of our Headquarters at Technical Training Command saying that Air Marshal Sir George Beamish was coming up to Wilmslow and wished to see me on a very confidential matter. The C-in-C was one of four Irish brothers who had achieved great distinction in the RAF and on the rugby field. A bachelor, Sir George had boxed for the RAF in his younger days and played rugby for Ireland and was known and admired throughout the whole of the Service. As a visit from the Commander-in-Chief was very rare and one at such short notice almost unprecedented, my Wing Officer and I awaited his visit with interest and some slight apprehension.

Arriving at Wilmslow we went at once to my office. Sir George came straight to the point and turning to Betty Parker said that he had decided to move all the WRAF down to Hawkinge on the south coast where the WRAF officers were already being trained. He went on to add that he knew that the one thing that all the girls would like would be to be together. Betty looking somewhat shaken turned to me for support and then summoning up her courage said, 'Sir, the one thing that we girls don't want is all to be together. We have joined a man's service and are proud and happy to be in it and it seems right that we should be trained together with the men with whom many of us will be working in the days to come'. The Commander-in-Chief looked at the floor and then at the ceiling and after a long pause said, 'I think

139

I'll have to take further advice'. I never heard the matter raised again.

For me this posting was a great change from Staff work on which I sometimes felt I was concentrating too much, although I never quite knew whether I enjoyed more being in charge of a big and active station, with all the human problems involved, or the more academic side of Service life for which, in many ways, I felt better suited. However, all this had to be left to a Higher Authority and since on the whole I was happy either as a Station Commander or as a Staff Officer I was content to leave my future in other people's hands.

With National Service now coming rapidly to its end, I received a telephone call from the Air Ministry one day asking me to report to London to talk about my next assignment. I found this a little intriguing since normally one had very little choice about postings and even less warning. On arrival I was told in great confidence that I had been selected as the prospective Air Attaché for the British Embassy in Athens with the acting rank of Air Commodore but that this must be mentioned to absolutely nobody since it would require, apart from my own assent, approval not only from the Foreign Office (which was considered to be something of a formality) but also from the Greek Government which in view of the prevailing difficulties over the future of Cyprus could not be taken for granted. I was fortunate in that the Assistant Chief of the Air Staff in charge of Intelligence – Air Vice-Marshal W M L MacDonald, another Irishman – had known my wife and me in Singapore when he had been in charge of the local Air Headquarters so, although he was good enough to take us to lunch and confirm that we knew our knife and fork drill, there was no great problem about my selection from the Air Ministry point of view. Nevertheless a great deal remained to be done.

It was pointed out, as I well knew, that my flying was by no means up to date so in July I was sent to the airfield at

140

Worksop near Sheffield to carry out a full training course on jet aircraft. I had flown Vampires briefly before in fine weather at Butterworth in Malaya but this time did a full conversion course which I did not find at all easy. Apart from being rather out of flying practice I much preferred large aeroplanes. The necessary preliminaries to the course such as jumping off the top diving board of a swimming bath in Sheffield complete with full flying kit, a 'bone dome', parachute, and Mae West amused me not at all, but fortunately there were a number of suitably dressed frogmen around to see that I wasn't drowned whilst endeavouring to extract myself from my parachute and get the dinghy suitably organised. There was also a requirement to see how well one could stand up in emergency to lack of oxygen at high altitudes, and trainees were placed in a kind of caravan which was gradually decompressed to see how long we could remain more or less compos mentis before passing out altogether. We were given simple tests and words and symbols to write but as the air got thinner and thinner my scribbling became more and more illegible and I couldn't compete with the simplest of sums. Fortunately there was always a medical officer looking in to see that we didn't pass out altogether, or if we did that we were revived pretty quickly.

The Vampire itself was a delight to handle although, flying alone in bad weather, I missed the warmth and comfort of a crew and, above all, of a navigator who most of the time at any rate had some idea of where we were.

After doing this jet course and being briefed on diplomatic life in High Commissions and Embassies and on certain intelligence matters I paid a whole series of visits to various aircraft companies who might wish to sell their equipment to the Greek Air Force at some stage, although in view of the diplomatic problems over Cyprus and the general poverty of that country few of their hopes in this direction seemed likely to materialise. There was no attempt to teach either my wife or me the Greek language since we were advised that the Royal Hellenic Air Force, like the Greek police, had been trained in the immediate post-war years by the British. They were now mostly flying American aircraft and their aircrew spoke very good English, although often now with a trans-Atlantic accent. In this respect, as I was to find out later, I was different from my USAF colleague who, with his wife, had carried out a very intensive course in modern Greek before taking up post.

We sailed from Bootle in a small cargo vessel, the *SS Pinemore* of the Johnston Warren Line, my family, which now included my small son, Desmond, who had been born at Warrington, with his nanny now taking up most of the passenger accommodation. We made various stops on the way and in the end our journey, in bad weather in this little ship, took so long that when we finally reached Athens we were told that the party given in our honour to introduce us to members of the Embassy and to the British Community in Athens had been held the night before whilst we were anchored just off Piraeus harbour waiting to disembark at dawn. Despite this slight set-back we began very soon to find our feet and to adjust to a new environment, thanks largely to the warm welcome we received from our diplomatic colleagues whose hospitality was almost overwhelming. Our new home, which we took over from my predecessor, was a comfortable house at Kifissia almost in the shadow of Mount Pendeli from whose marble the Parthenon had been built.

We were lucky too, in that the two other Service Attachés had arrived only a little while before us and we soon got to know Captain George Barstow RN and the Military Attaché, Brigadier Jimmy Johnson, and their wives and from then on we worked together happily as a team. That winter turned out to be bitterly cold and the whole of the Acropolis wore a mantle of snow which we were assured happened only about every ten or twelve years. Because of the problems over

Cyprus we were provided with a house guard by the Greek Government, but since we felt in no kind of danger they used to spend a good deal of their time seeking warmth in our garage where we fed them with hot soup from time to time. It was a pleasant sight to see these policemen playing with snowballs rather like children, and although the British Government was by no means popular with the local Press I did not personally feel any obvious anti-British sentiment, although I resolved in my dealings with the Greek Air Force to take things very easily indeed. I was reinforced in my feelings about this by my predecessor who before departing told me that he had not visited a Greek Air Force station because of the Cyprus problem, for almost two years. I hoped before my own time expired I could do a little better than that. In this I relied very much on the advice of our Ambassador, Sir Roger Allen. Both he and his wife had great experience of dealing with Service Attachés and knew how to handle us very well and I owed much to their advice and kindness during our stay in the Land of the Hellenes. It was perhaps more difficult for my wife Audrey than for me since she was expected to be more or less on parade whenever required by the Ambassadress whereas, working as I did for the Air Ministry as well as for the Embassy, I had every opportunity of getting around. I felt in no way bound to Athens or its environment apart from purely diplomatic occasions whenever I saw the opportunity to make a useful visit to some remote part of that most attractive country, although as a matter of courtesy I would keep Chancery informed whenever I left the capital.

There was one awkward moment soon after our arrival when I was asked to see the Head of Chancery – one Hamish Mackenzie. After wishing me every success in my new appointment he came straight to the point and said, 'Air Commodore, I understand you have a very unfortunate nickname'. Taken a little aback I suggested that perhaps he had suffered from one too, and, not denying this he went on to

143

say that he understood that mine was 'Turkey' and that this country, Greece, was practically at war with Turkey and I really could not go around Athens calling myself 'Turkey Rainsford'. I assured him that I never used that name and added that I had acquired it at school because a cousin of mine was called Chicken through a resemblance to a boy called Hen and, as they said I gobbled a lot, 'Turkey' seemed quite appropriate. He listened with great patience to this long saga and then said, 'Haven't you got any other names at all?' I replied, 'Yes, Frederick Fitzpatrick, but I answer to practically anything'. As neither of these names seemed to appeal to him any more than they have done to me he told me to call myself anything I liked and we soon became good friends.

I was serving now not only two masters – the Air Minstry in London and the Embassy in Athens – but had to keep in touch also with the Air Officer Commanding the Near East Air Force in Cyprus who was naturally interested in what was happening in Greece, and indeed in the Balkans generally. Once again I was fortunate. On my first appointment Air Vice-Marshal Sam Patch, whom I had known well in Singapore when he was the Senior Air Staff Officer there, received me very kindly and afterwards he was succeeded by Air Vice-Marshal Bill MacDonald who had been largely responsible for my original appointment to Greece. Not surprisingly, therefore, I took every opportunity to visit Cyprus and report to him in person but obviously since my job was primarily in Athens (and unlike my Naval colleague who was responsible for Israel as well) I had comparatively few opportunities to travel outside the confines of metropolitan Greece. Nevertheless, since the Greeks were becoming more and more involved in NATO exercises my contacts with the RAF in Cyprus were useful, and as time went by I found the opportunities of getting to know and assessing the capabilities of the Greek Air Force increased considerably. But this was a long and slow process.

In the early days of my appointment, at our weekly Staff meetings with the Ambassador, the Cyprus problem was high on the agenda. It had gone on for a long time but since, like everything connected with Greece, its history was fairly complicated and its solution depended largely upon the unpredictability of the Greek character, this question naturally took up a great deal of the time of the Ambassador and his staff. We Attachés could contribute a little by our own impressions of people we had met, and Sir Roger (referred to always as H E) was very willing to listen to us since by the nature of our jobs we travelled to rather different places than the Diplomatic Staff and met people that they would not normally have done. Indeed the problems of Cyprus were so very much in our minds it is perhaps worth attempting to explain in the light of Greek history how and why in the Year of Grace 1957 we had this intense emotional, and sometimes quite passionate, love/hate relationship with a people whom I've often heard called the Irish of the Mediterranean and whom, perhaps for that reason, I got to like very much indeed.

After the failure of the somewhat ill organised Crusades which had been launched with much religious fervour by the Pope in 1095, culminating in the capture of Constantinople by the Turks in 1453, what Mr C M Woodhouse in his excellent history of Greece has called the *Dark Age of Greece*, set in. It lasted from 1453 until 1832 and that long period under the sometimes cruel, thoroughly inefficient, and often corrupt rule of the Ottoman Empire had a lasting effect on the people, their culture and even to this day, their cuisine. The struggle for Greek independence largely under the stimulation and often the leadership of the Orthodox Church was much helped by the British Government and in particular by the Foreign Secretary Lord Canning whose name is still remembered gratefully.

At the time when the Greeks were struggling to throw off their Turkish yoke they received much help from the Royal

Navy and particularly from Admiral Sir Edward Codrington who, with the aid of the French and the support of the Russian Navy (commanded by a Dutch admiral), annihilated the combined Turko-Egyptian fleet at Navarino. The Greeks still talk about this great battle as though it was yesterday and although Admiral Codrington was removed from his command soon afterwards, ostensibly for having failed to carry out the order to prevent the deportation of Greek slaves from the Peloponnese to Egypt, he has remained to this day a great Greek hero. The Greeks, like the Irish, have long memories and they treasure the names of many famous Britons who over the years helped to restore their independence and their pride. It is a kind of affectionate special relationship which can turn from warmth and friendship to bitter anger at lightening speed and then the storm be almost as soon forgotten. It was important for any diplomat, whether a regular member of the Foreign Service or a Service Attaché, to understand something both of Greek history and of the Greek character and the experience of learning about both was one which I enjoyed. Every tourist to this day is pointed out the signature of Lord Byron on the seaside temple of Poseidon at Sounion, and to the Greeks his memory is far more than that just of a poet and a bon viveur!

This basic feeling of friendship for the British and for the British Services, reinforced by the help we had given in 1941/2 combined with a great hate for the Germans resulting from the treatment many of the Greek partisans had received during the war, was very evident in our association with ordinary people both in Athens and in the country, who were often very quick to recognise from what part of the world we came, even when I was not in uniform. Nevertheless they felt too, quite irrationally and most passionately, that we should hand over for them to incorporate in Metropolitan Greece the Island of Cyprus which, although it had been in its long history occupied by the Venetians, the Turks and the British, had never at any time been part of the Greek Empire. They were quite single minded about all this under the influence of the Cypriot Archbishop Makarios who, as the leader of the movement for ENOSIS (or union with Greece), was entirely in the Greek tradition. Although Makarios never openly supported violence against the British rule he gave tacit support to the rebel leader Grivas who did. Grivas was a guerrilla leader who made a name for himself by attacking firstly Greeks he considered unpatriotic and secondly British installations and, afterwards, the British garrisons on the Island and British civilians living and working there. Soon the word Enosis was on everyone's lips and the Greek Government, who were not particularly anxious to add the burden of administering one more island to the many they already had, were swept along and joined in the cry. The British Government were very much put on the spot, since Cyprus was demonstrably more prosperous under British rule, although four-fifths of its people spoke Greek and subscribed to the authority of the Greek Orthodox Church. However, there was a strong Turkish minority who had lived alongside their Greek neighbours for many years in a reasonably comfortable and sometimes almost symbiotic association. Once the Greek demand for Enosis got under way the Turkish Government quite naturally reacted and although they were happy enough with the status quo and had indeed showed no interest whatever in the Turkish minority in Cyprus since that island had passed under British control in 1878, they now laid a series of claims which were based more on emotion than on either history or reason. Indeed they were at some difficulty in arguing a case of either annexing the island or partitioning it and, as Mr Woodhouse has pointed out, in some negotiations the British seemed almost to be arguing the Turkish case before the Turks themselves had even thought of it! Not surprisingly their standpoint was given scant attention in the

Greek Press although our Embassy was well briefed on it both through diplomatic channels and in the newspapers arriving regularly from London. The British Government searching for some kind of a solution were genuinely afraid that if they abandoned Cyprus altogether there would be war between the Greeks and the Turks, as indeed had nearly happened in 1922.

When we reached Greece in November 1957 the abortive London conference on Cyprus (following a UN resolution urging the resumption of tri-partite negotiations) had only re-established already familiar positions. The Greeks still claimed to want Enosis and the Turks would, of course, have none of this. The British were quite happy to concede self-government to Cyprus if the Greeks and Turks would agree but here the deadlock was absolute. The Greek Prime Minister, General Papagos, who had done his very best over the years to reach some kind of a settlement over a dispute with which his government was getting increasingly disillusioned had died on the 4th October and was succeeded by Constantine Karamanlis who had been one of his loyal adherents. Since there seemed no solution to the problem and as Colonel Grivas' EOKA — the Cypriot Nationalist Association — was now moving from attacks against fellow Greeks who had for one reason or another earned their disapproval to Turkish Cypriots and British troops the situation was rapidly getting out of control. As by March 1958 no solution seemed to be in sight, Archbishop Makarios was deported to the Seychelles, the Greek Ambassador was re-called from London, and the Greeks appealed once again to the United Nations. This then was the background to my arrival to take up the post of Air Attaché and for all my time in Greece we Attachés were constantly being briefed on the latest development in this seemingly endless saga.

It was with some trepidation, therefore, that I made my first tentative approach to the General Staff of the Royal

Hellenic Air Force. I was determined to play it cool and to avoid any political discussions as far as possible. On my first call on General Margaritas, their Chief of the Air Staff, who had been partly trained in Britain, my reception was formal and correct although I sensed that the General would have liked to receive me more cordially if circumstances had been different. The Greek liaison officer, a Wing Commander 'Bobby' Dendrenos, spoke excellent English and made himself agreeable from the start but it was not he who held real authority. On asking him whether the Greek Air Force officers preferred to be called by RAF or American titles, and whether he would rather be addressed as Wing Commander or Lieutenant-Colonel, he replied with a disarming smile that since in Greek the word was quite different anyway he was happy to answer to either! I found that this was the general attitude of the Greek Air Force who, talking to British officers, were very happy to be referred to by RAF ranks which, since many of them had been trained in Britain, they understood very well. However, since military ranks had now become almost universal internationally amongst airmen they were usually referred to by Army titles and addressed as such on diplomatic occasions and at social functions.

On my first call I had said that I would like, in due course, to see something of the Greek Air Force in their own establishments and this request was noted without any commitment at all. A little later when I met some of the senior Greek officers on diplomatic and social occasions I mentioned again my wish to see something of their work and in due course received an invitation to visit one of the local Greek Fighter Stations near Athens which was almost certainly one that we had bombed from Egypt when it was occupied by the Germans in 1941. This first visit was revealing and talking to young Greek Air Force officers I realised that Service airmen have a great deal in common and as long as we kept off politics we could get on very well

149

indeed. I formed a firm impression then that with their good American and Canadian aircraft these Greek squadrons would give an excellent account of themselves in war, and I knew how bravely they had fought in 1941, but their reserves were lamentably weak both in terms of equipment and of manpower. Perhaps they thought this didn't matter too much as they had allies waiting in the wings. It was at least a good beginning and I felt that provided the political situation didn't become completely impossible I should soon be able to see more of the Greek Air Force at work. In the meantime I was greatly helped by my American colleague who since the United States provided most of the aircraft and backing for the RHAF were able to provide me with a great deal of information about the capabilities of the Greek Air Force at that time. Getting much further was obviously going to take time and depended to a large extent on the continual variations in the political climate and a solution to the Cyprus problem.

Away from politics we began to enjoy diplomatic life and seeing something of the country and its people. My wife, Audrey, took Greek lessons from a French woman resident in Athens and soon began to speak the language quite fluently and this proved useful on our visits outside Athens and even in the local market. We began to meet local people and found it quite usual for a Greek taxi driver if he recognised me as British (or in my wife's case Canadian), to charge us nothing at all and explain in pretty basic English that he had fought with the British either at sea or in North Africa. On the other hand, regrettably, if he thought we were American he would charge us about ten times the recognised fare, which I thought quite unreasonable since the Americans at that time were doing a great deal more to provide financial and other help to the Greek Government and the Greek Services than the British were able to do. But then I seem to remember a Latin proverb about how ungrateful people and nations tend to be to their benefactors!

They were certainly an excitable race. I remember once walking into a jewellers shop quite near our Embassy where an old lady was berating the proprietor. When they saw me at the door the shopkeeper smiled, the customer smiled, greetings were exchanged and my business was soon transacted, but as I left the furious argument started all over again. It was much the same with motor accidents and when we in turn had a minor one I was told by the insurers that they expected about two every year, although since the Greeks in Athens tended not to drive very fast, if often recklessly, accidents were seldom fatal. I was interested in this connection to be told that the Greek Police had been trained by a team led by the Inspector-General of the Royal Irish Constabulary, Sir Charles Wickham, who had been my father's superior in the old days in Ireland. It seems that because the Greeks can convey extremely offensive imputations about one's character, one's ancestors, and even one's legitimacy, by the use of fingers and hands the conventional traffic signs used by police in the United Kingdom had to be considerably modified as in their basic form they caused such anger amongst the Greek motorists that policemen were often assaulted by angry drivers and a very much stiffer and more stylised method of traffic signals had to be devised!

There was, of course, a great deal to be seen outside the capital and we had two relaxing family holidays, one at Xilokastron in the Peloponnese and another one at the wooded island of Thasos off the northern Greek coast where we saw the Medea performed by moonlight in a very old woodland theatre which had been so neglected that a tree had grown in the middle of the proscenium and the inevitable Greek chorus had to appear, disappear and change with only stunted shrubs and bushes for cover. In that Arcadian setting it seemed theatre at its ancient best, and it was an experience to treasure always.

On Sundays it was the custom of the small British

community and almost all our diplomatic staff to picnic on the beach at Marathon where we would set up little camps under the casuarina trees and sleep and swim until almost sunset. These were happy days and for some reason very few Greeks and not many Americans came there. Sometimes we would wander off and sit by the great mound where the heroes of that famous battle were buried. Greece was like that; history was everywhere and whether in Argos, in the huge theatre of Epidaurus or in some little valley in the heart of the mountains the two hundred years of Hellenic glory seemed to linger in the air, in the temple shades and even under the olive trees themselves. It was a wonderful country not just to visit but in which to live and it was impossible not to fall in love with the people, the climate, and the whole ambience of that ancient sunlit world.

One of my happiest memories is of an autumn day when, in accordance with custom, the whole Diplomatic Corps were invited to tread the grapes at a big vineyard on the outskirts of Athens. We went dressed either in shorts or in old clothes and, barefooted in a huge enclosure stamped on the grapes to the tunes of bouzoukia music with a glass of last year's wine, frequently replenished, in our hands. For a little while we felt part of the ordinary people of Greece and the sight of an eminent Ambassador doing a knees-up and happily stamping on the grapes with laughing Greeks and young diplomats from many other Embassies was one to remember, and perhaps showed democracy at its best. But then, as they were quite prepared to remind us, the Greeks themselves were the first democrats of all.

Once a year a wine festival was held at the Temple of Daphne. Visitors paid a nominal charge to enter the arena in which a whole series of stalls had been set up staffed by pretty girls in colourful Greek costumes, displaying wines from their particular district or island. We were given little glasses on arrival in which we could sample any wine that took our fancy and also a fairly substantial flask which we

152

were invited to fill up before it became time to close the bars. Towards midnight, on a little central stage, Greek dancers from the mainland, the islands, and, especially, thigh slapping knee breeched peasants from Crete performed for an hour or two whilst the audience sat and ate their sandwiches on the warm stones of the old theatre and often finally, if they had remembered to bring cushions, went to sleep where they sat. The Greeks on these occasions were at their convivial best sharing their wine, cheese, curiosity and conversation with all and sundry. Much later we roused ourselves feeling remarkably refreshed and not really tired at all as the sun rose to the north-east behind Mount Pendeli, and driving back we watched the city returning slowly to life.

We had many examples of the attitude of the ordinary people to the British at a time when relations between our governments were more than a little strained. On one occasion soon after our arrival my wife went into a small shop to buy bread and the assistant, like so many Greeks, was extremely curious to know exactly from whence she came. Although her nationality was Canadian she decided to declare herself as British and the shopkeeper, speaking quite passable English, said with a smile handing her the bread, 'Take this as a present from Makarios!'

During the first year or so I saw little of the Greek Air Force at work although when meeting their senior officers socially I formed the increasingly strong feeling that their affection for the Royal Air Force, in which so many of them had been trained, and indeed for Great Britain for historical reasons was undiminished but it was not easy for them to show this in public. However, we had plenty to do getting to know and understand something of the intricacies of diplomatic life and of its customs and behaviours. I had often heard that life in the Foreign Service was largely a matter of attending cocktail parties and for a while at least I almost believed that this was true.

In Athens the social life for a Service Attaché was almost continuous. We were involved of necessity in many receptions given by other Service Attachés on Armed Forces or National Days and these, of course, we attended in full uniform. There were many others given by the various Embassies to which we were also invited, and in addition to this the small but very high powered British community made us extremely welcome. Then there was the American Navy. At that time their Sixth Fleet was a constant visitor to Piraeus and we were invited almost every month to attend a reception given by the hard working Naval Attaché to welcome the latest ship to arrive. These were excellent parties, and since the American Fleet was always dry at sea I much preferred meeting their sailors on land but one really did need a cast-iron stomach. I had some useful counsel on this from my friend George Barstow, our Naval Attaché, who advised me that the thing to drink during a long evening was brandy (usually Greek brandy) and soda since, although it didn't taste of anything in particular, it was not unpleasant and kept one fairly sober! I did, however, realise fairly soon that there was some purpose to these continual social functions apart from increasing the profits of liquor manufacturers worldwide. We learnt a good deal from meeting not only our diplomatic colleagues but visitors from many parts of the world and for Service Attachés it was particularly helpful to receive the views – usually quite unsolicited – of others on the Cyprus dispute. The Russians played things a little differently.

At a reception a few months after our arrival I was approached by the Soviet Service Attaché, one Captain Chabanov, who represented all three armed Services in Athens. He was as always accompanied by another member of the Russian Embassy in civilian clothes and we were not quite sure whether he was his superior officer or a member of their Intelligence Staff. Captain Chabanov began by saying that it was high time I went and called on him and I replied, quite correctly, that since, in accordance with custom, on arrival I had sent official cards through our Embassy to all the other Embassies in Athens and as I had had the pleasure already of meeting him a number of times I considered a formal call was unnecessary. He answered that calling was a matter of diplomatic protocol and since this had been invented by the British he thought I should subscribe to it. I replied that I thought protocol was a French invention and as we used French in sending p.p.c. cards (meaning 'pour prendre congé') to our colleagues when we went on leave and when we sent them invitations we inscribed in the corner of the envelope the mystic letters e.v. (meaning 'en ville') France was the more likely origin. Brushing this aside he said that nevertheless he would like me to call on him at his Embassy.

I spoke about all this to Captain Barstow and together we went to see the Head of Chancery to seek his advice. He told us that there was no earthly reason we shouldn't go and call on the Russian if he wished us to, and no doubt we could handle ourselves appropriately. With this approval George and I set off in his car, with the Naval ensign flying, and made our way to the Russian Embassy. We were received by Captain Chabanov's assistant and welcomed with caviar and excellent vodka together with apologies for the Captain's tardy arrival. After a drink or two and being asked some rather simple questions about the equipment of our two Services, Captain Chabanov arrived beaming and apologising for being late and we sat down and had some more to drink and some more caviar. The questions continued on a very primitive basis touching nothing more than possibly confidential Service matters and after a while we decided it was time to leave. As we were making our farewells the door opened and in came the Russian Ambassador. It was rather like a stage play in that he had come in right on cue so again, as a matter of courtesy, we sat down had a few words with His Excellency, another glass of vodka and finally, feeling none the worse for wear, climbed into the Naval Attachés car. As soon as we had done so we remembered that it was the Fourth of July, American Independence Day, and we were both due at the American Embassy. Feeling quite cheerful we were mildly reproached for our late arrival by our American colleagues who were a little surprised by our excuse that we had just come from the Russian Embassy!

Diplomatic occasions varied a great deal and on two occasions I can remember, because of the number of parties in Athens on the same evening and the extraordinarily difficult and complicated way the Greeks numbered or failed to number their streets, arriving at the wrong one. Being in uniform I was readily recognised and my wife and I knew a number of other people there. It was only a day or two later when talking to some of my diplomatic colleagues who wondered at our absence that I realised that we had gone to the wrong address! Misunderstandings of this sort were not unusual.

The main requirement for a Service Attaché seemed to be, apart from a thoroughly adaptable stomach and the ability to change clothes quickly, a genuine liking for meeting people and some curiosity about their views on life and modes of living which were always varied, and often very different from our own. It was not difficult, without any feeling of disloyalty, to modify one's own feelings and views on British policy towards Greece in the light of some of their comments. However, since the Greeks themselves were so emotional and largely unpredictable it was quite likely that the views of those we met at these many social functions were themselves to be changed next day! There were many more formal occasions and in these the Greeks with their flair for the theatre and the love of ceremonial really excelled. Whether at the solemn funeral of Prince George of Crete or one of their National Days their organisation and timing could not be faulted. On these occasions the Diplomatic Corps assembled in the Greek Orthodox Cathedral and the service with the chanting of a hidden choir was always impressive. Whilst the congregation were assembling the Diplomatic Corps collected in an aisle and it was interesting to watch the Doyen who was Chinese from Formosa (now Taiwan) greeting his colleagues. He had been there for a long time partly because very few countries, including our own, at that time recognised Taiwan as a separate state since most of them had now established full relationships with Peking. Next in order of seniority was the Russian ambassador and when he arrived and sat next to the Chinaman it was noticeable that the Russian looked a little embarrassed and ignored his neighbour completely whilst exchanging courtesies with everyone else. The Chinaman seemed much more at home and appeared to look straight through the Russian while talking to other diplomats. It was a little private comedy observed with relish by us three Attachés and others in the Diplomatic Corps. The service itself, conducted by the Archbishop of Athens or one of his Bishops, was always attended by the King and Queen and at one stage the King would kneel and kiss the bible before the whole congregation.

The Greek Orthodox Church did seem to have a very real way of projecting the story of Christianity and at Easter time this was moving and evocative to a degree. On Good Friday all the women wore black and most men wore dark ties, the radio played solemn music all day and no parties of any sort were held. Written communications were heavily bordered in mourning black. On Easter Saturday it was much the same but on that evening the whole Diplomatic Corps and most of Athens gathered around midnight and a great candle-lit procession wound its way through the ancient streets. At the city centre on the stroke of midnight a great shout would go up and the cry of 'Christos Anesti!' (Christ is risen) and wild cheering would break out with everyone embracing their neighbours. Fireworks had once been common but because of various recent conflagrations they were banned before our arrival. I felt then as never before the real meaning of the Christian message – the knowledge that something quite dramatic had happened and that the whole world was rejoicing, like VE Day on an enormous scale, but this time not just for victory in Europe but for the salvation of humanity.

Other memories come flowing back – one of a farewell party at Heraklion in Crete given by the outgoing British Vice-Consul who, because of an economy drive, was not going to be replaced. The party was for some of his Greek and British friends and our host introduced my wife and me to a splendid piratical figure, looking a little like Long John Silver, who it seemed had led the partisans during the war from his stronghold on Mount Ida. As my squadron had sometimes dropped supplies to them en passant whilst bombing German airfields in Greece in 1942 I was particularly glad to meet him. When all this had been explained through an interpreter he got very excited and said that he remembered particularly the satisfaction he had felt one day when he had walked down the mountain and killed six Germans before breakfast! This was not a tale I felt I could repeat to my colleagues in the German Embassy in Athens but it did explain why this remarkable man was held in such high esteem and why, although it was said he owed a great deal of money to the government, he was unlikely ever to be forced to pay.

The Greek Royal family were a good deal in evidence and in the small, quite tight-knit diplomatic community in Athens we met them often. The coming of age ball of Prince Constantine at the Royal Palace was a truly magnificent affair. It was held in the open on a summer night in 1958 with a small dance floor in the floodlit grounds around which the whole Royal family, King Paul, Queen Frederika, the two princesses, Sophia and Irene, and Prince

Constantine sat and talked to their guests.

Constantine had invited his classmates from the Greek Naval Academy who were there in force together with their very pretty ladies. It was one of the most truly romantic evenings I can ever remember with everyone mingling freely and pink champagne flowing. We Attachés mixed with everybody, danced with the two princesses and walked in the moonlight under arches of roses. Although for that evening the Cyprus problem was forgotten we in the British Embassy had been advised to arrive singly not to draw too much attention to ourselves, and I heard afterwards that the King had invited Admiral Sir Charles Lambe to be his personal guest at a time when the British connection was being kept very much in the background. It was a brave and typical gesture from the monarch of a country that had never forgotten its real affection for Britain and particularly for the Royal Navy to which it felt it owed a lasting debt of gratitude.

The Greeks at that time were in a monarchist mood and the King was able discreetly to help in affairs of state and to support Mr Karamanlis who, in his record seven years as Prime Minister, did much to improve the general conditon of the country and its people. Crown Prince Constantine was particularly active and on one occasion at Easter time we Attachés were invited to the Greek Air Force Station at Tatoi where, when His Royal Highness arrived by helicopter, we took it in turns to crack coloured hard boiled eggs with him. It was a traditional Greek game, rather like schoolboy conkers, and whichever egg lasted longer was the winner.

Queen Frederika being German was a much more controversial figure and the Greeks, who did not like the Germans at all and only tolerated their tourists for their money, had considerable reservations about their Queen. We had the impression that Queen Frederika, who spoke perfect English, was anxious to do all she could to counteract this and she took a prominent part in all kinds of welfare

159

work. When I got to know the Greek Air Force better towards the end of my tour they liked to tell stories about her and in particular one about a certain Maison de Plaisir in Thessalonika. It was one of those Greek tales that could be varied according to the audience and both the circumstances and the details changed quite often in the telling. Basically it was a story about a visitor to this establishment who had much enjoyed himself. However, on leaving he thought the bill rather high and asking for it to be broken down he was told that forty percent was for madam, thirty percent was for the girl and twenty-five percent was for general expenses. Having added all this up he asked what about the other five percent and was told with a smile, 'That, of course, is for the Queen's Fund!'

During 1958 there was at last real progress in resolving the Cyprus dispute. Although at the end of 1957 the United Nations Assembly had passed a resolution calling for self determination for Cyprus it was with less than the two-thirds majority required to make it effective. Nevertheless the impetus for a settlement proved irresistible. The British appointed a new governor to Cyprus, Sir Hugh Foot (who afterwards became Lord Caradon), to take over from Sir John Harding and Makarios, since he was unacceptable in Cyprus to the British after his release from the Seychelles, came to live in the Greek capital. In August of 1958 Mr Harold Macmillan brought out to Athens a new plan for the joint administration by all three parties of the Island but the Greeks could not accept this since it admitted that the Turks should be involved. However, a change could no longer be denied. When in October Makarios suddenly announced he accepted independence for Cyprus instead of Enosis the end was in sight. Detailed negotiations went on in Zurich and in London for a year and finally even Grivas agreed that union with Greece was no longer practicable. By August 1960 negotiations had come to an end and a divided Cyprus became independent within the Commonwealth.

Once a settlement seemed to be in sight the Greek Government and people readily and almost dramatically became openly friendly again towards British people and the British Services. The Secretary of State for Commonwealth Relations, Mr Duncan Sandys, came on a visit and I stood with him on the roof of the control tower of the Greek Air Force Station at Eleusis where we witnessed an impressive display by Canadian-built F.86's of the Royal Hellenic Air Force. The station had laid out a great many Greek vases, urns, and other artefacts and before leaving Mr Sandys was invited to take his pick. He turned to me and said that he understood that the export of Greek antiquities was strictly forbidden and that he didn't feel he should take any. However, the Greek Colonel in charge assured me (whether truthfully or not) that everything on display had been dug up on the airfield very recently and was without great value. Finally we all took something and I ended up with two small tear vases which I have told my family to keep filled up in due course on my departure, although if their lachrymose glands run dry it may be that they will have to revert to aqua pura from the kitchen tap! A visit by an RAF Fighter Squadron to the airfield at Larissa was a great success and when Mr Sandys was asked at a press conference if the British Government had any intention of inviting a Greek Squadron to England he replied very quickly that we would always be delighted to see the Greek Air Force in the United Kingdom. A Naval visit followed soon and was led by the rather ancient cruiser Birmingham commanded by Captain Beatty VC who had won his distinction in breaching the lock gates at St Nazaire in the elderly ex-American destroyer *HMS Campbelltown*. The Captain and his wife, who had accompanied him in a Fleet Auxiliary, stayed with us a night or two in Athens. The whole atmosphere now was as if the sun had come out from behind Parnassus and all was well in this brave new Anglo-Hellenic world. The Greek Services were now our friends and we three Attachés felt free to go

161

almost where we liked, and during the latter part of my tour I visited almost every Greek Air Force station both on the mainland and in the islands.

Getting to know the officers of the Greek Air Force, who almost to a man spoke good English, was to realise what a delightful, uninhibited and extraordinarily courageous race the Greeks are at their best. One good friend of mine, Air Commodore Theodossaides, delighted in telling somewhat risqué stories and seemed to renew his fund of these continually since every time we met he had another one, which made me wonder sometimes if he was in direct communication with the famous story tellers of the London Stock Exchange! Like other Air Forces the Greeks rather enjoyed teasing their own army who were, of course, far stronger numerically and more powerful politically, and he rejoiced in telling a story about three retired Generals. It seems these three old soldiers were sitting out one day in the Zappeion Gardens in Athens lamenting the effect of old age on their various faculties and the youngest, who was in his late seventies said that he was going nearly blind and he could no longer rejoice in the sight of the children playing in the park and the lovely things there were to see in this new born world of spring. The second General, who was a year or two older, sympathised with him deeply and said that he, too, was feeling the effects of his years because he was getting deaf and he so loved to hear the sound of the birds and the voices of children and the glorious music of Wagner and Bach. He felt he was losing one of the major pleasures of his life. The third one, who was over eighty, paused a while and said, 'My dear friends my heart bleeds for you both but I am in far worse circumstances than either of you. This morning I was lying in bed with Daphne, my blonde friend whom you have both met, and who for all her eighteen years of age knows a great deal about how to make an old man happy. I turned to her as the sun was coming through the blinds and dappling the counterpane and I said to her on this lovely spring morning, 'Darling let's make love' and Daphne opened those lovely limpid innocent blue eyes of hers and looked into mine and said very clearly, 'You old goat, we made love a quarter of an hour ago!' He said, 'Gentlemen that's my trouble, I forget'.

By Christmas 1959 our tour was coming to an end and on Boxing Day for the last time we climbed Pendeli Mountain, a custom that the whole British Community had now adopted and was becoming almost a British tradition. The children ran ahead and my eight-year-old daughter, Kathleen, who had the legs of a Greek mountain goat was one of the first at the summit and then came back wondering why we laggards were tarrying so long. The rest of us, suffering heavily from overeating and our own and other people's hospitality, finally made it to the little shrine on the mountain top through a curtain of mist and when we got there we found that Captain Barstow's assistant had managed to get a jeep most of the way to the top and had lit a fire and brewed a welcome hot drink on the crest of that famous mountain. As we were enjoying this and trying to get our breath back a little platoon of Greek soldiers marched over the hill out of the mist into the clear air of the shrine and down the other side, the Lieutenant saluting us as he passed – another tiny etching on the pattern of a truly happy day.

Two months later our tour was over and after a series of farewell parties in which our Greek friends joined fully, glad that our relationships had been fully restored, we embarked again in Piraeus. It was not an easy country to leave but the warmth and kindness of those last few months lingered on although not until we reached the cooler air of Marseilles, our one port of call on the way home, did our bodies begin to recover fully from so much hospitality. Perhaps that is why they had warned me in London that the job of Attaché required an iron constitution and added that, since it meant being out of the main stream of Service life for quite a while, it was unlikely to further my prospects of promotion.

CHAPTER 9

Grey Funnel Line at Greenwich

On the journey home from Greece I began to wonder what the future held in store. It was a little unexpected. After being de-briefed at the Air Ministry, where I was assured that according to my Ambassador's reports I had not entirely disgraced myself in Athens and was offered the somewhat dubious consolation of being told that any damage to my liver had been incurred in an excellent cause, I was posted to the Directing Staff of the Naval War College at Greenwich. Although I did not know it at the time it turned out to be my last one in a Service which I had joined entirely by accident almost thirty years before.

The Senior Officers War Course (which has now been discontinued) was high powered with an intake of some twenty-one students of whom usually fifteen were from the Navy and three each from the Army and from the Royal Air Force. Most of these officers were of the rank of Captain or Commander or their equivalents in the other two Services. Although we completed the whole course in about five months it covered most of the syllabus of the Imperial Defence College (now the Royal College of Defence Studies) which took about a year to cover the same ground. The Directing Staff consisted of four officers only, the Commandant being a Naval Captain, supported by another Naval Officer, an Army Colonel and myself. The

164

administrative work was done by a Naval Secretarial Officer and a single clerk so the overheads were fairly light.

The course was an interesting one and since it was on a much higher and less detailed level than the longer one at Service Staff Colleges there was more time to study major international questions such as the Middle East, the Third World, the problems of nuclear war and the necessary economic limitations to defence spending in a peace time democracy. The weekly programme was quite leisurely, work starting at eleven o'clock on a Monday morning with Wednesday afternoon for sport which was quite undefined. The weekend began at lunchtime on Friday since the students mostly lived in Portsmouth or one of the Hampshire villages and although they lived in college during the week they nearly all went home at weekends.

Our studies were wide ranging and because of the immense prestige of the Navy and the convenience of Greenwich to Whitehall and also through the influence of senior officers (including Lord Mountbatten who visited Greenwhich frequently) we were able to draw on very high-powered lecturers. Many came down in the evenings and after dining in the college talked to us then. Since all the students and staff at the War College were individually cleared for Top Secret information they felt that they could really let their hair down and the discussions which followed were usually most illuminating. Apart from Government Ministers and officials we had talks from the Head of the BBC and the Chiefs of all three Armed Services. Although we did not travel abroad the course included visits to many Service establishments including HMS Excellent to study Naval gunnery and HMS Dolphin to learn about submarine and anti-submarine warfare. Regular visits were paid to Londonderry where Joint Air-Sea Warfare was taught and demonstrated.

Greenwich itself was a pleasant place in which to work and in the summer, following Naval tradition, we played bowls on the lawn and, in the winter, skittles in the alley between two of the main buildings. The Admiral President of the College when I reported there, was Earl Cairns, who afterwards became Marshal of the Diplomatic Corps and he was succeeded by Admiral 'Sandy' Gordon-Lennox who became Sergeant at Arms at the House of Commons after completing his tour at Greenwich. As I was the only airman on the War College staff, they made me very welcome and I enjoyed much of their hospitality, particularly when senior Air Force officers were visiting the College or when some dignitary whom I had met abroad was their guest.

On one memorable occasion I was invited to lunch with Queen Frederika and Crown Prince Constantine together with the two Princesses who were visiting England privately at the time. Prince Constantine told me that his father said that any visit to England must include one to the Naval College at Greenwich and as he himself had been trained at the Greek Naval Academy he was very glad indeed to follow this advice.

After an excellent lunch in the Admiral President's house Queen Frederika really let her hair down. She had the reputation, as I well knew, of being a tremendous extrovert and from time to time somewhat indiscreet but she was tremendous fun and as the Greek Royal family spoke English fluently, language was in no way a problem. She told us a story about Admiral Mountbatten when his ship had visited Piraeus at the end of the war and he had been received with great honour and much ceremony. She decided in a light-hearted moment that she would give him a surprise and when invited on his ship she went down with her lady-in-waiting to the Admiral's cabin and made him an apple-pie bed. Next day she said that she had sent a signal to him after his ship had sailed saying 'Admiral from Queen. I trust you slept well' and she said the answer came back quite quickly saying 'Yes Your Majesty, after certain very necessary adjustments had been made!' She had another story about General Montgomery who also had visited Athens and had sent his respects to the Palace saying that he would like to call on His Majesty. She said that she knew that Montgomery was a man of somewhat ascetic and indeed almost Cromwellian habits and she was not surprised when after the Royal invitation to dinner had been accepted gratefully, she had heard indirectly that Montgomery hoped it would be a fairly early evening. She could not resist this and sent him a further message saying that if the General would care to stay the night she would be happy personally to serve him dinner in bed! I cannot vouch for either of these stories but I have little doubt that they were very much in her character. It was not easy for a German Queen in a country which had been ravaged by so many of her countrymen to keep her end up but on the few occasions we met she seemed to have the happy knack of making everyone feel at home.

Time at the Naval College passed very pleasantly. The work was stimulating if undemanding and there was lots of time to think. In Greece I had taken at very short notice an examination for the Administrative Branch of the Home Civil Service when a few vacancies were being offered on a late-entry competition. This was open to members of the Armed Services up to the age of about fifty as well as the Colonial Service which was just beginning to run down. Although I had not passed sufficiently highly to be offered an appointment I had done fairly well and in 1961 I applied to take this examination again. I was informed by the Civil Service Commissioners that in view of my results in the previous competition I would be exempted from the large part of the examination which consisted of two days working on problems in syndicates of about six and I would now be expected to take only the written papers and perhaps face the Commissioners themselves. When the results of the written part of the examination had been assessed I was told that I would now be required only to meet the Selection Committee. My mind went back to the time thirty-five years earlier when as a Special Entry candidate for the Executive Branch of the Royal Navy I had faced my examiners before. The Board this time was presided over by Sir John Mallaby who had been High Commissioner in New Zealand and who had chaired the same Board when I had faced them at my previous attempt two years earlier whilst still serving in Athens. He put me at my ease at once and said that apart from himself and one other all my inquisitors had now changed and after a very friendly discussion on various matters, particularly about life in Greece and my views on the Irish question, I left feeling that I had done my best. However as I had not expected in face of the very heavy competition to be selected, and had done virtually no preparation for this examination, I had not told either the Air Ministry or my Admiral in Greenwich that I was competing amongst almost three hundred others for some thirty vacancies. Indeed I wasn't absolutely sure that I wanted one but in any case I didn't think I would have to make up my mind one way or the other. When the results were declared I was one of only nineteen candidates who were offered appointments and, having decided to accept, I had hastily to inform the Air Ministry that I would like immediate release from the Royal Air Force and also to assure the Admiral President of the College, who had been extremely kind to me, that a replacement would be found at very short notice indeed. Fortunately I had friends at court and Air Commodore Alan Deere who was on the Personnel Staff at Air Ministry and who had been on the same wartime Staff College course with me at Bulstrode came to the rescue and in a remarkably short time a replacement was found and the Admiral persuaded, without too much difficulty, that I was indeed in no way indispensable. Meanwhile I had much thinking to do.

In many ways I did not really wish to leave the RAF but

the die was now cast. Even if I was promoted again I did not
expect to serve much beyond the age of fifty-five and in the
Civil Service, although I might be forced to retire at sixty, I
could probably stay on until sixty-five. With children still at
school this was a major consideration, I had greatly enjoyed
my years of service and for many years the RAF had been
my life and, for long periods, my home as well. It seemed to
me that it owed its wonderful sense of comradeship largely,
in the commissioned ranks at any rate, to its very varied
methods of entry. We had officers who had been trained as
Halton apprentices and had come up through the ranks,
sometimes reaching the rank of Air Marshal, and there were
others who had come in on Short Service Commissions.
There was a considerable University entry and there were
the professional airmen who had joined the Cadet College at
Cranwell intending to make the Royal Air Force their
career. We all mixed happily together and very often one had
no idea whether one's brother officer had joined from a
university or from the ranks.

A friend of mine who had received a Permanent Commission from Trinity College, Dublin, told me a story about
university selection. He himself had been a medical student
and had obtained his commission on the strength of the Arts
Degree which was awarded automatically half way through
the course. He liked to tell about another medical student, a
contemporary of his at Trinity, who had been greatly
impressed by his friend's success in obtaining a Permanent
Commission. Finding his own progress at university more
than a little behind schedule he too applied when he had
gained his Arts degree after rather more than the scheduled
two years of study. He had the usual medical tests and
interviews but when he came before the final Selection
Board the President greeted him warmly and said that he
seemed in many ways to be a very suitable candidate indeed
for commissioned rank in the Royal Air Force but the Board
were somewhat intrigued by the discovery that according to

his medical report he was quite demonstrably pregnant! It seems that this young man knowing that he had diabetes had borrowed a sample from his girlfriend who presumably did not know at the time about her happy (or unhappy) condition, and the Board President went on to say that in all the circumstances he was afraid that the Royal Air Force would not after all be able to avail themselves of this applicant's services.

After talking it over with my very understanding wife and having made up my mind that I must now face up a little late in life to a new, if somewhat abbreviated, career in the Civil Service I was much concerned as to which Department I was likely to be assigned. I was in no way proud of my degree in Agriculture but as I had had to declare it on my application form I thought it was highly likely that I would be sent as a Principal to the Ministry of Agriculture and Fisheries, although I had stated that my first preference was for the Commonwealth Relations Office which I thought gave me some chance of being posted overseas to one of the Dominions. This degree which I hardly ever used seemed to haunt me. Many years earlier when it came to light as a young officer I had been placed in charge of the Officers' Mess gardens but unfortunately through confusing fertilizers and herbicides I managed to kill all the roses! I was then made Bar Officer and was rather more successful at this for a while until I tried to persuade my fellow officers to drink quantities of Guinness, the firm having been founded by an ancestor of mine whose descendant Sir Mark Rainsford (then Lord Mayor of Dublin) had made the great mistake of selling it on April Fools' Day 1759 to one Arthur Guinness, merchant, of Westmeath. As the weather got warmer consumption diminished and in the end I was very nearly compelled to either drink or pay for the unused barrels myself! It was of course a foolish thing to try to change other people's drinking habits and I hope it taught me a lesson.

I could only await now with considerable trepidation for my appointment to come through. It was with very great relief therefore when the letter came saying that, subject to the necessary security clearances, I had been appointed as a Principal in the Home Civil Service and assigned to the Defence Department of the Commonwealth Relations Office in Downing Street. This was beside the building in King Charles Street in which I had worked some years before when it housed the Department of the Chief of the Air Staff at the time of the Berlin Air Lift. Perhaps life wouldn't be so very different after all.

CHAPTER 10

Diplomat in India

I was lucky in my new boss – one General George Price, a distinguished soldier who had a long and intimate knowledge of Whitehall and its workings. He put me at my ease at once and was most helpful in introducing me to my new Department. Our role here was concerned primarily with supporting, and to some extent supplying, the Armed Forces of Commonwealth Countries and especially the newer ones who had just graduated from their previous Colonial status. We were dealing at one time with supplying submarines to Australia or Canada and at another with ground forces in the African territories, and although very few countries could afford or indeed appeared to need modern military aircraft it did not prevent many of them from asking for them! It was particularly noticeable that in the case both of ships and aircraft the inquiries we received nearly always stipulated that the very latest modern equipment should be made available. In some cases items requested were quite highly classified and had not yet even been delivered in any quantity to our own Services. In one particular instance tanks were asked for which we knew well could not possibly go over any of the local bridges.

During the summer of 1962 our attention in the Commonwealth Relations Office, and particularly in the Defence Department, was increasingly directed to tension on the Northern Frontier of India. A long simmering border dispute with China threatened to erupt, and in July shots were exchanged after the Indians had established some small outposts in the Ladakh area to contain continued Chinese infiltration. Things really came to a head in late October and hostilities broke out all along the long frontier between the two countries. Although the Indian Army made desperate attempts to contain the powerful Chinese invading force they soon were compelled to give up most of the disputed area. The Indian Government, and Nehru in particular, were taken by surprise since they had not expected war on this scale and the controversial Minister of Defence, Mr Krishna Menon, was forced to resign. The British Government was much concerned with these developments both for political and economic reasons and when an urgent request was received from the Indian Government for military supplies approval was quickly forthcoming. This was of course a job for our Department.

The first stated requirement of the Indian Forces was for a large number of the new FN rifles and ammunition. This was not all that easy to fulfil since supplies were fairly limited and the British Army were just now being re-equipped with this new weapon. However with the co-operation of all Departments, and no doubt largely through the influence of General Price, these rifles were made available. Getting them to India in a hurry posed something of a problem but a good friend of mine in the Air Ministry, Air Vice-Marshal Tommy Prickett, with whom I had served in the Western Desert in 1941, put two Britannias of Transport Command at our disposal at very short notice and the first delivery of FN rifles arrived in India on the 29th October 1962 only a few days after being requested. Further supplies were sent by sea. Our Secretary of State Mr Duncan Sandys was of course delighted and received many congratulations on this quick and timely delivery.

During the next year the supply of arms to India became a

major part of our task and as the pressure built up it reminded me of the Berlin Air Lift days again. Although the British Government agreed initially to make arms available as a free gift to the value of nineteen million pounds conditions were naturally attached. All weapons supplied were supposed to be for defensive purposes only but it was of course extremely difficult to decide in practice whether anti-tank guns, armoured vehicles, aircraft and other supplies were purely defensive or could in fact be employed just as easily in an offensive role. Since commonsense indicated that the distinction was necessarily blurred this did not worry us too much. What did become more of a concern was the problem of accounting for supplies since the Treasury seemed to expect everything to be supplied, shipped and paid for within the financial year and as much of the equipment required had not even been manufactured this was obviously impossible. Fortunately the experienced Civil Servants on our staff were able to sort this one out but it was a problem arising from the constraints of our budgeting system that I had known of old from Singapore days and I always found it frustrating.

Perhaps because my name had become associated with India, at the end of 1963 I was posted to the Deputy High Commission in Madras as the First Secretary. I realised at once how little I knew about modern India and particularly about the Southern States for which our Madras office was responsible and I had to learn fast. It was a nice change though to have been 'offered' the appointment and to know that, although I was not expected to refuse it, if I had any particular reason for not wishing to go a substitute could readily be found. I had no difficulty in accepting this assignment as India had always interested me and a number of my Irish relations had served in the Indian Army. I realised only too well that it was a country, or rather a sub-continent, about which one could read a lot and in which one could spend a whole lifetime and still come home without

174

any fairly clear picture of its varied life and peoples.

As it happened the Deputy High Commissioner in Madras, Mr W J M Paterson, was on leave in London and invited me to join him for lunch. Willie, as I soon got to call him, was a Scottish lawyer who, after serving in the Army during the war and becoming a Hungarian interpreter, had met and married a delightful Hungarian, Nori, who spoke many languages and was a tremendous success as the senior British memsahib in Southern India. From the start Willie and I got on well, as did our wives, and although I felt he applied a good deal of Scottish caution to our early meetings I sensed that when the time came for us to sail for India we had the prospect of working with delightful people who might well become real friends. And so it turned out.

At the time my posting to Madras came through my wife and I were still living in a little cottage at Mereworth near West Malling in Kent which I had bought when working with the Navy at Greenwich. I had expected then as a matter of course to live in a married quarter but the Admiral assured me on arrival that the Navy had not yet got down seriously to catering for matrimony and that, although one or two senior officers did live in married bliss within the College precincts, very few quarters were in fact available.

Audrey and I now set about the usual chores of arranging for packers, reorganising children's schooling and trying to let the house. Unfortunately I complicated matters considerably by developing what the local doctor diagnosed as a troublesome gall-bladder which needed surgical attention and I found myself very reluctantly agreeing to be admitted to hospital in Tunbridge Wells whilst at the same time endeavouring to persuade the Commonwealth Relations Office that my posting to Madras did not need to be cancelled. After a day or two in hospital the symptoms of the gall-bladder began to abate and when the surgeon came around for a pre-operational examination I told him that I was anxious to take up my appointment in India and that I was beginning to feel better already. He thought a little about this and then said that he was certain there were excellent doctors there who could easily whip out a gall-bladder, and although he did not in any way dispute the original diagnosis he felt that there was no reason I should not go after all. I discharged myself and told the Office that we could all sail as planned. In something of a hurry we sold our house quite readily at a small profit and prepared for another overseas posting – our first in the Commonwealth Service.

On the last day of January 1964 I sailed with my wife, eldest daughter Josephine, and my small six-year-old son Desmond on the P & O Liner *Orsova* for Bombay. As it happened Josephine, who was born during the war, was due to celebrate her twenty-first birthday almost immediately after our arrival in India. The journey out was the familiar one through the Mediterranean and the Red Sea and since we knew no one on board there was much time to read and to think. It was a pleasant change not to be sailing in a troop ship and to be able to treat the voyage as pure relaxation. I found my own thoughts instead of being concerned with India, about which I had read a good deal but knew very little, reverted very much to my youth and to the happy days I had spent in the RAF. The war was largely forgotten and as so often in life the good things seemed to stand out. Tiny quite unrelated incidents kept coming to mind.

After I joined the Faculty of Agriculture at Queen's University in 1931 we shared many First Year lectures with the big Medical Faculty. One of our subjects was Botany and our professor, one Dr James Small, who had written a very learned and expensive book on the subject which we were all expected to buy, was reputed to dislike medical students intensely. At any rate it had become a well established custom that he always began his inaugural lecture by declaiming 'Ladies, Gentlemen, and Medical Students'. At this point a great roar went up and it was the custom for us undisciplined young men and, particularly for those in the Medical Faculty, to release rats, mice, pigeons and miscellaneous livestock which were brought in specially for the occasion. I had a sneaking feeling that Jimmie Small's disapproval of medical students was by no means wholehearted and that he enjoyed the turmoil as much as we all did, but of course he gave no evidence of this whatsoever. The first sentence of his book remains in my mind always. It states 'A seed may be simply described as a ripened integumented megasporangium'! No doubt this is the perfect definition. Odd, I thought, that all this should come back to memory as we ploughed on through the tropical windless heat of the Red Sea.

Air Force memories, totally unconnected with each other and equally irrelevant came back too. One day when Orderly Officer at Driffield before the war I was summoned by the Control Tower to attend a small glider which had landed without any warning in the middle of the airfield. It was the first glider I had ever seen and I don't think anyone in the Control Tower had seen one either. When I drove out to meet the pilot it turned out that he was one Philip Wills, of the tobacco family, who had made many gliding records and on this occasion had flown from the Pennines, near Kinder Scout, to Driffield, having set off for this airfield rather as one might have done in a Tiger Moth. In doing this I think this time he broke yet another record for a planned flight and when we greeted him and took him to the Officers' Mess for a drink and lunch he said that his wife would be along presently with a car and trailer to collect the glider, and in the meanwhile he would appreciate it if we would take care of it on his behalf. I was to meet Wills once more after the war when he became a director of British European Airways – a company I nearly joined as a commercial pilot.

Another remarkable figure who arrived at our airfield shortly before the outbreak of war was a senior Group Captain who announced that he had come on behalf of

NAAFI to inspect our bar. As I was Bar Officer at the time it was of course my responsibility to look after him. I noticed that in addition to the King's and Queen's medals of the Boer War he also sported a black and yellow one of an even earlier vintage. After he had sampled the beer which he seemed to think fairly good I plucked up courage and asked him what this other medal was. He smiled and said 'Oh yes, yes of course that is the Zulu War'. I found out afterwards that he was well known to a much earlier generation of airmen as 'Zulu Bettington'.

Although my mind kept reverting to earlier days I found myself wondering how well I was going to cope with the responsibilities of my new post. I had learnt from the Commonwealth Office in London, and from Willie Paterson, that the job would be largely representational in that it would entail meeting a great many people of different races, colours and religions. There was too a considerable British community of planters, bankers and merchants in South India for whom we had Consular responsibility.

We arrived in Bombay in about two weeks, much refreshed by a very pleasant voyage. Although we had known none of the other passengers previously, we soon made friends on board and at Gibraltar we had been met by an RAF launch and taken ashore to explore the Colony as the guests of an old Air Force friend. We were fortunate too in Aden where Air Commodore Michael Le Bas, who had been a contemporary of mine on the Directing Staff at the Staff College at Bracknell, and Air Commodore Ian Lawson who had served with me in Egypt, afforded us warm hospitality. I realised then that although I had left the RAF for good it was a first class Club to belong to and that we still had friends all over the world. The timing of our arrival in Madras was just about right from a personal point of view. Under the regulations of the Commonwealth Relations Office I was only allowed to take dependent children at public expense under the age of twenty-one and Josephine, whose birthday is on February 21st beat this deadline by only five days!

In Bombay the *Orsova* was met by a representative of the Deputy High Commission there who handled with great efficiency all our problems of customs and disembarkation. Our immediate impression, and one which continued throughout our whole time in India, was of the enormous number of people who seemed to be everywhere. Wherever one went the streets seemed absolutely packed with dhoti-clad Indians and a fair sprinkling of smartly dressed merchants and foreigners. All along the sides of the roads, and very often up on the footpaths themselves, there were cattle lying and I realised then that as the animal was sacred to the Hindu they could not readily be disturbed. We were warned not to attempt to drink local beverages and for the first few days until we got used to the change of environment to be very sparing about eating local food. To back up this advice we were given enormous wicker baskets of food and cooling drinks as our rations for the twelve hundred miles journey to Madras. It was by far the longest and in many ways the most interesting rail journey any of us had ever undertaken. We travelled by steam train right across central India and although our carriage had somewhat primitive air-conditioning it became gradually hotter as we came further south. We were met in Madras on arrival on a Sunday evening by the entire European staff of our small office there. We had not expected more than a single representative to turn out on a weekend to take us to our new residence and it was extremely pleasant to find the whole party lined up, including welcoming wives, to greet us on arrival. Willie Paterson himself was on tour at Cochin in the western state of Kerala but would be back in a day or two and in the meanwhile our house was ready and spotless for our arrival. This turned out to be a very pleasant bungalow with quite a big garden near the Adyar Club and close to the sea. A whole team of servants under the somewhat nominal authority of the No 1 Boy Sammy were there to meet us. Although the bungalow itself had very noisy air conditioners in the bedrooms, we all felt that it would take a considerable time for us to get used to the heat and in particular the humidity which was almost one hundred percent. However we were in good spirits and first impressions were favourable.

Suitable clothing was our first major problem as although we had brought out lightweight garments from the UK it was soon clear that local cotton clothes in considerable quantity were needed for day to day living. Fortunately these could readily be secured and the Indian tailors were very good indeed at making garments up quickly. These included not only cotton shirts, trousers, and for ladies dresses, but also such items as thick towelling sweatshirts for playing games, and in a week or so we began to acquire quite a decent wardrobe of locally manufactured and tailored clothes.

Madras itself is the fourth biggest city in India and our Deputy High Commission there was a good deal smaller than the corresponding establishments in Calcutta and Bombay – all of which, of course, came under the authority of the British High Commissioner in New Delhi. Our office was quite comfortably housed and ample transport was available. We in Madras were responsible for British interests in the Southern States of Madras, Andra Pradesh, Mysore and Kerala, all varying greatly and each with its own local language. Several different religions were practised too. Within the Indian kaleidoscope nothing was simple – racial, ethnic and religious boundaries very often overlapping.

When Willie Paterson returned from Cochin and had briefed me on my general responsibilities as his deputy he suggested that I should, as soon as possible, see something of the territory for which we were responsible. I agreed readily and after my family had settled in during the next few weeks

I accepted his advice and set forth to visit a British-run coffee plantation at Chickmagalur in Mysore.

The long journey by road was somewhat alarming since my driver Krishna was a Brahmin and he seemed to think that everything, excepting, of course, sacred cows and monkeys, should get out of his way. He felt too that the optimum speed of the car was the maximum which it could reach with his foot hard down. Our route lay through Bangalore which at about 3,000 ft up was a welcome change from the heat and humidity of Madras. We night-stopped there at the West End Hotel and I took the opportunity to visit the Bangalore Club which has a long British military tradition. Two very elderly retired British officers lived there almost permanently and I was proudly shown the initials in one of the Mess books WSC showing that Winston Churchill himself had used the Club during his tour in India towards the end of the last century. The hotel was well established and remarkably cheap and I looked forward to the time when I could bring my wife and family on holiday to this cool, comfortable place where there was a good deal to see and it was not necessary to change clothes three or four times every day.

From Bangalore we pressed on through wooded rolling hills to our destination. In 1964 the coffee industry in South India, which had never been very large, was now almost extinct and most British planters and plantation companies had changed over to growing tea. This plantation in Mysore was one of the very few remaining ones and in many ways it reminded me of the coffee shambas in Kenya which I visited sometimes before the war. Although at this time of the year the coffee berries were not yet being picked I was able to see the layout of the whole plantation and was impressed by the attention given to the welfare of the native labourers who had their own sick quarters and a small school for their children. I got the impression that labour relations were good and there seemed no industrial trouble. Since prohibition was enforced in much of South India, and totally so in Madras State, I had been warned to take a gift from the supplies which we were able to import under diplomatic licence to Madras and this was well received.

The High Commission had its system of 'correspondents' in India which meant that if any trouble did break out, or if anyone was in real distress in their neighbourhood the correspondent, who was always centrally placed with good communications, would notify us at once so that we could take any necessary action either from a consular or purely welfare point of view. This system worked well and it was our habit on tour to stay with one of our correspondents who always welcomed us and usually laid on a small party of local British and Indian residents to meet us. Touring then was an important part of our responsibilities, and after this first extremely pleasant and friendly visit I realised that it was going to be a part of the job which I would enjoy immensely.

After a while my family and I began to settle down although the change of environment, of climate and of responsibility was greater than we had previously known. No longer was I supported by my Air Force friends and although Athens had given us both something of a taste for diplomatic life I had been glad enough to get back to the RAF. Working as a quite senior diplomat was obviously going to be in many ways very different indeed. We had much to learn – I about the country and its people, and for my wife the very practical problems of entertaining guests, some of whom would eat one kind of meat and some another, whilst many were more or less vegetarians. The various taboos and tastes of our guests were by no means the only problem. Indian servants, keen and willing as they usually were, often had real difficulty in understanding what a hostess wanted. This was well illustrated to us soon after our arrival. The young wife of a junior British technician found herself perforce entertaining a senior official of her husband's company who was paying a routine visit to

Madras with his wife. This lady, who was probably suffering from jet lag, showed few signs of enjoyment, eating and drinking very little. However, after dinner, rousing herself a little and no doubt for the sake of politeness, she accepted the offer of a liqueur – Green Chartreuse. After some considerable time when this had not been produced the servant (who had been engaged for the evening and was really a dhobi or washerboy) was told to hurry up. After still further delay he returned with a pair of pink knickers on a tray saying that he could not find any green short drawers but he hoped pink ones would do!

Compared to any job I had had in the RAF my responsibilities here were very much wider and in many ways less well defined. There were, in South India, such a bewildering mixture of people and races, religions and customs that it was very easy indeed to give offence, perhaps through serving the wrong food. Although the European community in that liquor-starved Madras State (which was then going through a period of total prohibition) were always delighted to be served alcohol in considerable quantities, most of the Indians were teetotal either by conviction, religion or, as in Madras, by law. Because of this local prohibition officials of the State Government in Madras had been to some trouble to get around the strict letter of the regulations on behalf of the considerable expatriate community with whom they had many social and commercial contacts, and I suspect also very often on their own behalf too. We in the High Commission, since we enjoyed diplomatic privileges, could import anything we liked for our own use but in local Clubs and hotels a special dispensation allowed members and their guests to drink together. It was decided, no doubt quite logically, that liquor was a drug and should only be prescribed by doctors and so liquor coupons were issued on the strength of a medical certificate. Diplomats were issued with these certificates automatically it being assumed that we all required them and the number that was made available was dependent on age, the reasoning being presumably that with increasing years rather more of this medicine was required! These regulations were quite loosely applied and it was not really difficult for anyone, whether a diplomat or not, to obtain a few of these coupons without a medical examination. In many ways it was all something of a joke but for a newcomer it could be annoying and it was not uncommon for thirsty visitors to travel across State borders for the purpose of obtaining liquid refreshment.

One day my daughter, Josephine, who was now working for the Trade Commissioner, told me that a friend, Simon Felton, with whom she used to ride in the early mornings in Guindy Park and whom she afterwards married, had frequently offered to buy her a drink, and as she wished to be able to return the hospitality occasionally she wondered if it was all right if she registered as an alcoholic! I assured her that I thought this was quite in order although in view of her very tender years the ration would be extremely small and I thought would in no way put a strain either on her budget or on my own. I myself found this practice embarrassing once, although not in India. When on leave in London trying to stand a friend a drink I found myself searching for coupons whilst my guest started to look in his pocket for money to pay the bill!

All this took a little getting used to but the job itself proved quite demanding. All the four States with which we were concerned varied tremendously. On the west the State of Kerala, with Cochin as its capital, was probably the most literate State in all India and its population was divided approximately in the ratio of a third each between Hindus, Moslems and Christians. There was also in Cochin a very small white Jewish community that had been there for many centuries and was heavily inbred. The State itself, a lush green land of coconut palms, lakes and lagoons boasts some of the finest scenery in all India and includes at Periyar a very fine wild life sanctuary. Here, from boats in the lake, elephants, leopards, deer and bison can be viewed feeding at close quarters.

In Mysore, the Maharajah's huge palace which had always been a great feature of the Indian scene was a strong attraction for tourists and visitors who came from far and wide. Although the power of all the great Princes had waned and very often been extinguished by now it was still possible to feel their influence. It was clear to even the casual visitor that the affection for the Maharajah and his big family was very genuine and very widely felt. Here was held annually a great Dassehra – a religious festival commemorating the victory of Rana over Ravana in Hindu mythology – over which the Maharajah himself presided. One of the most spectacular events of a very lengthy programme was always a huge procession, led by the Maharajah himself, including camels and gaily painted and caparisoned elephants, a spectacle which drew many foreign and Indian visitors, and it was customary for our Deputy High Commissioner in Madras, his wife or their representatives to be invited also.

In the *Diplomatic Service Wives Association Newsletter* of July 1965 my wife, Audrey, gave an account of her experiences at the Dassehra which she attended with Nori Paterson: 'We were Government guests and spent the first night in a seldom used Inspector's bungalow, where the staff had obviously been hastily recruited from the hills. They were delightful people and tried, without much success, to cater for our needs – no sheets, no towels, and mosquito nets that had seen better days: also a lack of other domestic items which one normally takes for granted. We decided to do without the nets but when, at bedtime, we saw the large overfed cockroaches, we changed our minds, dismantled the nets, took them outside and shook them. By this time we were badly in need of a wash, another problem since there was no bath, only a pint-sized cup and a bucket of cold water. Next morning we spent at the palace watching the blessing of the gaily adorned elephants, oxen, horses and Daimler cars belonging to the Maharajah. The palace, with its splendid carvings and pillars painted in colour combinations of pink and turquoise, was illuminated at night with thousands of tiny lights and looked like something from Fairyland. The Maharajah's throne is remarkable and dates from the 17th century. It is gold plate on ivory and carved with gold and silver Hindu mythological figures, adorned with countless pearls and emeralds. The golden steps up to the throne are each supported by female figures bearing gifts. Above the throne is a gold umbrella which is raised when the Maharajah ascends the throne so that the clusters of jewels on his turban won't become entangled with those on the inside of the umbrella!'

To the north of Madras, Andhra Pradesh, a largely Muslim State, was also our responsibility. It included most of the old east central State of Hyderabad whose ruler the Nizam, a good friend of Britain, had been most reluctant to accept the authority of the Central Government after Independence in 1947. In his huge palace lay fabulous treasures largely uncatalogued and often very badly arranged. Rubies and diamonds, emeralds and sapphires, great encrusted swords and the whole regalia of many centuries of princely rule were strewn everywhere. Now with its large and mixed population this State showed many signs of increasing prosperity. On the east coast of Andhra and about half way between Madras City and Calcutta at the northern end of our territory lay the Port of Vizagapatam. During one of my visits to this city when paying the customary courtesy call on the local Mayor I was interested to hear the story of a recent naval occasion. It seemed that the captain of a visiting destroyer, like many senior officers in the Indian Services, was an Anglo-Indian of very fair complexion and the Mayor told me with a smile that when the captain had called he had said that it was always a great pleasure to see the Royal Navy again. He had not, of course, realised that it was an Indian ship in the harbour, but the mistake was perhaps natural enough since in all probability the vessel was of British origin and probably at one time had flown the White Ensign.

Before leaving Vizag on that occasion I called on the local British-run oil refinery and was surprised to find that the Chief Engineer in charge had been a contemporary of mine at Queen's University in Belfast where he was a student of Chemical Engineering. He seemed equally surprised to find that a somewhat garrulous student in the Faculty of Agriculture was now attempting to represent Her Majesty's Government in South India!

Visits to these three very different States made a great and welcome change from working in the sticky heat of Madras but they were not really our primary concern although it was my own responsibility to report on any changes in their governments and on their relations with New Delhi and their often widely scattered British communities. We were much more intimately concerned with the affairs of Madras State itself which with its large Tamil population had not yet completely settled into the Indian Union.

Soon after our arrival in India large parts of the country were affected by a serious food shortage due primarily to failure of the monsoon. Madras State itself, which was normally a food exporting area, was badly hit. Prices began to soar and although aid was forthcoming from the United States of America and elsewhere the staple diet rice was not readily available in large quantities anywhere. Wheat, which was often substituted, was largely unacceptable to a peasant population traditional in their habits and with very few cooking utensils. I thought a little wryly how conservative in their tastes people are all over the world, remembering the dislike airmen in the Egyptian desert had for rice as a substitute for potatoes. Plus ça change ... These shortages although localised were in some districts really severe and were aggravated by the bad distribution of relief supplies

187

due partly to the Federal system of government and inter-state rivalries but largely also to inadequate storage, transport, and handling facilities – problems which have so often dogged Western aid to starving areas throughout the world. The situation became so serious that, in November 1964, after rioting had broken out in Kerala, a Food Minister, Mr Suramanium, was appointed by the Central Government in Delhi to cover the whole country. Rationing was introduced over a wide area but improvement was slow and patchy.

A more serious cause for concern and one which at one time threatened the very unity of India itself was the agitation which developed over the long planned introduction of Hindi as a national language. The background to this lies in the Indian Constitution and to the historian, with hindsight, the outbreaks of disorder which ensued may seem to have been predictable.

The Indian Constitution laid down that Hindi was to succeed English as the official State language after fifteen years. However, a special Bill provided for English to be accepted as an associate language in non-Hindi speaking States and Pandit Nehru, before he died in May 1964, had confirmed this dispensation. However, this was by no means enough for the Tamil population of the south and the extreme DMK party, which was in power in Madras State at this time, reacted strongly. Firstly, they demanded a separate southern State embracing all the three others in the area and when the Central Government objected they dropped this demand but re-affirmed their opposition to Hindi and asked instead for the largest possible measure of independence within the Constitution. Some DMK supporters went further and great numbers of copies of the Constitution were publicly destroyed. Several extremists even committed suicide by burning themselves alive. Students, who were particularly worried by the fear of being required to learn Hindi and thereby being handicapped in seeking Government posts, joined in and in February 1965 rioting broke out all over the South but particularly in the Tamil heartland, Madras State. Great damage was done to government and railway property and engine drivers coming down from the north with Hindi notices on their trains were murdered, sometimes being soused in petrol and burnt alive. Police, too, were attacked, largely by the hooligan element, and they opened fire in a number of areas killing over fifty people.

Mr Lal Bahadur Shastri, who had taken over only eight months before as Prime Minister after the death of the much loved Jawaharal Nehru, appealed for calm and assured the Southern States that the use of Hindi would not be compulsory for public office and that English would still be used as long as it was wanted. However, things were slow in calming down. In Madras City the Army was called in for a time and although we in the High Commission tended to go to work more or less as usual we felt the tension everywhere. Wives who were out shopping had their cars stopped and although Europeans were in no way the target of this agitation an awkward incident could very well have occurred at any time since the behaviour of Indian crowds was quite unpredictable.

In time things began slowly to return to normal and the students, who were somewhat mollified by government reassurances on their future eligibility for official employment throughout India, toned down their agitation and stated that they regretted that this had been taken over by anti-social elements. The Madras Government (whose Chief Minister Mr Annadurai had himself been briefly arrested) withdrew all prosecutions of student agitators and released two who had already been imprisoned. By the year's end a somewhat fragile peace had been restored.

In the cultural field, we in the Deputy High Commission aimed to encourage the excellent work of the British Council which ran a very successful school in Bangalore where teachers of all four southern states (supported uniquely by all four local governments) learned to improve their English. This language was, of course, still spoken as a lingua franca all over India amongst educated people, particularly in the major cities, and the British Council devoted a considerable effort to encouraging its use.

Much had been happening away from Madras. The loss of Prime Minister Nehru, who was greatly loved, was keenly felt, and is still felt to this day. Nehru was by any standards a very great man. He loved India and worked for it until his death, being determined to die in harness for the sake of the country he served so well. On his table lay the words of Robert Frost:

> 'The woods are lovely, dark and deep,
> But I have promises to keep
> And miles to go before I sleep
> And miles to go before I sleep'.

Shastri, who took over from him, had begun to make his name when he died tragically in Tashkent having, under Russian auspices, signed an agreement which included a no-war treaty with Pakistan. I saw him once in Madras – a tiny white clad figure addressing an enormous crowd on the maidan and as the language agitation was at its height it was a courageous thing for a Prime Minister, who was by no means popular in the South and who had drawn an audience more from curiosity than affection, to address this great throng. He, too, might have become a great leader had not death intervened.

In Madras, when life returned to normal, we got back to touring again and to contacting our British compatriots all over the south. I visited tea plantations in the Annamalais Hills, in the High Range, and in the Nilgiris where some British residents of an early generation had chosen to retire. At these high altitudes tea gardens were everywhere, largely run by big British companies like Brooke Bond and James

Finlay. Their managers lived in considerable comfort in these hill stations, usually in big bungalows on a hillside looking down over their estates. It was a lovely sight to see the early morning sun glinting on the dark green leaves of the tea bushes and to watch the women tea pickers with their great straw buckets and big straw hats moving slowly along the rows. That tea would be dried and packed on the same day. At most of these big estates management and staff were obviously on pretty good terms and the welfare facilities which I had seen earlier in Mysore were provided as a matter of course. Nevertheless, there were occasional reports of attacks by malcontents (often dismissed labourers) on planters and their families but these were always followed up very quickly by the local police.

Apart from these very pleasurable duty visits on which I could occasionally take my wife there were many other opportunites to see something of the country and its people and at the same time to enjoy ourselves. We spent one holiday in a bungalow at Wellington, near Coonoor in the Nilgiris, where the Indian Joint Services Staff College was now based and although there were no longer British Service Officers on the Directing Staff there were always three or four British officers from the different Services attending as students. I made it my business to go and see them as often as possible and took care to ensure that any visit to the Staff College was not an entirely dry occasion. The British tradition here, as elsewhere in South India, was very strong and just below the Staff College there was a small golf course on which students and Directing Staff battled continuously. In that cool air it was like being on holiday in the Highlands and it was for all of us a most refreshing change.

Back in Madras there were many purely social occasions. On one memorable one, two aircraft carriers paid a visit to the harbour, *HMS Centaur* and the Indian ship *Vikrant*, a rather smaller carrier which they had acquired from the Royal Navy. The weather being somewhat rough although the smaller ship managed to berth in the harbour the Captain of *Centaur*, no doubt wisely, decided to stay outside and a great deal of leg pulling ensued about the ship handling efficiency of the two Services. During the visit *Centaur* gave a delightful party to return some of the hospitality of local Madras residents but as the weather was pretty rough all guests had to be taken out in small boats and transferring quite elderly citizens in a fairly rough sea on the carrier was quite a feat both of balance and of seamanship. It got a good deal rougher as the party went on and finally it was decided, I thought very sensibly, that no more guests should be evacuated and quite a number spent the night on board. On another occasion the Submarine Depot Ship *HMS Forth* came into harbour at Cochin and I was able to lend the Captain my own car for a few days touring in the hills, a gesture which was reciprocated warmly in the hospitality I received on board. On leaving harbour the whole British community turned out to see *Forth* sail and the ship's company manned the rails as they moved out, giving us a farewell blast or two on the siren as they set out into the Indian Ocean.

Another maritime occasion did me no credit at all but provided a great deal of amusement to the British community in Madras. Sometime in 1965 a small 'A' class submarine, *HMS Astute*, paid a visit to Madras Harbour and as the Deputy High Commissioner was on leave in England at the time and I was acting in his place I was invited on board. Although I had been in submarines before I had rather forgotten how lavish the hospitality of sub-mariners can be and how very limited is their accommodation. On this occasion, as my wife too was away, I was accompanied by my eldest daughter, Josephine, in full evening dress and I was, of course, wearing a black tie. After being greeted by the Captain and entertained in the various very small messing areas on board, I was given a tour of the boat and almost everywhere we paused a glass was thrust into my hand

192

which, although I realised it might contain gin, I assumed
had been heavily diluted with something less potent. When I
finally emerged into fresh air I had some reason to doubt the
validity of this assumption and as I made my exit along the
narrow deck attempting to say goodbye to the Captain and
thank him for his hospitality I tripped and fell somewhat
heavily. Unfortunately in the fall my braces broke and as I
struggled to my feet endeavouring to maintain the dignity
suitable to Her Britannic Majesty's Acting British Deputy
High Commissioner and pull my trousers up I realised that I
had hurt myself quite badly. I am not quite certain how
Josephine (with whom my relations were for a little while
somewhat strained) managed to get me home but it turned
out next morning that I had fractured several ribs. The Navy
accepted full responsibility and as I was lying in my bed in
Madras insisted on bringing me English beer from their
stores and telling me funny stories which, when I tried to
laugh, hurt like hell. I began to think that perhaps it was a
good thing after all that I had not become a sailor all those
years ago.

Life was not of course, all parties, but I found in India as
elsewhere a fairly light-hearted approach did not prevent a
good deal of serious thought being given to the job in hand,
and my diplomatic colleagues on the whole seemed, even if
they took life a shade more seriously themselves, to
sympathise with this approach. India was full of problems
and as a visiting American said to me once, 'There is nothing
whatever to be done about India and the British are the only
people who can do it!'

A particularly interesting social occasion was a visit from
our High Commissioner in Delhi, Sir Paul Gore-Booth. Sir
Paul had been in India for some considerable time and was
greatly liked by everybody and when he came to Madras on
one of his visits he was greeted and welcomed by the whole
British community. As it happened Willie Paterson was
away and we had the pleasure of hosting an open air party for

193

Sir Paul and his wife. Amongst the guests we invited was a local British doctor who had served for many years in the Indian Army and was in practice now in Madras. During weekends he tended to hand this over to an Indian assistant and as he had had a stroke some time before this visit of Sir Paul's, he was very glad to sit in a chair on the lawn. He was a fellow countryman of mine with a medical degree from Trinity, which he claimed was, in his case, somewhat unusual as the Dublin Roman Catholic Archbishop at that time was reluctant to allow any of his flock to go to what was still to some extent a Protestant and Anglo-Irish university. Jack did, of course, know his Irish history and he was well aware that Sir Paul's cousins had lived at Lissadell, made famous by W B Yeats in some of his writings. After the party had been going for some little while and whilst Sir Paul was surrounded by high dignitaries, including most of the Consuls and Consuls General in Madras and a great many Indians, Jack, who had been sitting by himself quietly in his rattan chair, stumbled to his feet and picking his way through the throng addressed the High Commissioner somewhat as follows, 'High Commissioner, isn't it true that your aunt was Countess Markiewicz and that she was sentenced to death for high treason after the 1916 rebellion but was afterwards reprieved?' In any other circumstances I think this opening gambit would have caused a major sensation but Sir Paul knew Jack and Jack knew Sir Paul and the High Commissioner, who was a little short-sighted, after blinking a moment or two said, 'Yes indeed, Jack, yes indeed, the old girl was very lucky to get away with it!' Having made his point in front of that varied international gathering Jack returned to his chair and sat down again quite happily. Oddly enough nobody seemed embarrassed and I did not even feel it necessary to apologise, but I think in any other place and in any other circumstances I would have wanted to sink into the ground.

As it happened this was the High Commissioner's last

194

visit to Madras as he was now at the end of his tour and was shortly to be replaced by John Freeman who paid us a visit soon after his arrival in New Delhi. The new High Commissioner decided that he should get acquainted with all his outposts early in his tour and after a short time at his office in the Indian capital visited Calcutta, Bombay and Madras where he stayed for a few days with us getting to know our problems and meeting some of the British community. As it seemed appropriate I arranged for a Press conference for him in the Deputy High Commissioner's office. Since he had been the Assistant Editor of the New Statesman under Kingsley Martin as well as making a great name for himself with his Face to Face programmes on TV, we were not surprised when the local media turned up in force. When we sat down Freeman took the initiative immediately and said that he knew the local Press and radio people were very interested in his past journalistic background and he would be happy to answer any questions about that on this his first visit to Madras but he hoped that next time they would be more concerned with Indian problems and British reactions to them. A little taken aback by this they asked him very little indeed about his previous connections with the media and only a few tentative ones about his first impressions of India and about Anglo-Indian relations generally. The High Commissioner fielded these with ease and we thought the whole meeting had been a tremendous success. The British community were equally impressed, although being on the whole highly traditional in their customs and beliefs, they had been a little suspicious at first that somebody who was not a professional diplomat was to be our new High Commissioner and since most of them were probably Tories at heart they could not quite see why an ex-labour MP and a known friend of Harold Wilson should have been appointed! However, on meeting His Excellency they realised at once that he had a completely open mind and had already taken some trouble to study the problems of British citizens in India and particularly the commercial and taxation questions with which many of them were faced. This pleased them greatly and from then on I heard only praise for our new master in New Delhi.

In 1965 the very important Plowden Report on British representation abroad had been published and its effects were felt throughout our posts worldwide. It was recommended and agreed by the Government that the Foreign and Commonwealth Services should be amalgamated and that the Trade Commission Service of the Board of Trade should also be brought in. The conditions of service were roughly that, while all Foreign Service people naturally stayed in this new Service, we in the Commonwealth Relations Service, which was theoretically home-based, had the chance to opt out and join one of the Home Departments, and several of our friends elected to do this for personal and family reasons. The Trade Commission Service of the Board of Trade had to apply to join and many of them who had a taste for living overseas did this although their acceptance was not automatic. I had no difficulty at all in making up my mind but I did feel conscious of my own limitations as a diplomat, particularly as I was in no way a linguist and tended, even when speaking French, to break into kitchen Swahili!

The normal tour of duty overseas in the Foreign Service varied considerably according to climate, and Madras, which was considered a fairly hard lying post, rated a tour of about three years with intermediate leave after eighteen months or so. When getting towards the end of my tour one day and changing sets of tennis at the Madras Club, I was handed a telegram which had just come in from London stating that I was to proceed as soon as possible to Korea since somebody had failed a medical examination in Tanzania. I was playing at the time with my new boss, Clifford Heathcote-Smith, who had recently taken over from Willie Paterson in Madras. He was not prepared to let his deputy leave at very short notice if he could help it and this suited me well enough since two of my own children were due out on their summer holidays in a week or two. The necessary signals were exchanged and London finally agreed that whilst the posting must stand I should leave at the earliest convenience of the DHC and of myself. All this was, of course, something of a surprise and although I had been quite prepared to go abroad again after long leave at home I had not expected an immediate transfer to another and, in this case, very remote overseas post quite so soon. However, there was nothing to be done about it and Audrey and I soon made up our minds to enjoy Korea as much as we had Southern India.

The usual domestic problems immediately arose and as we were all equipped with the lightest possible tropical clothing I did not feel inclined to go to Korea with its extreme continental climate without acquiring some warm clothing. We arranged, therefore, after the summer holidays, to sail from Ceylon and after flying to Colombo from Madras, where most of the British community seemed to be at the airport to see us off, we prepared to embark on the *SS Laos* of the Messageries Maritime Line for Yokahama. Just before doing so a telegram arrived from the Ambassador in Seoul saying that he was retiring in five or six weeks and would I please get a move on as I would be taking charge of the Embassy soon after arrival. I telegraphed back that in view of the urgency I would now disembark at Hong Kong and fly direct to Seoul leaving my wife on board to follow me later from Japan. Beginning to wonder now what on earth had hit me, why London had not told me, and how after just four years in the Foreign Service, much of which had been spent as a civil servant in Whitehall, I was going to cope with running an Embassy, we duly set sail from Colombo for the Land of the Morning Calm.

Chapter 11

Land of the Morning Calm

We were sorry to leave Madras where we had made many friends amongst both the British and the Indian communities. We had both learnt a little – only very little – about the southern area of the Indian sub-continent and we had been living there through some exciting days. In a way looking back it seemed to be a sort of afterglow of the Raj on which the sun had set only some fifteen years before.

For the considerable British community in South India it had been a time of great change and we knew that from now on they would be much reduced in number. In 1966 the rupee was substantially devalued and as many of the British citizens, and particularly British planters and merchants, were paid largely in rupees they suffered severely since they had many expenses in the UK, particularly for educating their children. Some of the bigger companies were able to make up this shortfall for a while but the general tendency was to reduce European staffs as quickly as possible especially on the tea plantations where at the time we left the number of young planters coming out from home had fallen quite dramatically. Since a few of us, and this included of course the staff of the High Commission, were paid in sterling with local allowances only in rupees we stood to benefit while living in India, and staying in Indian hotels became very cheap indeed. However since many of our friends were suffering considerable financial hardship we tried as far as possible to avoid dwelling on this.

There had been a great deal to see in Madras and going to church on Sunday in St Mary's Church in Fort St George we were worshipping in the oldest Anglican Church in all Asia. The fort itself had been built by Francis Day in 1640 and in the big graveyard outside the church lay the remains of many gentlemen of The Honourable East India Company. Amongst them lay the grave of Admiral Hood who died in Madras on Christmas Eve 1814 after a fever lasting only three days. Here, as all over the East, many had died at a very early age and probably more foreigners had succumbed to fever than had perished in the incessant colonial wars. In this church of St Mary, Robert Clive had been married in 1753 to Margaret Maskelyne from Wiltshire, the record of the marriage being still preserved in the India Office Library.

At Fort St George history was all around us. Elihu Yale whose benefaction had secured the struggling college in Connecticut that blossomed out into a full university bearing his name in 1745, had served here as Governor on behalf of the East India Company. Here, too, Arthur Wellesley – the victor of Waterloo and later the Duke of Wellington – had served in the barracks still called after him. Coming to Madras in 1796 he fought in various Indian wars making a great name for himself as a Lieutenant-Colonel in charge of the baggage train for the battle of Seringapatam at which the cruel Tippo Sultan met his downfall. Wellesley served in India – mostly in Madras – until 1804 and finally came home in 1805, after a most distinguished career. Although he had commanded up to fifty thousand troops – mostly local Sepoys – at one time during his long service in India, his real fame was yet to come.

All over India, as indeed all over the East, we had seen signs of the colonial past of the great European powers. Fishing at Pulicat on the Madras coast we passed by the remains of a large Dutch graveyard. Pondicherry, which had been French until after Indian Independence, still had a few French citizens living there and enjoyed a fair degree of local automony which allowed it, inter alia, to relax their liquor laws. On the other side of the coast, although not within our area, the substantial Portuguese colony of Goa had been occupied forcibly and after some bloodshed by Indian Government troops.

Our tour in India had indeed been a great experience and I felt proud of what Britain had achieved there over the centuries. The Indians were proud of it too – perhaps more so in the South where the British tradition remained still quite strong. In Madras statues of Queen Victoria and George V still occupied prominent positions. At a cocktail party in honour of a visiting American warship I heard a US Naval Officer asking an Indian Official why so many colonial relics still seemed to abound in the city and why portraits of British Governors in full uniform still occupied a place of honour in Government House? The Indian's reply, 'This is a part of our history and we are very proud of it', seemed to say it all.

As we sailed east in this comfortable ship calling at Singapore, Bangkok and Manila I thought how wise it was of the Foreign Office to allow, and indeed encourage, us to travel by sea whenever possible. This was particularly useful for an officer taking up a new post as it gave him a chance to unwind and if, as in my own case, proceeding direct from one overseas posting to another without home leave it was a great comfort to be able to relax. It gave an opportunity also to read about one's next assignment and often from talking to fellow passengers gave one some idea of what was in store. I must admit though that in the case of Korea I got very mixed reports from the various people who had visited that country already.

We got to Hong Kong on the 5th October 1966 and I left my wife on board to carry on to Yokahama and then join me in Seoul by air from Tokyo. After spending a night in Hong Kong and buying some badly needed warm clothes for the harsh Korean winter, which would soon be upon us, I flew direct to Seoul where I was met by the Consul from the British Embassy who seemed a little surprised to find that I had not obtained an Entry Visa. This was entirely my own fault as I had rather assumed that travelling as a diplomat (if indeed I had thought about the matter at all) no visa would be required, but this, of course, was normally a formality that would have been arranged by the Foreign Office in London. Fortunately the Koreans made no objection to my arrival and in a day or two, after meeting my new ambassador Sir Walter Godfrey and being shown the very comfortable flat in which we would live within the Embassy Compound, I started a round of calls on the various Heads of Mission, of whom there were about a dozen or so. Sir Walter was punctilious about this and although I had a hand-over of only four or five weeks before he left for home and retirement I think we got around nearly them all.

After a week or so my wife duly arrived from Japan and as I was fortunate enough to have a pleasant flat and three good servants to welcome her, settling down was not too difficult.

The British Embassy Compound in which we lived has a history going back to 1884 and it is still the only piece of land in Korea owned by the British Government. The quite substantial Number One house and the adjoining Number Two (which was divided into flats which I shared with our Consul) were in the grounds of the old Duk-soo Palace. The American Embassy was close by and at one time the Russians were represented here too. We worked in a long single storey building close to both the number one and number two houses and just over the wall was the fairly new Anglican Cathedral which was built in Romanesque style in the mid 1920's. Although the British were now represented by a small Embassy we had started with a Consulate General before graduating to Legation status.

I found it interesting to read in a report of the Consul-General, Walter Hillier, who was in charge at the time in 1884 when the main buildings were constructed, the following statement referring to the interest of the then ruler King Kojong. It seems that on completion of the work which His Majesty had watched from his adjacent palace Mr Hillier had shown him plans and photographs of the building and he wrote home as follows:

'These latter have so taken his fancy that he has requested me to invoke Mr Marshall's assistance in constructing a similar building in the palace grounds undertaking, if Mr Marshall will arrange a contract with Shanghai workmen for its erection, to lodge the money with a bank, to be drawn on from time to time.'

Mr Marshall was, of course, the man in charge of the work but, although the Office of Works were gratified by this unexpected tribute, they decided that they had too much to do to get involved in building for the King, but Mr Marshall was allowed to offer plans and advice to His Majesty.

The flat in which we lived was one in which I was informed soon after our arrival the notorious spy, George Blake, had once occupied, and who was still remembered by some of the small British and foreign community living in the Korean capital.

The business of calling on the Heads of Mission took quite a time and when Audrey arrived she was involved with Lady Godfrey calling on their wives. The doyen of the Diplomatic Corps at that time was a Monsieur Chambard who had played rugby for France but surprised me a little by saying that the game had deteriorated since his day and for this, and indeed almost everything else, he seemed to blame the Americans! He and Sir Walter were good friends and as they both spoke each other's languages perfectly it was pleasant to hear them going so easily from French to English and back again. I wished that my knowledge of that language had been matched by rather more experience in speaking it.

Although Sir Walter Godfrey was due to retire very shortly he gave me a very thorough handover in the few weeks before he left. As he had been an Inspector at one time in the Foreign Service he was extremely keen on accounts and I spent many hours with him going through the Embassy books but I was glad of the experience since figures have never been my strong point. He assured me that my appointment as Chargé d'Affaires *ai* would come through as soon as he left and I had cards printed accordingly. I wondered what the *ai* meant but my Latin wasn't unduly stretched when I was told it meant 'ad interim'. There was only one other Chargé d'Affaires *ai* en poste in Seoul at the time, an Israeli, and when I called on him I was a little surprised when he showed me a Tommy gun in his desk together with a spare magazine which he assured me was a useful thing to keep for an emergency! I noted the advice but I have no reason to believe that any other Embassy or Ambassador was similarly armed.

The staff of our Embassy at the time consisted of only about eight or ten British officers, not all of whom had full diplomatic status. We were fortunate in having the services too of a Defence Adviser, one Brigadier Bancroft, who had fought with his regiment – The King's Own Shropshire Light Infantry – in the Korean War and knew the country quite well. He had a kind of dual or triple role being the Ambassador's adviser on defence matters and the Officer responsible for the small British contingent of troops which has continued to serve in Korea ever since the Korean War which ended with an armistice and not a full peace treaty. He had a small supporting staff of Commonwealth Officers from Australia, Canada and New Zealand and one of his jobs was to keep in close contact with the Korean military, and more particularly with the Americans who had about 50,000 troops in the country, many of them on or close to the De-Militarised Zone (DMZ). Whenever there was an incident on the frontier between North and South Korea (and these happened very often) a meeting would be called by one side or the other at Panmunjom and the Brigadier would be in attendance backing up the American spokesman. Because of the limited space in our compound only very few of us lived in official quarters, but the Brigadier and the other officers were on the whole reasonably well housed in local accommodation, although the rents for these were very high.

I had not realised before that the Koreans are such generous people. Although I knew that the Chinese are in the habit of giving frequent presents, on special occasions and to say farewell, Audrey and I were astonished when the time came for the Godfreys to leave at the enormous number of parcels and presents that kept arriving at the Embassy. Indeed during the last couple of weeks the Korean hospitality, in which we necessarily got involved, was almost overwhelming and as practically every member of the small Diplomatic Corps in Seoul gave a party for the outgoing ambassador I had not much time to settle down to work. This did not worry me unduly as meeting my colleagues was obviously important and, as in Athens, I found that over a drink or two one could learn a great deal about the country, the capital and the political situation, more particularly the extent of the threat from the North.

When, in due course, I was accredited in my new appointment I did not think it worth moving into the Ambassador's house although the name of Sir Walter's replacement had not been announced, and indeed I do not think was known at that stage at the Foreign Office. I wrote home at once saying that I would like to drop my Air Force rank which I had used as a matter of course in the Defence Department in London and, more hesitantly, in India since I was dealing largely with the British community. In writing about this I mentioned jocularly that so far as I knew the Office had never confirmed me as a regular member of the Diplomatic Service and it must be a little unusual to have a

Chargé d'Affaires who was still on probation! I got an immediate apologetic reply saying that this slight oversight had been corrected and from now on I could in all senses be regarded as a confirmed and accredited diplomat. I still felt that I was a slightly unorthodox one, but if the Office knew that, as presumably they did, they took it in their stride.

First impressions of Korea (once called The Hermit Kingdom), its capital and its people were varied and often contradictory. Seoul, which I had last visited fourteen years previously, was now a huge thriving city with a population of about eight million and boasted no less than twelve universities including two for women, one of which, EWHA, was one of the biggest female academies in the world. Many modern buildings had been erected and others were going up fast; the whole city seemed in a state of rapid development and there was activity everywhere. Some of this was no doubt due to the approach of winter but a great deal of it stemmed from the natural industry of a people who in that way greatly resembled the Japanese, although they really had very little time indeed for the inhabitants of the Land of the Rising Sun. This aversion probably originated in the Japanese occupation of their country in the early part of the Twentieth Century and although many of the older Koreans, including officials in Government and senior officers in the Services, had learnt to speak Japanese at school and in some cases while attending Japanese academies, they were reluctant to admit that they knew the language at all. However, there are many signs still of Japanese influence – in the architecture of the railway stations, the railways themselves having been built by the Japanese, and in the design of many Government buildings. Korean Buddhist temples resemble greatly those to be seen in Kyoto and other cities in Japan. It was interesting when talking to visitors from Tokyo (with whom the Koreans of necessity did a good deal of business, particularly in consumer goods) to note that very few Koreans were willing to admit any understanding of the Japanese language. In these circumstances business tended to be conducted in rather basic American English, and although no doubt many of the Japanese knew quite well that their Korean opposite numbers understood their language there was no way to make them give way on this.

After I had been in Seoul for a little while and had completed the Annual Report to London, which Sir Walter had been good enough to leave me largely in draft, I decided it was time to see something of the country and one of my first visits was to Panmunjom. At this time incidents were happening on the border between North and South Korea, frequently calling for full scale meetings of the Armistice Commission. To observe fair play neutral observers had been appointed, on the North Korean side from Czechoslovakia and Poland and on our side from Sweden and Switzerland, all four countries being represented in accordance with the terms of the Armistice agreement by senior officers. On this, my first visit to Panmunjom, my wife and I travelled up in the office Princess with the Union Jack flying as guests of the Swiss representative who was a retired senior officer of both the Swiss army and Diplomatic Service. The journey north from Seoul over rough country, bare brown relieved by green patches of paddy and ginseng, to Freedom House at Panmunjom took only about an hour. It was here that on July 27th 1953 at 10.00 o'clock in the morning the armistice had been signed after no fewer than two hundred and fifty-five meetings, spread over two years, between General Mark Clark, Commander of the United Nations Command, and Kim Il Sung of the North Korean Peoples Army supported by Peng Teh-Huai for the Chinese Peoples Volunteers. The terms were unique; for one thing the Republic of Korea never signed it and the agreement was binding on the military forces of North Korea, the 'Volunteers' of Communist China and the sixteen United Nations members who furnished combat forces. Although the Republic of Korea is not a signatory and the ROK Government participated in the peace talks only as an observer it fully supports and observes the agreement quite strictly to this day.

Panmunjom itself is a little south of the 38th parallel, which roughly forms the boundary between North and South Korea. The de-militarised zone winds one hundred and fifty-one miles across the Korean Peninsula and the zone itself is marked by no less than twelve hundred and ninety-two intermittently spaced markers printed in Korean and English at the line of ground-contact between the opposing sides at the moment of cease fire. The Armistice Agreement created the 'DMZ' and required the withdrawal of all military equipment and forces, but each side is allowed one thousand civil police in its half of the Zone at a time. Three hundred American, seven hundred Republic of Korea Military Personnel selected for this duty make regular patrols in the southern half of the zone and very often these patrols encounter and, sometimes capture, North Korean communists attempting to infiltrate into South Korea. They are quite enterprising at doing this and have been known to tunnel right under the de-militarised zone which is 4,000 metres wide, and on other occasions small coastal parties have attempted sea landings in the far south of the peninsula.

At the time we went to Panmunjom a fairly routine meeting was being held over a border incident in which one or two people had been killed. The United Nations Command was represented by a senior member, a post which rotated every six months between the United States Army, Navy and Marine Corps, and was supported by Brigadier Bancroft and his Commonwealth advisers. On the other side four officers from the North Korean Peoples Army and one from the Chinese Peoples Volunteers represented the Communists but in fact very often the Chinese didn't bother to attend. The senior members are the only spokesmen allowed for their side and at the early meetings a great deal of wrangling went on about the agenda to be discussed and particularly about the size of the flags which each side was allowed to display on their tables. I am told that these from being quite miniature rose almost to the ceiling as each side tried to outdo the other! The representative speaks in his own language and each statement is translated into Korean and Chinese after the United Nations position has been made clear, and into English and Chinese after the North Koreans have had their say. To watch all this going on was quite fascinating but we ourselves were well aware that we were also being watched. It was very obvious travelling in the official car that we were being photographed at close quarters and we were warned by the burly American military police that if we walked into the wrong side of the Panmunjom Compound we could easily be abducted into North Korea and not too much could be done about it.

Freedom House, in Panmunjom itself, was designed in the Korean style as a unique structure dedicated to the support of the United Nations Command as a historic symbol for the peaceful reunification of the divided nation and in front of it is a statue of the Korean General Ul Chi Mum Dok who defeated an invading Japanese Army of the Sui Dynasty in 612 AD. The Koreans, we discovered, have long memories and they love to celebrate battles by land and sea of long ago. On this occasion Audrey and I, as guests of the Swiss observer, watched the proceedings with interest and were lavishly entertained to lunch afterwards. The meeting like a great many of its kind seemed to produce no decisive result, each side blaming the other and I didn't feel anyone was very surprised, and since our Brigadier represented the British Government, I did not feel it was in any way my duty to attend another one.

On February 11th 1967 my time as Chargé d'Affaires came to an end when our new Ambassador, Mr Ian

Mackenzie, flew out from home. Ian had been a Commercial Counsellor in our Embassies in both Stockholm and Oslo and he was very interested indeed in commercial matters. Soon after arriving in Seoul he told me that in his opinion the thing that mattered most was promoting British business in that part of the world and that this should be the principal task of the Embassy. When I protested mildly that I didn't really know the difference between the Board of Trade and a Bill of Lading he said that perhaps I ought to find out and since I was now overdue for home leave I was posted in June to attend a crash course on commerce in the City of London College, which I managed to combine with my leave. The course was an interesting one and although I felt a bit old for absorbing fairly intensive lectures on such subjects as Banking, the Euro-dollar and the Brussels Trade Agreements I managed to learn quite a lot and when I returned to Seoul I found myself, for the rest of my tour, extremely busy on commercial work.

At this time Korea, as we reported to London, was in the state in which Japan had been twenty or thirty years earlier and although a poor country it was full of determination to build up a strong and prosperous economy backed by its enormously industrious people. My task was to encourage British business in every possible way and, when the representatives of British firms came out, to introduce them to senior Koreans, very often at the level of one of the two Deputy Prime Ministers who was concerned with commercial matters. This usually involved drinks in our house and attending kisaeng parties given by the Koreans. These were on the lines of Japanese geisha parties although a good deal more relaxed since the hostesses were very often Korean university students from one of the colleges in Seoul. These entertainments were great fun and involved drinking quantities of the local beverage chumjung (a form of sake) and dancing to both Korean and western music and they were an essential part of the preliminaries to any big business deal. I learnt very soon that it is quite impossible to hurry the East and I met a Canadian who had discovered this a good deal earlier. He represented a big American insurance company and he told me that he had done little except play golf for about six months before managing to secure a quite enormous deal.

This was more difficult with British businessmen who knew little about Korea and very often, after a visit to Japan, had stopped in just for a night or two, but as long as we knew they were coming we were usually able to give them at least a few contacts. Sometimes, of course, their visits were quite hopeless from the start. On one occasion a representative arrived without notice selling gnomes and pixies for garden lawns and when I told him that the Koreans didn't have garden lawns he was a little surprised! Another one came in with samples of excellent writing paper but here again Koreans either made their own or imported it from Japan. Their major requirements were in the line of capital goods, including equipment for roads, railways, textile factories and power stations and some very useful contracts were secured by British companies.

During this time, with much help from my Ambassador, we were able to assist Cathay Pacific Airlines in securing an agreement allowing daily flights to Korea from Hong Kong, as opposed to the one or two weekly ones that they had been allowed before. We managed also to persuade the Export Credit Guarantee Department in London to raise considerably their ceiling for cover for business in Korea since it was apparent that opportunities were enormous and although there was really only one British firm acting as agents in Korea for the quite extensive trade that was beginning to develop it obviously needed the maximum possible support from home. For my part I had, of course, to be careful not to seem to favour one firm against another since our job was simply to promote British trade and if representatives of companies in the motor or textile business came out and wanted to be introduced to appropriate Korean officials, without whose support no business could be done, we had to be prepared to give similar treatment, a little later, to another company selling a rival product. All this involved my small staff and myself in a great deal of paper work and a good deal of entertainment, although it was comparatively seldom that we saw the results of our labours.

There were, of course, many lighter moments. During the winter months the Koreans organised an International Hunting Competition (using the American term for shooting) in the Island of Cheju-Do off the south coast at which teams of five or six nations set out to shoot pheasants which were extremely plentiful both on the island and on the mainland. We usually flew in an aeroplane loaned by an American Admiral and the small British team was led by our Brigadier who was an excellent shot, supported by some of us who were a great deal less skilful. The Governor of the island, who had been head of the Korean Army Provost Branch, entertained us royally and at the end of the competition the Japanese, who sponsored it, gave us all second prizes. The participants consisted usually, apart from the Japanese, of the Americans, the Taiwanese, the Koreans and the British and it was always understood that the Koreans should get the first prize. This they supported by producing very large numbers of pheasants although we had some slight doubt as to whether they had all been shot on that particular day! The competition always took place in mid-winter in quite bitter weather but the Governor gave a tremendous party afterwards in which huge stone baths full of boiling water were shared by everybody and afterwards Korean hostesses were laid on for our entertainment. It was always a pleasant few days and we returned home refreshed by the exercise and laden with pheasants which we had not necessarily shot ourselves!

One day, about halfway through my tour in Korea, our

young Consul reported to me before going on leave and mentioned that I had authority to conduct marriages. I was more than a little surprised by this and although I had known that for some reason in the Diplomatic List there was a small 'm' after my name I had not bothered to inquire about this although I vaguely thought it had something to do with my sex! However, Fred Kempson assured me that it was extremely unlikely that I would ever have to marry anyone, but he did suggest that if I did have to while he was on leave I should study the regulations rather carefully since although I had this power to marry people there was no way I could unmarry them. Having duly warned me Fred went off on his well earned leave and as I was by now acting as Commerical Secretary I rather forgot about our conversation.

However, a few weeks after our Consul had departed an American GI in uniform asked to see me and when he was brought into my office said that he wanted me to marry him to a Korean girl. I told him that although I did have authority to marry Canadian as well as British citizens, since the Canadians had no embassy in Seoul, there was no way at all that I could marry Americans. He countered this by showing that he was in fact a Canadian serving in the American Army. This shook me considerably but I told him to come back again and we would see what we could do for him. Hastily thumbing through the regulations I found that a notice had to be prominently displayed giving the name of the bridegroom and his fiancée and that when the marriage was being conducted witnesses must be present. All right so far. The actual wording of the ceremony was not unlike that in a Registry Office at home but it included some words which had to be translated into Korean such as consanguinity which I did not think were likely to be readily understood either by the GI or his Korean bride. However, after due time had elapsed and the necessary warnings had been given I opened my office for the wedding ceremony and as my wife at that time was still a Canadian citizen I thought she had better come along to see that justice was done. It all went off very well and I was not too surprised to see that the brightly clad little Korean lady and her husband, when he was not on the DMZ, were already living together in Seoul. We gave them a glass of sherry afterwards and I was greatly relieved that the whole affair seemed to have gone off satisfactorily.

However, this was not to be the end of the story. A week or two later another GI turned up requesting me to marry him to a Korean and before long yet a third. I wasn't quite sure whether it was the glass of sherry or the novelty of being married in the British Embassy that accounted for this sudden outburst of matrimony. A few days later on meeting the American Ambassador, Mr Winthrop Young, at a diplomatic gathering I told him that I was spending half my time now marrying American GI's to Korean girls and asking him what he proposed to do about it. He thought I was pulling his leg until I explained that two of the three GI's were Canadians caught up in the draft while living in the States and the third had been a volunteer. His Excellency, who had come from Saigon quite recently, was most interested in all this and asked me if I thought Korean girls would make good wives. He said that in Indo-China he had spent a good deal of time trying to prevent unions of this sort but I told him that, although my experience was extremely limited, I thought the Korean girls probably would make good wives and we had already met a number of extremely pleasant ones who seemed to have more individuality and to be less dominated by their husbands than the Japanese wives, delightful though these ladies obviously were.

There was a pleasant sequel to all this some months later. Brigadier Bancroft had as his deputy a Major John Serjeant, RE, who had fallen heavily in love with a very high class Korean girl. His tour of duty was normally a year but he had it extended for six months to woo this charming lady (who told me in excellent English that she had the nickname of Pumpkin because her family thought she looked like one!) and in due course she agreed to marry him. I had real pleasure in marrying them and my Ambassador, Ian Mackenzie, gave a champagne party on the Embassy lawn for the happy couple. Last time I met them the gallant Major was serving at Chatham and had two young children and I felt that this was one marriage that was going all right.

During my time in Seoul the animosity between North and South varied in intensity and although a tentative attempt was made to reach a limited agreement, for the economic advantage of both countries, this did not succeed. Both sides continued to be very heavily armed, the South Koreans being massively supported by the Americans and the North Koreans enjoying the rather distant support of the Russians and the somewhat closer, if intermittent, backing of the Chinese. Evidence of the continuing British commitment to the defence of the Republic was, of course, given by our 'Honour' Guard and the presence of our Brigadier and his Commonwealth staff. There was always a danger that hostilities could break out again and we were constantly reporting on this. On two occasions during my tour in Seoul the temperature on our side of the border rose almost to boiling point.

One Sunday evening in late January 1968 sitting in our Embassy flat we heard a loud crackling noise not far away. We were puzzled at this but I suggested that the Koreans might be letting off fireworks, Chinese fashion, although this was not a great habit of theirs. Interspersed with this noise of small explosives were a few loud bangs. In the morning we discovered that a party of about thirty highly trained North Korean officers had infiltrated the DMZ and had attacked the nearby Presidential Palace in an attempt to kill President Park Chung Hee. They had very nearly succeeded but after killing several of the guards the alarm had been raised and quite a battle had ensued in which a number of soldiers, police and unfortunate civilians caught in the cross-fire had been killed. One or two of the North Koreans were captured but one who was taken away for interrogation had managed to conceal a hand grenade and blow himself up in front of his captors. Although several of the raiders managed to escape very few are believed ever to have got back to North Korea. The South Koreans naturally reacted strongly and were quite prepared to mount a massive raid on the North which could have easily escalated into a full scale war. Fortunately their Allies kept their heads and the American Ambassador and their Four-Star General in charge, General Bonesteel, a Rhodes Scholar, managed to calm the Korean military and took steps to ensure that insufficient fuel was available for them to launch any major offensive. There was always the danger though that some young Korean Officer, perhaps in their Air Force, would on his own inititative take his squadron in a death or glory revenge attack on the North and for a few days things were very tense indeed. Since we in Britain were still pledged to support the Korean government in any unprovoked attack we naturally watched these developments with considerable concern. An even greater danger to peace was to follow almost immediately.

On the 23rd January 1968 a North Korean attack on the American ship *Pueblo*, after a running battle in which one of the American ship's crew was killed, ended in the *Pueblo* surrendering and being taken in triumph to the North Korean capital Pyongyang. This capture of an American Naval ship – the first since the Anglo-American war of 1812 – caused tremendous anger in the United States and amongst American forces everywhere, and since a strong element of the South Korean Services were always ready and willing to have a go at the North the situation looked very dangerous indeed. As rumours began to filter through of the ill treatment of the *Pueblo* crew by their Northern captors, American anger almost reached boiling point but short of a full scale war, or a major and probably unsuccessful raid on the prison camp itself, there seemed little could be done. We began to think seriously about having to evacuate the Embassy and I was glad that at Singapore, on passage from Madras, I had discussed this possibility with Air Marshal Sir John Grandy the Far East Air Force Commander-in-Chief. The Americans, too, were making tentative plans, and if the worst happened we arranged to travel with them. We packed a few basic necessities, enough for a 24 hour journey, and hoped for the best. We were assured that measures would be taken to ensure that if war broke out the main bridge over the Han would not this time be blown up too soon, leaving us on the wrong side of the river, trapped in Seoul. However, someone would have to stay behind in our Embassy and the finger seemed to point to me. I had no wish whatever to be taken prisoner as our Minister Captain Holt had been at the start of the Korean War and I tried to put this possibility to the back of my mind.

The crew of the *Pueblo* remained in North Korean hands until 22nd December 1968 during which time there seemed little prospect of any reconciliation between the North and the South, and by the time they were released we ourselves had left for home.

For my family, and especially the children who came out regularly over the North Pole for holidays, there was much to do and see in Korea and it made a great contrast to life in Southern India. The country itself is wild and largely mountainous reminding me in many ways of the West of Ireland or the Highlands of Scotland and only about a third of it is suitable for agriculture. In winter, from about November until the quick Spring thaw in early April, the land is frozen solid. It was customary, before the really cold weather set in, for open spaces to be flooded and when they froze they were used as skating rinks. It was a pretty sight in

216

the middle of this bustling city to see hundreds of Koreans, including many children, in their multi-coloured clothes laughing and skating in the quite bitter weather. As the winter intensified a strong wind blew down from Siberia and with it came wild birds, including many species of geese and wild duck. For the sportsman, in addition to the plentiful pheasants which came sometimes almost up to our door in wintertime, shooting of wild duck and geese on the East Coast made a pleasant excursion. As the terrain was largely inaccessible we usually went by air with American friends who flew us in one of their light aircraft. There was little game fishing although small salmon were caught off the West Coast and from time to time appeared in the shops.

In the summer, the surrounding hills clad in wild azaleas, we swam and picnicked by a big reservoir north of the Korean capital, but on the whole there were not so many opportunities for family travel in this still fairly wild country as we had enjoyed in India. Ancient ruins and temples abounded and sometimes the traveller would come across a Korean funeral party, the men in their traditional long white robes, wispy beards and black horse hair hats heading for a grave which they had most carefully positioned for the benefit of their ancestral spirits. We did not think the Koreans, who were usually at least nominally Buddhists or Confucians – religions or philosophies which they combined with worship of ancestral spirits – a particularly religious people, although there was a small Christian community and quite a few Christian missionaries, mostly Canadians whom we looked after in Consular matters. Indeed the first two Presidents of the modern Republic – Syngman Rhee and Yun Po-sun – were both Christians although in 1948 only about four percent of the population professed allegiance to that faith. On the whole outside the capital the Koreans were a poor peasant people living in small wooden or mud houses roofed with straw and subsisting in the winter on very primitive rations, including the famous kimshee which they had made in the summer from mixed vegetables and spices and buried in great pots for winter use. These houses seldom had more than three rooms and the family slept in the same one removing the bedding during the day and storing this in wooden chests. They were heated by a fire in the ground in the centre of the house with mud or concrete ducts running from this under the floor. Wood was usually burned and the poorer people even used twigs and leaves. The heating was effective and indeed could be extremely hot as the Brigadier's wife and mine found out once when touring. Since there was nowhere to stay at their destination their driver found someone to put them up. They were given the third room and what appeared to be new blankets. It was so hot sleeping on the floor that the ladies put all the blankets under them. In the morning they were given an enormous breakfast of kimshee (the mild cucumber kind) and raw fish and fortunately their hostess did not watch them eating it. They washed in the kitchen with madam and all the children looking on, and went on their way. It had been a rare opportunity for a foreigner to experience Korean hospitality at its simple, heart-warming best. In spite of a generally low standard of living the Koreans remained a proud people conscious of their ancient culture (they claim to have invented printing even before the Chinese) and have a recorded history going back to about 200 BC.

Social life for us was largely confined to our diplomatic contacts, there being few foreigners resident in the capital but there were one or two Naval visits also. On one occasion I dined on board the British frigate *HMS Falmouth* making a courtesy visit to Pusan on the other side of the Peninsula whilst my Ambassador was the guest of a larger ship visiting Inchon.

In the summer of 1968 I was busy on commercial work, trying to encourage and promote the rapidly growing British commercial interest in this developing economy but unfortunately working under high pressure I became quite ill and ended up in the American Military Hospital in Seoul with a pulmonary embolism which could easily have proved fatal. After making a good recovery I was treated as 'tour expired' and sailed home a little early, once again on the *Orsova*, in late September.

Since the Suez Canal was still closed we made the long voyage around the Cape visiting South African ports, Madeira, Lisbon and Rotterdam on the way. By October we were home again at the end of our third tour East of Suez – three different countries Singapore, India and Korea – with very different peoples, but we had enjoyed them all.

Of the three, Korea had been the most challenging. In India we had had no real language problem; here it was very different. The quite savage climate took getting used to and walking heavily muffled with a Russian type fur hat complete with earflaps into the bitter wind I sometimes longed for the heat of India. Contact with Koreans had taken longer to establish too, partly because of the language difficulty and partly because it is not easy to obtain a real rapport with a people of so very different a culture and language living at the other side of the world. Although Western influence, and particularly American influence, was beginning to be widely felt Korea, no longer The Hermit Kingdom, was still a fairly backward country. With their energy and adaptability the Koreans were catching up fast and it was touching to notice how much they appreciated meeting and talking to British people. Quite often I would be telephoned at night by some university student or even lecturer saying that they wanted to talk to an English Englishman because, although they had a great respect for the Americans who were there in considerable numbers, they wanted to go back to the fount of the language. Although I found this quite flattering I was not at my best talking English English to some eager student at two

219

o'clock in the morning! All this was behind us now and I knew that in a little while all these memories would begin to mingle, and be woven into the colourful mosaic of our very varied life.

Chapter 12

A Bite of the Big Apple

In 1968 we were home again for Christmas, the first time in four years and we spent the festive season in a house in Kent which we had bought on leave and subsequently let. It was good to be back and although as a family we were still pretty rootless our new neighbours were welcoming and friendly. Nevertheless, I soon began to feel restive again and asked for another overseas assignment. The Foreign Office, as always, were sympathetic and promised to post me abroad as soon as possible but the doctors were inclined to think that a few months more at home would do me no harm, so I was given some temporary work in London whilst I tried to curb my growing impatience. By the spring of the New Year I felt fully fit again and was told by the Postings Department, who had borne my importunities with great patience, that they had in mind a posting for me to North America. Since various clearances were required, they could not yet disclose the destination.

All this put the entire Rainsford family into a state of considerable excitement since my wife saw prospects of seeing something of her own family in Montreal, and having paid long visits to the Pentagon in Washington, whilst working in Air Ministry, I too relished the prospect of a posting across the Herring Pond. I managed to extract from the Foreign and Commonwealth Office the information that it would be a consular appointment and not to the Embassy in Washington and I immediately had visions of San Francisco or Los Angeles – preferably the former which I had visited briefly on one occasion whilst returning to Seoul via North America. Since Korea was almost the other side of the world from the UK the air fare whether by the East or by the West routes varied very little, and it made a pleasant change to return via North America and the Pacific. In March, after the necessary approval had been given to my appointment by our Ambassador in Washington and my new boss, I was officially appointed as Deputy Consul-General in New York.

Leaving my long-suffering wife once again to pack up, let the house and sort out the children I sailed in great comfort from Genoa on the Italian ship *Michel Angelo* for New York where we finally arrived on the 18th April 1969. We had left Genoa intending to make a brief call at Naples but soon after reaching that port the crew declared a one day strike. Although the passengers were told that all necessary safety arrangements and minimum catering would still be assured, most of us took the opportunity for a day ashore. The unexpected day in Naples proved a pleasant break although it did mean arriving a day later than scheduled in New York Harbour. Although I had long since ceased to use my Air Force rank in the Diplomatic Service, perhaps because it still appeared on my passport I was agreeably surprised when the Purser said to me on leaving Naples, 'General, we would very much like you to take over a spare cabin that has just become vacant'. I told him I was quite happy in my present accommodation but he pressed me to look at a perfectly magnificent VIP suite containing three or four rooms which he invited me to have as the guest of the Italia Line. I was assured that there was no question of my having to pay for this quite undeserved luxury which was way above my own Civil Service entitlement. The palatial accommodation included a private bathroom and enough hanging space to accommodate a huge wardrobe. It contained also a well furnished cocktail cabinet and I realised that for once my Royal Air Force rank – irrelevant as it was to my present circumstances – had proved extremely useful!

I was seated at the same table as Signor Annigoni, the Royal Portrait Painter, and I was interested to note on the first night that although he joined in bingo with great enthusiasm the Maestro, as he was always called, did not take part in the evening ballroom dancing. However, his very lovely travelling companion, whom he introduced variously as his secretary or his model and whom I believe he subsequently married, always did, but on the stroke of midnight looking at her tiny watch she said goodnight and like Cinderella disappeared from sight. Signor Annigoni – a solid slightly florid Florentine – was excellent company on the voyage and he loved to talk about the famous people he had painted. He had just finished his second portrait of the Queen. A remarkable trencherman he did full justice to the excellent food provided and always managed to finish the whole bottle of wine that was provided for every passenger at each main meal. He was good enough to invite me to the private viewing of his new exhibition in Manhattan.

On arrival in New York I met the Consul General, Sir Anthony Rouse, who had been knighted a year or two previously for his distinguished work looking after British interests in our wide consular area and, as I was soon to find out, he and his wife were extremely popular. He told me that since his outgoing deputy had not yet vacated his official apartment, arrangements had been made for me to stay with a senior member of our Trade Office there, Ewen Fergusson and his wife Sarah.

I was lucky in my time of arrival. The brief spring was almost upon us and walking in Central Park with trees bursting into leaf the change from winter was quite dramatic, and the fresh champagne-like air of uptown

Manhattan was invigorating indeed. Most of the British Government Offices in New York City were situated on Third Avenue in a large block shared with many other, mainly commerical, offices. Sir Anthony assured me on arrival that my work would involve a great deal of entertaining, speech making and getting around an area which covered most of New England, a prospect which suited me admirably.

Although I had done a brief and intensive course on consular work before leaving London I was much relieved to find that on our staff we had several UK-based Vice-Consuls and locally engaged Pro-Consuls to handle the very heavy day to day routine work. Most of this was fairly straightforward but there were always problems of Britons running out of money or concerned with marrying American citizens and still wishing to retain their British nationality. On the whole though they were not as complicated as in Madras where one would sometimes have a passport application from (say) an Englishman born in Ceylon whose father had first seen the light of day in Burma with a grandfather born in a princely Indian State, whilst his mother was Irish and his grandmother came from Ayrshire! Since immigration rules were all the time becoming tighter these cases were a great headache but fortunately they seldom came my way in New York. Soon after arriving in the 'Big Apple', as the New Yorkers loved to call their city, I realised the truth of what Sir Anthony had said to me about my new responsibilities.

Ewen Fergusson and his wife had gone away for a few days, leaving me in their comfortable flat in central New York and the Consul General was also out of town, when I was reminded that the mammoth *Daily Mail* Air Race between the Tower of London and the Empire State Building in New York was due to take place in a few days. It was hoped that I would give a reception for the participants in the various categories and particularly for the many New

Yorkers, including the Police, Customs and Harbour people who were co-operating magnificently in facilitating this event. As I had only been in the city about a month and my wife had not yet arrived I was somewhat taken aback but the Fergusson's apartment was large and my own office was able to help in organising plentiful supplies of food and liquor, as well as issuing invitations to all and sundry on my behalf. Fortunately I had had necessary invitation cards printed before coming out from home. I had still met very few people in New York and although it was perhaps a good chance to remedy this it was not quite the kind of introductory gathering that I had envisaged. My thoughts turned rapidly to pretty girls and I realised that young airmen (and some not so young) would like feminine company and I approached the managers of both British Overseas Airways and British European Airways whom I had only just met and asked them if they would invite some of their air and ground hostesses and office staff, and although a little surprised at the shortness of notice they did this very willingly. The party seemed to be a success and although very few of the guests realised that I was supposed to be their host I don't think this greatly mattered, and since all this came under the heading of Official Entertainment I didn't have to foot the bill!

This party was one of very many during the three years that we spent in New York, and particularly when my wife arrived we were greatly concerned with public and semi-public functions and private entertaining, and we met an enormous number of usually very friendly people.

At this time New York City had begun to settle down after the recent student riots, but Harlem was still an explosive spot since race relations between Whites, Blacks and Puerto Ricans could become very tense indeed. The aftermath of the Vietnam War was still very keenly felt and we met many Americans who had lost close relatives in that bitter, long drawn-out, futile struggle. It was a moment in history when the United States, having felt top dog since the end of the Second World War, was now suffering from the bitter humiliation of their failure in Vietnam, and the sense of frustration which prevailed seemed likely to turn from a mood of self-searching and self-criticism into one of withdrawal from world affairs and into a kind of anguished neutrality. Americans everywhere were questioning their own values, praising the British system of democracy, and wondering how on earth they had got themselves into this awful mess. It was, of course, a passing phase but it was sad to see and have to report on so great a nation questioning some of the basic values on which the Union had been built.

New York City was as exciting as ever and seemed to have changed little since I had passed through it once or twice twenty years earlier when visiting the Pentagon in Washington. We lived in a well furnished apartment belonging to the British Government on East 57th Street, quite near the UN Building and the East River. This was a quiet part of the city only about ten minutes walk from our office on Third Avenue. With high rise buildings all around it took a little while to get one's bearings but the almost obligatory boat trip around Manhattan Island helped a great deal and gave a fair idea of the layout of the whole city. It was not at first an easy place to get out of by car since the traffic was so heavy that it was quite possible to miss a particular bridge or tunnel leading from Manhattan Island and to find it almost impossible to get back. It took a good while to get used to driving under American conditions but after a time one realised that in fact it was very easy to get from downtown Manhattan to quite lovely country in New Jersey up the Hudson River in well under an hour. Even the journey through Queen's into Long Island became fairly painless when the houses and traffic began to thin out after an hour or so. Sometimes on a weekend we would drive perhaps half way down Long Island past some of the splendid residences of the rich and stay at small motels alongside the sea. They were plentiful and comfortable and it was easy to find a good sea food restaurant where in season one could dine off soft shelled crabs, and at any time on freshly caught clams or lobsters at a price that was not prohibitive for an occasional evening out.

Much has been written about the violence of New York and our many visitors would frequently ask us how dangerous the city really was. There was no very easy answer to this one and although during the three years I spent in the city three British citizens were murdered, considering that at any one time there were many thousands holding British passports in our Consular area, some living there permanently and others visiting relatives or travelling as tourists, the number was not perhaps so very great. There were plentiful stories of muggings and of robberies, as in any big city, and in our office we not infrequently had to help British citizens who had suffered in this way.

One day in the vestibule of the Consulate General I noticed amongst a group of people waiting to see one of the Consuls a gentleman dressed in full Highland regalia looking remarkably unhappy. I wondered for a moment if he perhaps had been suffering from an overdose of his country's favourite beverage and I asked one of the Vice Consuls, who was a Scotsman himself, to investigate. The story he brought back fully explained both our caller's unusual attire and his very obvious distress. It seems that this gentleman was the representative of a Scotch Whisky Company and on leaving his hotel he had been robbed of a briefcase containing almost all his money, his passport and a list of all his potential customers. He had pursued his assailant unsuccessfully and I couldn't help feeling that the sight of this flying Scotsman must have aroused some interest even amongst hard-bitten New Yorkers who were not easily surprised by anything they saw or heard. He now needed money to pay for overnight accommodation, a flight home and a new passport and we followed the established

227

routine of providing him with all this, and with a passport valid for a single journey, renewable only when he had refunded the money that we had lent him from the Public Purse. There were other examples of this kind. On one occasion we were telephoned by a visitor over two hundred miles away in Upper New York State saying that he was spending his last few dollars on this phone call and needed help urgently.

My own family had two experiences of the dangers of trusting strangers too readily. In New York, as elsewhere, children of Diplomatic Service parents serving overseas were flown out at public expense twice a year for holidays and the first time my twelve-year-old son came out he was the victim of a very simple confidence trick. With his elder sister, Kathleen, he decided to go skating at the Rockfeller Center, no great distance from our own apartment. Arriving there without mishap they both queued up for their skates and boots. Whilst doing this a pleasant spoken American came up and started talking to them saying that he had been in England during the war and after they had talked for a while he turned to Desmond and said, 'Here, you don't have to line up like this, I'll get your skates for you'. They gave him their money, thanked him warmly and waited and waited but the man never came back, leaving two very disillusioned children and the whole Rainsford family a little the wiser.

An experience of my own was even more revealing. One day whilst walking back to the office on Third Avenue after a good lunch I was approached by a very pretty young woman who asked me if I would help her to read a notice in an adjoining office block. She motioned towards the entrance and asked me to help her to identify the names of the various occupants of the building. She pointed rather vaguely to one and when I read this one out to her she asked to borrow my pen so that she could write it down. I didn't see anything very unusual about this but since she seemed in no hurry to note the address I was getting a little impatient when another girl came up to me and they both started to proposition me in very basic terms. Alarm bells rang loudly and I realised at once that these were two New York hookers whose company was definitely beginning to pall. I immediately demanded my pen back but the second girl started hugging me and saying, 'If you don't like my friend perhaps you would prefer me'. I disentangled myself as quickly as I could from her embrace, snatched my pen back, and as I walked back to my office a little shaken by this unexpected encounter I looked to see if my wallet was still intact. Fortunately this had not been touched and it was not until I was sitting at my desk again that I remembered that I had cashed that morning one hundred dollars and placed them in my waistcoat pocket and when I looked for this money it had all gone. This taught me a real lesson but I did not think it worth reporting the incident to the police nor indeed to any of my colleagues for a considerable time afterwards.

After a while one began to feel like a New Yorker and although we had been warned not to walk on the inside of the pavement in case there were muggers lingering in doorways, or on the outside either in case of being robbed from a passing car we all managed to walk around the town fairly freely, although, perhaps unconsciously, a little more alert than in an English town. The New York police were not, in our experience, over friendly, and perhaps because they were more concerned with major crime than with tourists they were not particularly helpful to visitors asking the usual questions that are directed daily at the British bobby. I heard one story of a senior British official walking in Central Park who, getting a bit bemused, asked a passing cop the best way to get to Macy's, the big downtown store. The officer we were told took the cigarette out of his mouth, rubbed his head, spat on the ground and then said, 'Buy a map, Dad. Buy a map'. We never doubted that the story was true.

I had heard a great deal about riots a year or two earlier in Harlem at which, walking almost alone, Mayor John Lindsay had greatly distinguished himself and living, as we were, in midtown Manhattan, it was an easy enough place to visit. However, I was strongly warned about going there alone even in the daytime. Driving through Harlem it was easy to visualise its past as a small, quite prosperous American village with elegant brownstone houses now largely taken over by Blacks and Puerto Ricans. The rents being high, tenants had, over the years, taken in more and more lodgers and overcrowding and the gradual deterioration of property had led to frequent outbursts of anger and violence often triggered off by some quite trivial incident; it was not in the nineteen seventies a place to linger in the daytime, and I would not like to visit it by night.

New York was full of surprises. On one occasion I was invited to a philatelic gathering to accept an award on behalf of a distinguished British stamp collector and to make a suitable acknowledgement on his behalf. This involved some frantic research on the origin of stamps and stamp collecting and I was interested to discover that Benjamin Franklin had apparently been one of the originators of the postage stamp in the USA. Another time I was asked to present certificates from the Outer New York Critics Guild to British actors and actresses including Anthony Quayle, Keith Baxter and, I think, Claire Bloom. Both Anthony Quayle and Keith Baxter were playing in 'Sleuth' on Broadway at the time. After the formalities were over we had dinner in Sardis, a restaurant much frequented by stage and literary folk.

In Manhattan there were still some remarkable old fashioned clubs – one being The Coffee House Club based on 18th century London where members and their guests sat together at a long refectory table and everyone talked to his neighbours. Another time my wife and I were invited to watch old time tennis – a game I had never seen anywhere in the world – played in the middle of New York. I found it surprising that this bustling modern city still managed to find time and room to remember, and even to revere, its early Dutch and British colonial history.

One of the more pleasant duties of the British Consul General in New York was to inform British citizens of any Honours and Awards that were coming their way in the next Honours List. This practice began when an honour, which had been approved, was declined by the recipient and so it is now customary to ensure in advance that any award would be gladly received.

At this time the Metropolitan Opera House was in charge of Rudolph Bing who had made a great name for himself at Glyndebourne and at the Edinburgh Festival, and although of Austrian origin he still retained his British citizenship whilst living in New York. He was always very good to the Diplomatic Corps and he used to invite its members in turn to use his own private box at the theatre from which my wife and I witnessed many glittering performances, notably a quite breath-taking one of Aïda.

One day we heard from London that it had been decided to recognise Mr Bing's very distinguished services to music by offering him a knighthood and I had the pleasure of going to see him, in the absence of my Consul General, to ask him if he would be prepared to accept it. I telephoned his secretary and made an appointment to call on Bing whose guests we had already been. When I arrived at the Opera House I found this small, friendly man seated at a big desk at one end of a huge room which reminded me of a story I had heard Bob Boothby tell about an interview he had with Hitler before the war. When the Führer had greeted him, hand raised, declaring 'Hitler' Bob had replied in that fruity voice of his 'Boothby'!

After exchanging the usual courtesies and as I was about to come to the point of my visit the General Manager turned to me and said, 'And now Mr Acting Consul General what have you come to see me about?' I replied at once that I had the great privilege of asking him if he was prepared to accept a knighthood from the Queen. Mr Bing paused and was silent for a moment and then he said in a voice near breaking point, 'This is the greatest honour of my whole life'. It was a truly emotional moment for both of us. I had to say then that until the award had been announced he must tell absolutely nobody and he replied rather like a schoolboy, 'Please can I tell my wife?' Feeling that this was inevitable in any case I told him I was sure that this would be all right but please would he make a point of making quite sure that absolutely nobody else was informed, and he promised to do this. Afterwards he took me on a tour of the Metropolitan Opera House which reminded me almost of a factory. The area was vast and there seemed to be carpenters and mechanics everywhere, assembling huge pieces of machinery, painting backgrounds and making stage furniture. It was obviously an enormous undertaking to be in charge of an enterprise of this kind and apart from handling temperamental performers from all over the world he had to be responsible for a huge labour force whose frequent demands for better pay or working conditions were publicised in the New York Press, and on one or two occasions caused a complete shutdown until a new contract had been agreed.

Every day in New York seemed to be different from the previous one and the most unexpected invitations came our way. Quite soon after arrival I found myself invited to represent the Consul General at a big gathering of Scottish clans from all over North America. Having already sampled American hospitality I decided to arrive just before dinner, leaving time to meet my host and have a single drink before we all sat down. The big hotel room was absolutely packed and we had the fairly standard American meal of a shrimp cocktail, a very large piece of beef and either ice-cream or fruit salad to follow, all these being washed down with a copious supply of iced water. The food and company were agreeable enough and seated at the top table I was beginning to enjoy myself until glancing at the back of the menu for the names of the speakers I found that I myself had been put down to make the principal speech of the evening. This was a complete surprise as I had very little warning of the dinner and no one had even suggested that I should have to sing for my supper.

When the time came for me to get to my feet I started by saying that although I had too imperfect a knowledge of Scotland I had a great regard for its inhabitants and especially for the splendid amber liquid which they distilled so readily north of the border. I think I may have laid this on a bit thick because before I had finished I was passed a note by the Chairman of the evening saying, 'My heart bleeds for you but the presiding minister is a rabid teetotaller. I hope you will join me afterwards for a wee doch an dorris'. I paused to read this and wished I had time to send a reply saying that it wasn't afterwards but now that this reinforcement was urgently required. However, I seemed to have got away with my address since in the gent's lavatory a visiting Canadian asked me if I was prepared to go up to Canada and talk to them there, to which I replied that in no way was I prepared to address Canadians or anyone else with my tonsils petrified by iced water, but he assured me that this was purely an Amerian custom and that in Canada something much warmer would be provided.

Another memorable occasion was a visit to a small town in New Jersey at which General Pershing and his American troops had assembled during World War I before entraining for New York and the battlefields of France. Since it was a semi-military occasion I was supported by an RAF Wing Commander who was on exchange to the American Air Force, and the French Deputy Consul General had a French ADC also. We were met by local representatives of the American Legion and set out in a fleet of automobiles for the assembly point. The procession proceeded at a snail's pace and on my car I flew a large Union Jack and a smaller American ensign, with a young American cadet trotting beside my car whilst another one accompanied my French colleague. The whole town was en fête and many people cheered us from the steps of houses, and sometimes from windows and balconies, whilst occasionally a Union Jack would be waved. Basking in this reflected glory I was a little startled when a very angry American came up to the window of my Daimler and shouted at me that I had no right whatever to be flying a Union Jack in New Jersey and that in any case my flag was much bigger than the American one, and he threatened to tear it down. He was obviously not an Anglophile and for a moment I thought he might have to be removed by the local police.

When we eventually arrived in the town centre and took our place on a newly erected stand we all stood to attention whilst the Marseillaise and God Save The Queen were played by the local band. There was then a long pause while we waited for the American National Anthem. Finally, the Master of Ceremonies went up to the Band Master and asked him what on earth had gone wrong, to which the Band Master replied, a little testily, that they had all been practising hard on the British and French National Anthems but had not brought music for their own! Since this conversation was conducted within the hearing of the guests the situation was becoming a little embarrassing until an appeal was made through the loudspeaker asking if any of the several other bands present could play the Star-Spangled Banner? This cri de coeur was answered quickly by the leader of a New York pipe and flute band of young girls who, dressed in green with saffron kilts, looked very smart indeed. No doubt the honour made their day although I think the Town Band must have been teased unmercifully for their inability to play their own National Anthem on so important an occasion.

Although consular and representational activities were

234

our main concern, political reporting too was important and this, of course, we did directly to our Embassy in Washington. It was not easy to get the feel of a city in which over a million inhabitants were of Irish origin, another million or more were Italians and probably there were at least a million Jews also. Another big ethnic group was the Poles, and the Blacks, who were moving northward in search of work, were continually increasing in numbers. Last, but by no means least, came the WASPS – White Anglo-Saxon Protestants – whose influence in commerce and industry and in the general administration and running of the city was often predominant. The Mayor, John Lindsay, was a typical WASP and he claimed an ancestry that was partly Scottish and I think partly Dutch also. In our reports we always began by saying that New York was sui generis and was in no way representative either of America as a whole or even of New England.

Of all these various groups it was only the Irish, or those who claimed to be Irish, who caused us any serious trouble. On St Patrick's Day the huge traditional procession through central New York and past the Roman Catholic Cathedral was a very special occasion and a small group of militant Irishmen nearly always assembled outside our office. Being on the eleventh floor of a high rise building they were more trouble to the other occupants than to ourselves but we thought it wise for this one day to remove the Union Jack outside our building and if things looked at all menacing to close the office and let the staff get home a bit early. Once the procession had dispersed and the marchers had duly tanked up almost anything could have happened. Other British offices – banks and airlines – being on street level were more vulnerable; on several occasions they had their windows broken.

All this was almost routine and since we all had ample warning it was more or less endurable although a bit of a nuisance on the day. However, things sometimes became a good deal more troublesome.

During the early seventies the New York Irish – mostly descendants of emigrants fleeing from the Famine of 1845, with few who had even been to Europe – under the influence of NORAID, the organisation raising funds nominally for Irish charity but probably also for the IRA, became more militant. The increasing disturbances in Northern Ireland were their primary causus belli and served to release a good deal of pent-up and ill-informed anti-British feeling. This agitation developed from collecting money in public houses and on the streets to the attempted occupation of British Government offices in New York, Chicago and elsewhere. In New York small groups arriving individually and posing usually as ordinary members of the public lined up just before closing time saying that they would not leave our office until the last British soldier left Northern Ireland. Outside they would have Press and TV crews waiting to record the eviction of innocent Americans by the brutal British. These invasions began to become something of a nuisance and since we did not wish them to interfere with our work or cause us to close we took it in turns sitting up with these protesters as we had no wish to ask the police to remove them in front of the media. I sat up most of one night with a group of these unwelcome visitors, most of whom seemed quite well educated and not particularly prone to violence. Until well into the morning I talked to them about their grievances and discussed and quoted Yeats with a young girl student who a little before dawn – suffering perhaps from a surfeit of politics and poetry – developed a severe tummy ache and persuaded the others to take her home. We were beginning to miss our sleep and to feel the need of adopting rather sterner measures when a similar group invaded our Embassy in Washington, and to the great relief of all our offices the Ambassador decided that enough was enough and had them all removed swiftly in Paddy Wagons. The Officer-in-Charge of the New York Police

Precinct just across Third Avenue from us, one Donovan by name, had assured me repeatedly that his men – Irish in origin to a man – would be extremely happy to take similar action if we ever needed their help.

For me there was a small postscript. Debating one day on a New York TV station about the problems of Northern Ireland with Patrick MacKernan of the Irish Consulate General in New York, who was a good friend of mine, we both thought that we had managed hopefully to make at least some of our listeners realise that the problems of a divided nation were not quite as simple as many seemed to believe. Walking across Second Avenue next morning on leaving my home a stranger said to me that he had recognised me on the screen last evening, and feeling that my Dublin colleague and I had acquitted ourselves fairly well I replied that I hoped that he had enjoyed watching the programme. His rejoinder that I would be lucky to be alive by tomorrow gave me food for thought on the walk to our office in Third Avenue.

In April 1971 my Consul General Sir Anthony Rouse left for home on retirement and as Audrey and I had formed a very great regard for both Tony Rouse and his charming wife, Tim, we missed them a lot. Since his successor did not arrive until September, for the whole of the summer I found myself the Acting Consul General. This entitled me to the use of one of the very few Daimlers in New York – a vehicle which always excited much interest although Rolls Royces were fairly common. It also, of course, involved a good deal more responsibility.

One of the more pleasant annual engagements of the Consul General was always to meet His Royal Highness the Duke of Windsor and the Duchess during their annual visit to New York where they spent a few weeks in the Waldorf Astoria before going on to Florida. These peregrinations were always notified in advance and it was the custom for either the Consul General or his representative to attend the

Royal couple on their arrival by sea. On this occasion, after the Duke had settled in to his suite in the Waldorf, we were a little surprised one morning when at quite an early hour the telephone beside our bed rang and my wife answering it heard a voice saying, 'This is the Duke speaking'. Although for a fleeting moment she thought someone was pulling her leg she rallied quickly and we both gladly accepted the invitation to come and call on HRH in his Waldorf apartment, bringing with us our daughter, Kathleen, who was now working as a secretary in our Trade Office. When we arrived at the Waldorf the Duke received us warmly but unfortunately the Duchess was indisposed. HRH asked us what we would like to drink and my wife and I settled for the standard American drink of a Martini, which is, in North America, a fairly powerful cocktail. My daughter Kathleen asked for a Dubonnet which did not happen to be available and to save any embarrassment she too changed to a Martini, a drink that she had never even sipped before. Both her mother and I looked at her with some alarm when she raised it to her lips but fortunately she had the sense to handle it extremely gingerly. His Royal Highness spoke with nostalgia of his wartime days in the Bahamas and when I said that I would be at his disposal when he left on the next stage of his journey he asked if I wouldn't much prefer to spend the day playing golf!

A great deal of our time in New York seemed to have been spent at Kennedy Airport meeting and greeting visitors from all over the world. When the Labour Government was out of office we had visits from Harold Wilson, Denis Healey and Tony Benn. Meeting Harold Wilson one day at Kennedy Airport, when he flew in to lecture in the city and I think to help also in promoting a book he or his wife had written, I escorted him with airport officials to a VIP lounge while the necessary customs and immigration formalities were being carried out. When I commented favourably on his arrival on schedule Mr Wilson replied instantly, 'But not as good as Transport Command'. I was really surprised that someone on his staff knew not only that Sir Anthony Rouse was no longer in charge of our New York office but also that I had served in the Royal Air Force. After we had settled down for a few minutes in the lounge a member of the airport staff came and asked Harold Wilson if he would be willing to see some Press men who had assembled in the next room. He readily agreed to do this and suggested that I should accompany him. When the reporters asked him some pretty pointed questions about his opinion of our Ambassador in Washington and of the new British Government he replied instantly that he had a great admiration for the Ambassador and that although he would have a lot to say about our Government when he got home he had no intention whatever of criticising it when abroad. Next evening he was the principal speaker at a huge gathering of middle rank American Trade Unionists and labour officials and gave an impressive tour de horizon about world events which seemed to go down well, but meeting both the Wilsons in the lift afterwards he said with a smile, 'That was pretty dull stuff wasn't it? But come and hear the next one because that should be more fun!' This was not, of course, an invitation that I could easily accept since our bailiwick, large as it was, was confined to the New England States.

On two occasions we were invited to the opening of new buildings at Kennedy Airport. In the spring of 1970 TWA completed a fine airport terminal to handle the new Jumbo 747 Jet traffic. At the opening ceremony, after a great deal of quite lavish American hospitality and meeting many guests and TWA staff, I was invited to the tarmac in front of television cameras to greet the first British passenger to step off the 747 which had just arrived. As I was representing the British Government I wasn't entirely sure whether this was the right thing to do but taking a chance I stood at the bottom of the gangway with the Press all around and asked a number of tired passengers, as they put foot on American soil, if they happened to be British. The reception I received, although polite enough, was by no means enthusiastic but fortunately a genuine Briton soon appeared and assured me, in front of the microphones, that he had indeed had a very pleasant flight. I could not help wondering though what BOAC would say in due course when they heard that I had been promoting an American airline!

A more important occasion, from the British point of view, was the opening of the new BOAC/Air Canada Terminal at Kennedy Airport by Princess Alexandra on the 24th September of that year. Accompanied by Angus Ogilvy she was welcomed by Sir Charles Hardie, the then Chairman of BOAC, and was presented with a ceremonial key. After addresses by the Chairman of Air Canada and by the Chairman of the Port of New York Authority the party undertook an extensive tour of the new terminal and its facilities. The inscription on the plaque which Princess Alexandra unveiled reads:

'These stones, from three famous landmarks, symbolise the air bridge between Europe and North America. The lower stones were taken from London Bridge and Brooklyn Bridge whilst this cross-piece is from Signal Hill, Newfoundland, the point from which Marconi transmitted the first trans-Atlantic wireless signal and close to the point from which Alcock and Brown commenced the historic first trans-Atlantic flight'.

Everything had gone according to plan and once again I felt that the Special Relationship with the United States really did mean something and that (to paraphrase Bernard Shaw), even if the two nations were divided by a common language, the gap was not awfully wide!

For some reason which I have never discovered, our New York office was, and presumably still is, responsible for consular affairs, i.e. for the protection and welfare of British subjects, in the French Islands of St Pierre and Miquelon near the mouth of the St Lawrence. When I inquired what this responsibility amounted to in practice I was told that no one from our office seemed ever to have been there and it was doubtful if any British citizens now lived in the islands, but presumably if a British ship went aground or an aircraft came to grief in that area we would have to spring into action. All this passed from my mind until in the early spring of 1971, being now the Acting Consul General in New York, I decided to look into it a bit further. I asked our office to dig up any papers we had on the matter and found that we had none. I decided that it would be fun to go and visit these rather remote islands and after obtaining permission from Lord Cromer (who had now taken over as Ambassador in Washington from my late boss in India, John Freeman), I wrote to the French Governor at St Pierre reminding him that the British Consulate General in New York had consular responsibilities in his area of which he was doubtless aware, and I asked him if it would be convenient for me to come and call on him. I imagine this letter caused some surprise since I cannot think that the welfare of any British subjects in the territory was one of the Governor's main concerns. Indeed, I very much doubted if he had any idea at all that our New York office had any consular jurisdiction in his area although doubtless this had been agreed many years before with the French authorities. The Acting Governor replied that I would be very welcome. I wondered then how to get there.

I put this task to our Travel Section and though they did not find it at all easy they set to work with a will. In the end they booked me from New York to Halifax in Nova Scotia, where I spent a night or two amongst friendly folk the Canadians like to call the Blue Noses before taking a somewhat infrequent scheduled flight to St John's in Newfoundland. From here there was an occasional service to St Pierre when weather permitted, but fog rolling in from the Grand Banks, as it so frequently did, very often made flying impossible. The weather wasn't too bad this time, and after a night in St John's we took off in an ancient Dakota for the little Island of St Pierre where I had a most friendly reception from the Acting Governor and his staff – the Governor being on leave in France. He told me at once that to the best of his knowledge there were no British subjects at all on either of the Islands although he was very pleased to see me. There were, however, several Canadians of both sexes living there and the language was not a great problem although, not surprisingly, my host preferred to speak in French. After an excellent lunch I was given a brief history of the Islands; they had been French for very many years and although St Pierre was much the smaller of the two it had a considerably bigger population than Miquelon, its main industries being connected with fishing, principally for the large cod so prolific in those waters. The Island of St Pierre, His Excellency assured me, had once been known as the Island of Five Thousand Virgins but both the population and the hymeneal count had fallen a good deal since then. The islanders I met seemed a tough and hardy lot, and due to the frequent visits of ocean going fishing vessels they were well in touch with the outer world.

My host soon said that he thought we should dispense with formalities and on the second evening of my visit he took me down to a crowded local discotheque where the wine was flowing and Spanish and French fishermen were competing for the attentions of some very pretty local girls. The Acting Governor suggested that we too joined in and although we each managed to get a dance or two we soon withdrew from the somewhat unequal contest and concentrated on restoring and improving the entente cordiale which became even more cordiale as the night went on. As this was not that long after General de Gaulle had called briefly at St Pierre on a French Warship and declared

242

'Vive le Quebec libre', it was not perhaps an entirely wasted exercise.

Next morning the fog had begun to come in and I had to wait a further day or two before the weather was fit to fly back to St John's. In due course visibility was restored by a howling gale in which we took off on a very rough flight indeed during part of which time I was handed the controls as the pilot was not feeling at all well. Being well out of flying practice and not feeling on top of the world myself I was exceedingly glad when he took over again and landed us safely at our destination.

After returning to New York I thought it wise to write some account of this visit, especially as it had taken rather longer than I had expected. I sent this as usual to our Embassy in Washington and copied it to London and to Paris as well since I thought the Embassy there might like to know. In due course I received a reply from the French capital saying that they had found my trip extremely interesting but perhaps on another occasion I would warn them in advance as they thought the French Government might like to be informed also. I must admit that I had thought of doing this before taking off but had the horrible feeling that although the visit was quite legitimate, and was covered by authority from our Embassy in Washington, objections might be raised from some other quarter.

A year later our time in New York had almost come to an end. We had seen quite a bit of New England – sometimes lecturing to the English Speaking Union in Rochester and Syracuse, visiting Boston and Philadelphia, or week-ending in little New England country towns some of which had been founded almost three hundred years before. The signposts could be confusing since sometimes Bristol or Warwick seemed to be in quite the wrong direction but although the white painted, often wooden, houses were very American much of the countryside reminded me of the south of England and the rolling Sussex and Hampshire

Downs. There was little crime anywhere and visiting country churches and the rich museums with which even quite small towns seemed to be endowed, we were told that there was no need to lock up anything. It made a pleasant change from Manhattan where doors were double locked and peep holes provided to check on visitors at all times of the night or day.

By May 1972 it was time to leave. It had been for both of us a memorable tour and as Audrey's parents still lived near Montreal we had been able to visit them quite often and to enjoy long vacations in their country home in the Laurentian Mountains west of the city. It had been a very pleasant way to end the ten years I had served in the Diplomatic Service, or more correctly in which we had both served because the role of wives was almost as important, and sometimes more important, than that of their husbands. In mid May, after the usual series of farewell parties, we sailed for home on the QE2, in a cabin heavily laden with flowers and champagne, for Southampton and retirement. It was to prove an exciting voyage.

About half way across the Atlantic, after we had settled down to a relaxing and comfortable journey, we were startled one late afternoon by an announcement from the Master, Captain William Law, saying that he had been informed that there might be a bomb on board and that, whilst no one need feel alarmed, as a precaution the ship was going to heave to and parachutists would be dropping alongside to see if they could find any explosives. Although the sea was fairly calm there was a cloud base of under a thousand feet and the visibility was not good, being perhaps no more than about a mile. The passengers took this announcement extremely well; some made for one of the many bars, others started to write letters and a very few donned lifejackets. After an hour or two an RAF Nimrod flew past quite low and circled the ship a few times and was then followed by a Shackleton which after flying up and down quite close to the QE2 disappeared into the low cloud and dropped three or four parachutists. Conditions for this kind of exercise were far from ideal and Captain Law said afterwards that he was fortunate in being able to pick them up in a boat which when lowered might be too small to show up on his radar screen. Although all were safely retrieved by no means all the equipment they carried was salvaged. I shall not readily forget the sight of this great liner, almost stationary, with its little boat speeding back and forth picking up these very brave men, one of whom told me afterwards that he had been airsick in the air and seasick in the water and thought there must be some easier way to earn a living! The outcome of this story is well known and after a very exhaustive search of the more vulnerable parts of the ship we were assured that any danger had passed. I don't think the originator of the hoax was ever discovered although I did hear the story that a somewhat deranged cobbler in New York had been responsible.

Shortly before reaching Southampton passengers were all assembled in the First Class Lounge and were thanked by a Director of Cunard for their forebearance on the trip. An American woman, much moved, replied saying how wonderful the British were and how magnificently the affair had been handled. 'In no way would we Americans have done as well'. That night we all received champagne from the Company with a note thanking the passengers for their fortitude on a somewhat unusual voyage.

With the excitement beginning to die down and the flowers in the cabin beginning to fade I began to wonder what my life had all been about. I had spent ten happy years in the Diplomatic Service and longer than that in the RAF and what had I achieved? Perhaps in the span of one lifetime one couldn't achieve a great deal. We had both been rewarded by many lasting friendships, meeting a great many people all over the world, and I had never had a posting that I didn't enjoy.

Life in the Foreign Service had been very different in many ways from the RAF. In the Diplomatic Service I had felt much more continually on parade in that at all times and in all places one was representing our country and the Queen. In the RAF off-duty one's loyalties were the same but as one airman amongst many others one was accepted primarily as a member of the British Armed Services and not as a representative of one's country. Perhaps the experience of being an Air Attaché had been a useful prelude to my slightly amateurish career as a diplomat, but I felt, now that both careers had ended, my life had not been entirely wasted. I had met so many people, Greeks, Chinese, Indians, Koreans, Americans and a host of diplomats from just about everywhere, and I had come to the not very original conclusion that all over the world people tend to be very much alike even if their manners and mannerisms are quite different, although like our own, changing all the time.

I remember once meeting in New York, Peter Ustinov, who said that in Japan he had talked to our current Ambassador who told him a little story about how even in the East things were changing very fast. His Excellency had said that in the old days, at a Japanese party after dinner, the host would be apt to say, 'Would your most noble Excellency be kind enough to place his honourable posterior on my miserable and unworthy sofa?' Nowadays a modern Japanese host was far more likely simply to invite you to sit down. As my father had said many years ago the pace of change (he did not like to call it progress) was quickening all the time and having lived through two wars and their aftermath I knew how right he was. In the Foreign Service I had been treated far more kindly than I had expected, or than I probably deserved, having joined as a very late entrant and with a different background to most of my colleagues.

It had taken Audrey and me a little while to get used to Diplomatic protocol and we had made our fair share of

246

mistakes, although perhaps if I had read the official manual on all this a little more carefully we might have avoided some of them. Shortly after arriving in Korea we had found ourselves hosting a farewell party to Sir Walter Godfrey and his wife on their retirement and we, of course, had invited the senior members of the Diplomatic Corps including the doyen, Monsieur Chambard, the Australian Ambassador, their wives, and quite a few others. We had barely begun to settle down and I think this was fairly well understood. After a few drinks when we went into the dining room I seated myself at one end of the table with my wife at the other having paid some little attention to the seating plan for the others. The meal went well enough until the ladies retired, while the men lingered over their port and cigars. Unfortunately the women were ushered into one of the bedrooms where our servant, Mr Park, had turned back all the covers and prepared the beds, thereby exposing a great deal of unpacked and semi-unpacked luggage which had only just arrived, and this was duly noted in the morning when the Ambassadress, after thanking my wife for the party, pointed out that this had been somewhat unfortunate and that, even more unfortunately, I had failed to place His Excellency at one end of the table with my wife at the other. I had assumed that as host in my own house I sat at the top of the table with the senior lady on my right but it was laid down – no doubt for very good reasons – that even if you are entertaining in your own house your own Ambassador, as the British representative, must always be placed at the top of the table whilst you as host located yourself strategically so that you could keep an eye on proceedings generally. This was a lesson easily learnt but no doubt we should have learnt it in advance. There were other occasions of this kind too but as you got to know your fellow diplomats you realised that many of them had had similar problems. In India it was quite common at other people's dinner parties to find one's own cutlery or glasses appearing, and on occasions when the cook dropped the main joint somehow a meal would be conjured up, probably from next door, and it was very difficult ever to find out afterwards how this miracle had been achieved. The important thing was never to be surprised and to avoid seating senior diplomats (foreigners, of course!) at the same table as their ex-mistresses, particularly if their wives happened to be present.

All this was behind us now and I wondered again what the future had in store. I wondered too where to live. For me the call of my homeland was very strong, but although I had two sisters still living in Ireland – one in the North and one in the South – my children were all in England; like so many Anglo-Irish I was pulled both ways across the Irish Sea. I was drawn one way by my love for the land of my birth and by the memories of a happy childhood, and the other way by my children and the wish not to lose contact with the many friends Audrey and I had made all over the world who now lived in the United Kingdom.

On an early summer's day we came back to the house in the Kentish village we had bought five years earlier whilst on leave from Korea. The world seemed at its best. Through broken clouds a shaft of sunlight lit up the Church tower and moved on, irradiating the dark red tiles of 16th century houses. The village was quite perfectly beautiful – old, tranquil, well established. It had absorbed so many foreigners – Normans, Danes, the prisoners and refugees of countless wars who had elected to stay – could it absorb one family more? I thought of Yeats, 'I will arise now and go to Innisfree; and a small cabin build there, of clay and wattles made . . . ' and I wondered if the Weald of Kent at the end of the day could be Innisfree for me.

We walked down the hill again. The Canada Geese were honking on the pond and, watching the resident ducks undismayed by the northern invaders, I remembered William Allingham's lines:-

Four ducks on a pond,
A grass bank beyond,
A blue sky of spring,
White clouds on the wing;
What a little thing
To remember for years –
To remember with tears!

The sun came out as we wandered into the Vine and when a warm voice in a village that seemed no longer strange bade us welcome I thought again that home is where you make it. This was a place where one day one might belong. I felt that perhaps, and only just perhaps, this wandering Anglo-Irishman might begin here to put down tiny tendril roots. I wondered how long they would have to grow.

Index

Arnhem, 46
Army, 116, 123, 125, 149, 173
Army in Berlin, *see* British Garrison
Army Staff College, 116
Astana, 132
'Astute', HMS, 192
Atcherley, Air Cdre David, 100, 105
Athens, 38, 140-163, 182, 204
Atlantic, 21
Attlee, Earl (Clement), 112
Auster, aircraft, 121
Australia, 31, 37, 38, 49, 59, 127, 129, 172, 203
'Autobiography of a Rebel', 67
Auxiliary Air Force, 21
Avent, Sqn Ldr, 80, 81
Avro, aircraft, 18, 21

B
Baird, Flt Lt The Hon RAG, ('Jock'), 39, 40, 86, 87, 88
Baker, Air Marshal Sir Brian, 113
Balkins, 144
Ballymoney, 5
Baltic, 90
Bancroft, Brigadier D R (Dawney), OBE 203, 204, 207, 208, 211, 213, 214, 218
Bangalore, 181, 189
Bangkok, 200
Bantu, *see* Africa, 10
Bardia, 47
Barker, Dudley, 102, 111
Barossa Valley, 130
Barstow, Captain George, RN, 142, 144 154, 155, 163
Bassingbourn, 30
Battle of Britain, 72
Baxter, Keith, 230
Beamish, Air Marshal Sir George, 139
Beatty, Captain, VC, 161
Beirut, 45
Belfast, 5, 18, 50, 64, 74, 187
Belgium, 74
Benghazi, 34-37, 44, 45, 47, 61, 62, 79
Benn, Tony, 238
Berlin, 73, 79, 92, 96, 101-103, 106-108, 110, 111
Berlin Airlift, 103-113, 114, 171, 174
Bettington, Group Capt ('Zulu'), 178
Betty, Brendan ('Bread and Butter'), 15
Bing, Sir Rudolph, 231, 232
Birmingham, 21, 117

'Birmingham', HMS, 161
Bitter Lakes, 33, 119
Blackpool, 30
Blake, George, 202
Blenheim, aircraft, 62
Bloom, Claire, 230
Bombay, 178-180, 195
Bonesteel, General, 215
Boothby, Flt Lt R ('Bob') MP, (later Lord Boothby), 67, 68, 69, 231
Boothby, Lady, 68
Boothby, Lady (Wanda), 69
Bootle, 142
Borneo, 132
Bracknell, 114-116
Bramcote, 98
Briggs, Lt Gen Sir Harold, 126
Brisbane, 131
Bristol Freighter, aircraft, 110
Britannia, aircraft, 173
British Broadcasting Co, (BBC), 165
British Civil Aviation, 101
British Commonwealth, 111, 115, 172
British Council, 189, 190
British East India Co, *see* East India Company
British Embassy, Athens, 140-163
British Embassy, Seoul, 201-219
British European Airways (BEA), 177, 225
British Garrison Berlin, 101-104, 108
British High Commission, New Delhi, 180, 183
'British Hussar', 55, 63
British Overseas Airways (BOAC), 225, 230
Brooke Bond Tea Co, 190
Brunei, 132
'B' Special Constabulary, 5
Buckeburg, 103
Buckingham Palace, 113
Bulstrode, 70, 72, 115, 168
Burlington Gardens, 6
Burma, 127
Bury St Edmunds, 28
Bushey Park, 98, 101, 104, 107
Butterworth, 125, 129, 141
Byron, Lord, 146

C
Cairns, Earl, Rear Admiral, 166, 168, 175
Cairo, 16, 33, 40, 44, 51, 52, 53, 54
Calcutta, 180, 186, 195

253

INDEX

INDEX

259